THE BOOK OF
MUSICAL DOCUMENTS

The Book of
Musical Documents

BY
PAUL NETTL

GREENWOOD PRESS, PUBLISHERS
NEW YORK

ACKNOWLEDGMENTS

This book is an anthology of documents pertaining to music history. It contains quotations from theoretical works, letters, memoirs, poems, archives, newspaper and magazine articles, etc.

Its original model was Hermann Unger's "Musikgeschichte in Selbstzeugnissen", a book to which I am greatly indebted.

I wish to express my deepest gratitude to Mrs. Frida Best, who is responsible for the English version of a great part of documents originally written in German or French. I also wish to thank for her generous helpfulness, Mrs. Margaret Bush, who was instrumental in finishing the manuscript and reading proofs. Finally, I should like to thank Dr. Dagobert Runes of the Philosophical Library for his deep interest and understanding.

Paul Nettl

Preface

Music is one of man's most sensitive means of expression. It reflects his thoughts and emotions to a surprising degree and from time immemorial has been intimately connected with his inner and outer life. Just how music sounded in former days is largely guess work. Until the invention of the phonograph it was impossible to record sound and, though music was noted down, we do not know exactly how it was performed or imagined by composers. The written word, on the other hand, is not so dependent on performance. Prose, as the *Bourgeois Gentilhomme* discovered, is spoken by everyone and language is less subject to personal interpretation than notation. Words are used as a medium to explain the whys and wherefores of society and are a vehicle by which man expresses his views about life as well as about music. A great deal has been written concerning music and most people have not been shy in praising or condemning it according to their likes and dislikes, temperament or training. Neither the art nor the science of sound have had a peaceful evolution. Innovations have been attacked and jealousies between composers and performers have been frequent.

Now we can enjoy music without understanding a great deal about it, but the more one knows about a field the more pleasure one derives from it. Reading about music, therefore, is a legitimate way of increasing one's knowledge.

Paul Nettl's *Book of Musical Documents* shows what an extraordinary range the field covers. The author has chosen examples primarily from original sources. Musicians tell us of their hopes and fears, the shortcomings of their contemporaries or the power of music. We learn a good deal about the economic side of the art and find that theory and practice are frequently far apart.

The opportunity to become acquainted with the ideas of some of the great masters of music gives one an insight into their characters. Also, comments of lay observers are really illuminating. Reading these pages takes one into the greenrooms of music history. We rub elbows with Socrates, Attila, the Minnesingers, Castiglione, Shakespeare, Lessing and Jean Jacques Rousseau. Gabrieli, Monteverdi, Bach, Handel, Haydn and Mozart are quoted, now in an official, again in a private capacity. One of the most touching documents is a letter of Haydn about Mozart

> "If I could imbue the mind and soul of every music lover—and particularly those on high—with the same great musical understanding and the profound feeling I have for his inimitable works, the nations would vie with one another for the possession of so precious a gem. Let Prague keep the rare man but let it reward him, for, without this, the history of a striving genius is a sad one, and gives little encouragement and incentive for further striving to posterity. So many promising spirits are dejected for the want of it. I am indignant that this one and only man has not been engaged by some royal or imperial court."

The section on Beethoven gives an excellent picture of music's greatest Titan. Selections from letters, the Heiligenstadt will, quotations from the Notebooks, the Conversation books and comments by those who visited him—all are there, together with Grillparzer's moving funeral oration. Nearly a third of the book is devoted to the 19th century—a period extremely rich in documentation, especially as literary elements played an unusually important role in the music of the romantic era. It is natural to find the names of Heine, Nietzsche and Tolstoy here and to recognize the dual gifts of such men as Schumann, Berlioz and Wagner who were almost as distinguished in literature as in music. Weltschmerz also begins in earnest:

> "My productions are the outcome of my understanding and my pain" said Schubert. And "Life's burdens weigh down

on me heavily. How happy I would be to fly from life to art, but as art lives only in life, and life only in art, both combined, continue to harass me," wrote Weber.

Schumann, calling attention to the fact that Beethoven "on the title page of the C major Overture uses the expression "Gedichtet von" instead of "composed by", urged musicians to read good literature. This was the period of the LIED and the intimate song as opposed to the impersonal solo cantata and the classical aria; Schubert, Brahms, Duparc and Debussy have left us pieces for voice and piano in which the fusion of words and music are unsurpassable. It was an age of contrasts—Niccolo Paganini and Franz Liszt brought the career of the virtuoso to hitherto undreamed of heights, Bizet's Carmen was at first a fiasco in Paris; while in Boston, of all places, Johann Strauss conducted 20,000 people in the Blue Danube Waltz assisted by 100 sub conductors.

It is gratifying to find an anthology with voluminous quotations on the music of today. Discussion of quarter tones, twelve tone scales, mechanical music, jazz and the like are welcome. The final section: Music in a Degenerated World takes up Nazi practices and theories. Few ideas are more foreign to Americans than the complete submission of music to the state. The principles for which we have struggled in modern times: Liberty, Fraternity and the Pursuit of Happiness are opposed to censorship and aesthetic rules dictated from above.

Nevertheless music from earliest times has been controlled more than we realize and, in the past, the totalitarian approach to art has been the rule rather than the exception. Art for Art's Sake is a relatively modern idea—definitely frowned upon in communist countries today—for excessive individualism is considered anti-public. Subjectivism, innovation, and abstract tendencies, often referred to as "formalist trends", are considered harmful and "alien to the principles of socialist realism." Two world ideologies are face to face today the one stressing individual freedom, the other social control; naturally they affect the creative processes of music. The place of the composer in the new world is by no means ideal but we have not reached the point where the Administration of Propaganda and Agitation has been asked to correct the situation, liquidate the shortcomings of composers and provide for the development of music "along realistic lines".

Writings of Musicians and thoughts about music will always be used as documentary supplements to notation. It was a happy idea to make this *Book of Musical Documents*, for such an anthology, besides being interesting to the scholar is both instructive and pleasing to the layman.

CARLETON SPRAGUE SMITH

Table of Contents

List of Illustrations

PRIMITIVES AND
ASIATIC PEOPLES

Work and Song
The Music of the Sotho Negroes

WORKMEN like to sing when at work, and work is often accompanied by singing, provided the work permits a beat of time. The melody of the solo song usually begins on a high tone, and irregularly descends. The text is entirely optional.

Dance is always accompanied by singing in chorus, as is all work, adaptable to the beat of time.

Then there are solos with accompaniment by the Kxoro, which are mostly sung to basket-weaving, tanning of hides, sewing and similar occupations. The lines of the text are arbitrarily split up by the solo singer so that, at times, he begins in the middle and brings the beginning of the piece at the close. Single lines are torn to pieces and very often one line is repeated over and over again. The accompanying chorus opens the introduction with "dya, oé, dya, oé, é" or "ha, oó, ho ho ho ho ho o, ho, ho" or similar sounds. Some times two choruses are formed, of which one begins the cadence in deep tones, whereupon the other tunes in, in a higher one. This is done several times in succession. Then the solo singer starts his song while the chorus continues its part. The continued singing of the chorus between each pause of the solo forms, so to say, an interlude. With the beginning of a new stanza, the soloist often tunes in in another key which is followed by the accompanying chorus. There can, of course, be no question of harmony. The notation of the melodies is difficult since the Sotho scale consists of whole tones only. There is no rule and never are two performances alike.

Missionary K. Endemann
From the "Review on Ethnography" VI.

3

Music of the Japanese:

ALTHOUGH the Japanese like the Chinese have a systematized theory of harmony, we are unable to understand their musical productions, which to us seem singular and grotesque. Japanese music, insofar as it is of a profane character, always serves as an accompaniment to a song, a theatrical or a pantomimic performance. Thus, odes and ballads are executed to the tones of a four-stringed lute, called the BIWA. Some of these BIWAS are of great value and are therefore preserved by their owners in cases of brocaded silk. As far as I know the BIWA virtuosi are the most honored and best paid among Japanese musicians. I heard only one of these BIWA players who, while on a tour, gave a performance at Nicco. After having properly seated himself, he closed his eyes and with horrifying grimaces proceeded to give his performance. He sang with a high nasal voice and manipulated his instrument with a broad three-cornered block of wood, at times plucking the strings, at others, pressing on the strings from below, and letting his fingers glide over them with such rapidity, that their movements could hardly be followed. The long KOTO (a harp), as well as the SHAMISEN (a three-stringed guitar), are preferably used by the female sex, and mostly for the accompaniment of lyrical and dance songs. The KETTLE-DRUM (tympano), which is placed on the left shoulder, and a DRUM, beaten with a heavy drum-stick, are put into use by the "NO PLAYERS" and for dance music. The wood instruments, the SANG (also well known in China) and the FLUTE (shawm) are also employed by the NO PLAYERS. The flute, as in China, is played by the blind in the streets to arouse attention and pity. Many of these unfortunates prefer to earn their living as teachers of the KOTO and SHAMISEN while others have chosen the profession of masseurs.

From "Travel Reminiscences" of
Prince Rupprecht of Bavaria.

4

The Miraculous Power of Music

A Chinese Legend

WHEN Siang played the cither, the birds circled above him, and the fishes leaped out of the water. Music Master Weng heard him. He left his home and followed Master Siang in his wanderings. For three years he twanged the strings with his finger without evoking a melody. Master Siang said to him: "You had better go back home".

Master Weng laid the cither aside, sighed, and said: "It is not that I do not know how to play the strings,—that is not the reason why I cannot bring forth a melody. What I have in mind does not refer to the strings. What I am striving for, does not refer to the tones. So long as I have not attained what is in my inmost heart, I cannot from without express it on my instrument. Therefore, I dare not raise my hand to play the strings. But give me a little more time and then see what I can do".

Not long after, he again came before the Master Siang. Siang asked him: "How is it now with your cither?" Master Weng answered: "I have attained what I have been striving for; now judge my playing". Thereupon in the time of spring he struck the Shang string to the accompaniment of the reed-pipe, when suddenly a cool breeze sprang up and all the plants and trees bore fruit. Thus when autumn had come, he struck the Güo-string and had another reed-pipe give answer. Gentle zephyr breezes began to blow mildly, and all the plants and trees unfolded their splendor. During the summer he plucked the Yü-string and had the eleventh reed-pipe accompany it: and hail and snow fell together and the rivers and lakes suddenly became hard and glassy. In winter time he struck the Djee-string and had the fifth reed-pipe answer. The sun became burningly hot, and the hard ice melted at once. Finally he let the Gung-string resound, and united it with the four other strings, and sweet breezes blew and rustled, auspicious clouds swam through the skies, brilliant dew drops appeared on green leaves and the springs purled briskly. Master Siang beat his breast, arose, and said: "Your playing is marvelous; even Master Kuang with his melodies, and Dson Yan with his flute could do no better. Let them follow you: one the cither under his arm, and the other with the flute in his hand".

"LIA—DSI" — "The True Book of the
ever-flowing primordial source".

Ethical Effect of Music

HARMONY is the power that aims to bring heaven down to earth. It instils into man the love of good and a sense of duty. If you want to know whether or not a realm is well-governed, whether or not the customs are good or bad, examine the kind of music it cultivates.

A Chinese Chronicler.
(A. Kraus Figlio on the Music of Japan).

Music — A Regulating Power

MUSIC comes from within, the customs of the peoples have been ordained from without:
Since music comes from within, it brings peace.
Since customs have been established from without, they produce a mode of living.
Truly great music is always simple.
Truly great customs are always moderate.
And the customs affect the outer man,
While music affects the inner.
Customs aim to keep man within proper bounds.
Music aims to fill the heart with noble feelings.

6

Customs keep man within proper bounds, and at the same
  time incite him to action.
This power constitutes the beauty of customs.
Music fills the heart with noble thoughts and at the same
  time tempers the passions.
This power constitutes the beauty of music.
If customs were to moderate without animating they would
  soon disappear.
If music were to kindle without mitigating it would soon
  become licentious.
Custom thus becomes a gift, returned by the giver.
Music thus serves to mitigate the passions.
A sense of obligation to the customs creates joy.
The mitigating effect of music creates peace.
The twofold practice of music and customs serves but one
  purpose: Perfection.

From the Li-Ki "Book of Ceremonies".

A Hindu Legend

ONCE upon a time, a young girl was unthinkingly singing
a melody to herself, the significance of which was unknown
to her. When, however, the skies overhead suddenly became
overcast, she realized that she was singing one of the Ragas,
the miracle working airs. A violent storm broke loose, con-
jured up by the magic of these tones. The phenomenon was
all the more surprising as the country had been suffering
from a long drought, without the smallest cloud ever dim-
ming the glaring light of the heavens. Now a violent cloud-
burst refreshed the earth and the girl had saved her country
from a famine.

Combarieu, "La Musique et la Magie".

7

HELLENIC AND
EARLY JEWISH CULTURE

Egyptian Origin of Greek Music

ORPHEUS has taken the form of the hymns from the Egyptians. It is well to remember that the inspiration for the music of the Greeks (in strongly mythical coloring) who, according to the assertion of the ancient priest to Solon, were but children, compared to the Egyptians — has been derived from the age-old culture on the Nile. So the statement that Greek music is a daughter of Egyptian music, is not merely a baseless conjecture.

Plato, "Timaeus".

Music and Ethos

Dialogue of Socrates and Glaucon

Socrates: Then now, my friend, I said, that part of music or literary education which relates to the story or myth may be considered to be finished; for the matter and manner have both been discussed.

Glaucon: I think so too.

Socrates: Next in order will follow melody and song.

Glaucon: That is obvious.

Socrates: Every one can already see what we ought to say about them, if we are to be consistent with ourselves.

Glaucon: (laughing) I fear, that the word "every one" hardly includes me, for I cannot at the moment say what they should be; though I may guess.

Socrates: At any rate you can tell that a song or ode has three parts — the words, the melody, and the rhythm; that degree of knowledge I may presuppose?

Glaucon: Yes, so much as that, you may.

Socrates: And as for the words, there will surely be no difference between words which are and which are not set to music; both will conform to the same laws, and these have already been determined by us, have they?

Glaucon: Yes.

Socrates: And the melody and rhythm will depend upon the words?

Glaucon: Certainly.

Socrates: Were we saying, when we spoke of the subject matter, that we had no need of lamentation and strains of sorrow?

Glaucon: True.

Socrates: And which are the harmonies expressive of sorrow? You are musical and can tell me.

Glaucon: The harmonies which you mean are the mixolydian and such like.

Socrates: These then, I said, must be banished; even to women who have a character to maintain they are of no use, and much less to men.

Glaucon: Certainly.

Socrates: In the next place, drunkenness and softness and indolence are utterly unbecoming the character of our guardians.

Glaucon: Utterly unbecoming.

Socrates: And which are the soft or drinking harmonies?

Glaucon: The Ionian and the Lydian; they are termed relaxed.

Socrates: Well, and are these of any military use?

Glaucon: Quite the reverse; and if so, the Dorian and the Phrygian are the only ones which you have left.

Socrates: Of the harmonies I know nothing, but I want to have one warlike, to sound the note or accent which a brave man utters in the hour of danger and stern resolve, or when his cause is failing, and he is going to wounds or death or is overtaken by some other evil, and at every such crisis meets the blows of fortune with firm step and a determination to endure; and another to be used by him in times of peace and freedom of action, when there is no pressure of necessity, and he is seeking to persuade god by prayer, or man by instruction and admonition, or, on the other hand, when he is expressing his willingness to yield to persuasion or entreaty or admonition, and which represents him when by prudent conduct he has attained his end, not carried away by his success, but acting moderately and wisely under the circumstances, and acquiescing in the event. These two harmonies I ask you to leave; the strain of necessity and the strain of freedom, the strain of the unfortunate and the strain of the fortunate, the strain of courage and the strain of temperance; these, I say, leave.

From Plato's "Republic"
(Translated by B. Jowett, M.A.,
Oxford University)

Miriam's Song of Victory in Egypt

AS Pharaoh's army went down into the sea, and Miriam, the prophetess, took a timbrel in her hand, all the women went out after her with timbrels and with dances.

And Miriam answered them: "Sing ye to the Lord, for He hath triumphed gloriously; the horse and the rider hath He thrown into the sea."

Moses II — XV

Healing Effect of David's Music

AND Saul's servants said unto him: "Behold now an evil spirit from God troubleth thee."

"Let our Lord now command thy servants which are before thee to seek out a man, who is a cunning player on the

13

harp: and it shall come to pass, when the evil spirit of God is upon thee, that he shall play with his hand and thou shalt be well . . . ."

And it came to pass, when the evil spirit from God was upon Saul, that David took the harp and played with his hand: so Saul was refreshed and was well, and the evil spirit departed from him.

Samuel I — XVI

The Orchestra of the Temple of Jerusalem

THE orchestra of the Temple of Jerusalem consisted of the following instruments: NEVEL, the big harp, originally without resonant body; KINNOR, the little lyre or harp, the Semitic form of which was square, and the Phoenician and Assyrian form of which was mostly triangular. The KINNOR had no resonant body. Both were string instruments. Their difference lay in the number of strings as well as in size, as the Talmud explains. These two instruments were the most important ones, without which no public religious ceremony could be held. As to the number of their strings we have no definite information. Whether SHEMINITH indicates eight and ASOR ten strings, cannot be proved. We do know, however, that in Egypt and Assyria the number of the strings of the harps and lyres, etc., varied from three to twenty-two. Neither have investigations been successful in finding out the tonality, the range and pitch of the string instruments in Israel or Egypt. We are rather more informed of the quality of their tone. The tone of the KINNOR is described in the Bible as "sweet", "tender", "soft" — lyrical. The KINNOR was popular among the more cultured classes in Israel. The tone of the NEVEL was naturally stronger because the instrument was larger than the KINNOR, especially

14

after it had received a resonant body. According to Josephus, the NEVEL had twelve strings and the KINNOR ten. And from him we know that on the NEVEL they used to play with their fingers, whereas for the KINNOR they employed the plectrum. However, it is reported of King David that he played the KINNOR with his hand — which means fingers.

There were likewise two kinds of wind instruments, one of which was of no musical value, serving only for signaling purposes. To this class belongs the SHOFAR — ram's horn (in Assyrian "shapparu" — wild mountain-goat). It produces a few tones approximating c-g-c, or any other equivalent intervals, e.g., 1-5-1, 5-8-8, 1-4-8, and so on. The pitch, naturally, depends on the size of the SHOFAR and on the construction of its hollow. The instrument lends itself to the production of various rhythmical forms, from long notes to 32 shorts. But it is impossible to produce on it any melody whatsoever. Indeed, the Bible applies the terms "blowing" — tekia, meaning long notes, and "shouting" — terua, meaning short notes in staccato or tremolo form, but not "nagen" — producing musical tones. It was used chiefly for announcements and signals, not only in secular life, but also in religious ceremonies to call on the God to remind Him of His duties to His people, or to wake Him from His sleep. To the SHOFAR was also attributed the magic power of frightening and dispersing evil spirits and gods of the enemies who helped their people in battle. This belief was current among all primitive tribes, and it was likewise, accepted in Israel, as many Biblical stories and phrases testify. The blowing of the SHOFAR was even attributed to Yahve Himself, in order to frighten His enemies and to gather the scattered remnants of His people to His sanctuary. Thus, Zachariah says: "And the Lord God will blow the horn . . . The Lord of Hosts will defend them". Later, after the Second Destruction, the idea of blowing the "Shofar of Redemption" was transferred to the prophet Elijah, who is supposed to announce the coming of the Messiah.

15

During the latter part of the period of the Second Temple two types of SHOFAROTH were in use: the curved (male) ram's-horn and the straight (female) mountain-goat's horn. The latter form with a gold mouthpiece was used in the Temple on New Year, whereas the first form, with a silver-covered mouthpiece, was used on fast-days. After the destruction of the Temple no luxurious decorations were permitted.

The SHOFAR is the only instrument that retained its position in the Synagogue throughout the Medieval Ages up to the present day. On New Year's Day the SHOFAR was blown to remind God of His promise to Abraham, Isaac and Jacob, and especially of Isaac's sacrifice and of the ram that substituted for him. Later, Jewish philosophers, such as Saadia (tenth century), tried to interpret the custom of SHOFAR blowing by giving it a higher human idea, namely, that the sound of the SHOFAR stirs the heart to awe and reverence, and its purpose, therefore, is to remind us of our duties to God. In like manner, Maimonides speaks of this custom.

Of all musical instruments, it was the most unmusical of them, the SHOFAR, that was retained. Because of the religious reasons just mentioned, it was carried into the Synagogue. The term "tekia" of the Bible and Mishna was in the third century explained as a "long note", whereas concerning the term "terua" difference of opinion arose as to whether it meant short staccato notes or a tremolo on one sustained note. Finally, in the fourth century Rabbi Abahu in Caesarea (Palestine) made a compromise that both ways should be used, the staccato (shevarim) and the tremolo (terua), and thus it remained to this day.

From "Jewish Music in its Historical Development"
by A. Z. Idelsohn.

"The Voice of Israel"

An Expert on Jewish Music

THE Jewish people have created a special type of music, an interpretation of the spiritual and social life, of its ideals and emotions. In this music we find the employment of particular scales, motives, modes, rhythms, and forms, based on definite musical principles. These run through the music like a golden thread. Elements which do not conform to them have no hold on the music and consequently vanish from the body of that song.

Jewish song voices the spirit and the history of a people who for three thousand years has been fighting bitterly but hopefully for its existence, scattered in thousands of small groups among the millions having diverse tongues, cultures, and creeds. Its history has shown Jewish music always to be a genuine echo of Jewish religion, ethics, history, of the inner life of the Jews and of their external vicissitudes.

Wherever a Jewish group maintained Jewish spiritual culture, there Jewish song was cultivated. Wherever the group upheld its historic integrity, Jewish song flourished. It is a song created by the people of Semitic-Oriental stock, the same who created the other Jewish spiritual values and upheld them. It is the product of those imbued with the fundamental and genuine elements of that song. I have often recounted of musicians of foreign origin as well as of Jews without knowledge of Jewish music, who were unable to create music genuinely Jewish. That great song, born of Jews, preserved by them, and in the course of centuries developed by them, can continue to grow only through musicians, born Jews, reared in Jewish environment, steeped in Jewish folklore, and folksong, vibrant with Jewish emotion, sensitive to Jewish sorrows, joys, hopes, and convictions — faithful sons of Israel.

A. Z. Idelsohn.

Antiphonal Singing of the Jewish Sect
'The Therapeuts' — About 50 A.D. in Alexandria

AFTER a recitation, one of the members rises to sing a hymn in praise of the Lord. It is either a hymn, invented by himself, or by one of the poets of olden days, for many were the songs left by these poets, written in three-foot verse, to be sung at feasts of thanks-giving, at sacrificial ceremonies before the altar, and to be executed by a choir in unchanging metre, and in measured alternating strophes. At the close of the chant, to which members had given silent attention, men and women raise their voices to join in a final prayer.

After a simple and devout meal, they all rise to group themselves in the centre of the dining room — one group consisting of men, the other of women. Each group has a precentor. They sing paeans to God, in manifold metre and melody, now with the full, now in harmonic alternating choruses. After each of the choruses has given vent to its jubilant feelings, they join together in unison song, imitating the example of the Red Sea: the 135th Psalm where each verse ends with the chorus refrain: "Quoniam in misericordia ejus aeternam" at the time when the people had gathered — men as well as women — and, inspired by general elation, formed one chorus to sing the praise of the Lord, their Savior. Moses led the male, Miriam the female singers as they tuned in, responsively, first one, then the other and as the low voices of the men blended with the finer ones of the women, the Therapeuts succeeded in producing a truly harmonious symphony, entirely conforming to the rules of music.

Philo of Alexandria.

Jewish Origin of the Ancient Egyptian and Greek Music

A CLOSER investigation of Jewish melodies discloses that they are constructed tetrachordally, and modally. Tetrachordal: the melodies are enclosed in the span of a fourth, of which two combined, form the octave. It is striking that in the Hebrew melodies the modi change with the character of the pieces. Epic melodies (narratives from the Pentateuch) are Dorian; Lyrics (laments) are Phrygian; Jubilations, Lydian. And that too corresponds with the Greek usage. It is the same language of tones with the same signification. No wonder, then, that the Greeks ascribe the doctrine of the ethical, purifying power of music (the Katharsis) to the Egyptians.

Curt Sachs, "Music of Antiquity".

The Gregorian Chant is Linked to the Ancient Jewish Music

IT was in Palestine that we, for the first time, got a vivid conception of the music of the ancient Orient. Since Z. Idelsohn has demonstrated that melodies of the Jewish-Babylonian and the Jewish-Yemenite communities who, as early as the period of the Kings, seceded from the old tribes, — accurately corresponded with those of the present Catholic church, it necessarily follows that they have all of them faithfully preserved the treasure of melodies of the ancient Jewish cult and that we must form from them our conception of temple music.

Curt Sachs, "Music of Antiquity".

19

THE MIDDLE AGES

Cultivation of Music at the Court of Attila

IN the evening, the torches were lighted. Two barbarians, stepping up to Attila, and facing him, sang songs suitable to the occasion, wherein his victories and martial virtues were extolled. The guests sat quietly gazing at them; some of them enjoyed the poems, others, remembering their exploits, were elated, and others again bemoaned the loss of their wild courage, and wept because their bodies had grown feeble.

The Byzantine Priscus, on his visit to Hungary.

Propagation of the Gregorian Chant

OF all the peoples of Europe, it was the Germanic or Gallic races, who again and again endeavored to acquire the sweetness of the chant. But they were not in any way suited to accomplish this kind of singing, partly because they heedlessly added their own products to the Gregorian Chant, and partly because of their innate wildness. For, while with their powerful bodies, they combined fine, strong voices, they could not reproduce the melodies heard, in soft tones, but — owing to their toper-gullets — instead of singing them sweetly — roared them out, much as a heavy cart rolling down a mountain side would jolt, bump and rumble, and, instead of pleasing the senses, were deafening and confusing in sound.

Johannes Diaconus, in his Biography of Gregory I.

Report on the Instrumental Tone System
of the Middle Ages
The C Major Scale of the Organ

LET it be known that there are only seven degrees in the melody of the voice. Virgil calls them "seven divisions of tones", and the last is of the same quality as the first. Therefore the lyres, as well as the rottas (kind of a harp) have seven strings. On these, as well as on other instruments, the alphabet goes no further than the first seven letters: c d e f g a b. Of these seven, four — namely d e f g — are the final tones of all songs. Those of the first and second tone close on d; those of the third and the fourth on e; of the fifth and sixth on f; of the seventh and eighth on g. And if a melody descends from its tonic to the fifth and ascends to the ninth degree, so that its range is up to thirteen (as in the antiphone, on the first tone, Cum fabricator mundi), — there must be added over all of them the first six of the whole alphabet: c d e f g a, and below this, the last three, which makes sixteen since older musicians considered fifteen strings to be sufficient.

Notker Labeo (died 1022)
(Gerbert, Scriptores, I, 96, ff).

Organum

THE organum consists of voices of various timbres and keys, which, now, separated from each other, in wide intervals, move in a perfectly measured relation, and, following rational rules of music, conformant to the various church modes, now come together, thus forming a natural pleasing concord.

Scotus Erigena (about the middle of the
ninth century) in
"De Divisione Naturae".

THE MIDDLE AGES

"De Harmonia Institutione"

CONSONANCE is the logical harmonious mixture of two tones, which can only be brought about when two tones, stemming from different sources, form a concord, i.e., when the voice of a boy and that of a man sing together, or as in the so-called organum.

Hugbald, Monk in the Monastery St. Amand sur l'Elnon, Flanders, around 900.

Another Treatise on the Organum

THE Diaphonia or Organum, as is well known, is based on the consonance of the fourth, inasmuch as two voices moving together laterally, retaining this same interval, finally mingle. This brought about the following rules:

First rule: that tone for tone these voices preserve the interval of a fourth.

Second rule: that at the close of all the melodic sections, the individual voices meet on one and the same tone,—namely there, where the end of a phrase takes place on the final tone of the scale or on one of its neighboring tones, be it the upper or lower second. But in order that the voices may properly conjoin, at the close, a third rule must be followed, i.e.: wherever at such intervals (interpunctuations) at the main part, or the cutting in, the main voice descends to the closing tone (or to one of the above mentioned neighboring tones), the accompanying voice (the organum) must not go lower than the tone which forms the lower second of the final tone. Furthermore it must be noted, that we distinguish between a middle, a higher and a lower organum. The middle organum moves around

25

the final tone; the high one around the upper fifth; the low one around the lower fourth. All three are justified. Should it happen that an organum must be set into thirds and seconds because the interval of the fourth cannot be used, then the result would be an irregular organum. The organum, at all times, requires a careful well-measured tempo, and can well be used for church music.

From the "Cologne Tract de Organo"
(10th century).

Musical Tract of a German Minnesinger

READ nineteen tones by Guido's hand
Of hexachords consisting.
Eight church tones therefrom were found,
Drawn from harmony of spheres.
These master well and quickly.
The single note sounds simple
But wondrous rings when multiple,
When three and four enter the ring,
The shells of heaven are singing.
If this advice you follow well
Your road will e'er be sure and simple. .
Of course, the practicus wiil laugh,
And spite of me criss-cross will write.
Beware of false repeating!
And in correct cadenza ever close!
And also in the middle parts
To rules show proper reverence.

Heinrich von Meissen, called
Frauenlob, (died 1318)

English Origin of Polyphonic Music

T HE Britons do not sing in unison, like the inhabitants of other countries, but in many different parts. So that, when a company of singers among the common people meets to sing as is usual in this country, as many different parts are heard as there are performers, who all at length unite in consonance, with organic sweetness. In the northern parts of Great Britain, beyond the Humber, on the borders of Yorkshire, the inhabitants use the same kind of symphonious harmony; except that they only sing in two parts: the one murmuring in the bass, and the other warbling in the acute or in the treble. Nor do these two peoples practice this kind of singing so much by art as by habit, which has rendered it so natural to them, that neither in Wales—where they sing in many parts—nor in the north of England—where they sing in two parts—is a simple melody ever well sung. And, what is still more wondrous, their children, as soon as they attempt using their voices, sing in the same manner. But as not all the English sing in like manner, but only those of the north, I believe they had taken this art at first, like their language, from the Danes and Norwegians, who used frequently to invade, and thus to occupy, for a long time together, those parts of the island.

Giraldus Cambrensis: "Descriptio Cambriae"
(12th century).

Early English Organ Playing

I T is miraculous, how with all this, and with the great rapidity of fingers, they could keep the music so well-proportioned, and how, with great art, despite the many winding melodies and intricate runs, perfect harmony was obtained, which is

27

arrived at by a suave rapidity as well as by retaining the even in the uneven, and the single beat intact in the many.

"Descriptio Cambriae" (*12th century*).

Medieval Teaching of Phrasing

IT is of the utmost importance, in the study of singing, to know how the notes are combined. For, as in language, generally two or three or four letters, a-mo, tem-plum,—so in music also one single tone sung, or two, three or four combined, form a unit which we can designate as a musical syllable. And as a single syllable, or two or three or four, form an integral part of speech: a word, a succession of one or two or more musical syllables (f.i. the seconds, fourths, or fifths,) form a musical phrase.

"Musicae Artis Disciplina"
(*12th century*).

Ars Antiqua — Ars Nova

England as the Model for French Music
of the Middle Ages

Tapissier, Carmen, Caesaris,
N'a si pas si longtemps si bien chantèrent
Qu'ils esbahirent tout Paris,
Et tout ceaux qui les frequentèrent,
Mais onques joue ne dechantèrent,
En melodie de tels chois,
Le m'ont dit cela qui les hantèrent,
Que Guillaume Dufay et Binchois,
Car ils ont nouvelle pratique

De faire frisque concordance,
En haulte et en basse music
En fainte, en pause, et en nuance,
Et ont pris de la contenance
Angloise et ensuis Dunstable
Pour quoi merveilleuse playsance
Rend leur chant joyeux et stable.

Tapissier, Carmen and Caesaris
Have of late so well sung
That they have charmed all of Paris,
And all who them have haunted.
But ne'er before has such a choice
Of melody rung out (so I've been told
By them who them have heard)
As of Guillaume Dufay and Binchois.
Of a new mode the've taken hold
To make a frisk concordance,
In music high, in music low,
In fainte*, in pause, and in nuance.
Of English music too they've taken count
And Dunstable's marvelous plaisance,
Which their music renders now
So joyous and so stable.

Martin le Franc (*about* 1440)
in "Le Champion des Dames".

Inscription on the Grave of John Dunstable

JOHN Dunstable, an Astrologer, a Mathematician, a Musician and What not . . .

Musicus hic Michalus alter, novusque Ptolomeus
Junior ac Athlas, supportans robote celos,

* Musica ficta (Chromatic, use of accidentals).

Pausat sub cinere, melior vir de muliere
Nunquam natus erat; vicii quia labe carebat
Et virtutibus opes possedit vincus omnes.
Cui exoptetur sic optandoque precetur
Perpetuis annis celebratur fama Johannis
Dunstapil, in pace requiescat, et hic sine fine.

Here lie the ashes of a musician, who was another Michael, a new Ptolomeus. Like Atlas, by his might, he upheld the heavens. No better son was ever born to a mother, for he lived ever free from faults or guilt; all gifts of virtue were bestowed on him. If love followed him in life, may a prayer go down to posterity, may the ages forever laud the name of John Dunstable, Rest in Peace. May your fame on earth be without end.

John of Whethamstede after
"Weever's Funeral Monument" (1631)

A Medieval Poet on Music

ME thoughte thus, that hyt was May,
And in the dawninge, ther I lay,
Me mette thus in my bed all naked,
And loked forth, for I was waked,
With smale foules, a grete hepe,
That had afrayed me out of slepe,
Thorgh noise, and swetnesse of her songe.
And as me mette, they sat amonge
Upon my chambre roof wythoute,
Upon the tyles all aboute;
And songen everych in hys wise
The moste solempne servise
By noote, that ever man, I trowe,
Had herd. For somme of hem songe lowe,

Somme high, and al of oon acorde.
To telle shortly at oo word,
Was never herd so swete a steven,
But hyt hadde be a thyng of heven,
So mery a soun, so swete entewnes,
That, certes, for the toune of Tewnes,
I nolde but I had herd hem synge,
For al my chambre gan to rynge,
Thorgh syngynge of her armonye;
For instrument nor melodye
Was no-her her yet half so sweet,
Nor of acorde ne half so mete,
For ther was noon of hem that feynede
To synge, for eche of hem hym peynede
To fynde out mery crafty notys;
They ne sparede not her throtys.

> *Geoffrey Chaucer from the*
> *"Boke of the Duchesse"*

English Origin of the *"Ars Nova"*

A
ND it so happens, that in our time, the possibilities of
music have had so wonderful a growth, because it seems to
be a new art, which, calling it by its name "Ars Nova", from
all accounts has its source and origin in England, where Dunstable has of late emerged as its leader. Contemporary with
him were Du Fay and Binchois, in Gallia, and their immediate
descendants were the moderns Okeghem, Busnois, Regis, and
Caron, the most prominent masters of music that I have ever
heard.

> *Tinctoris in "Proportionale musices editum*
> *de magistro Joanne Tinctori"*
> (about 1445-1511).
> *(Coussemaker, Script. IV).*

The Blind Organist Francesco Landini

W HEN Francesco was old enough to understand the sound of a melody, he at once began to practice music seriously, first with the voice, then on string instruments and the organ. Although he could not see he made astounding progress on all musical instruments and played with such skill that the lack of eyesight was never perceived. He proceeded with great sweetness and artistry to play the organ, his hands moving with greatest rapidity, but always keeping correct time,—so that he soon, to the astonishment of every one, by far excelled all organists ever known. This must be reported, although it seems incredible.

The musical instrument, the organ, is composed of quite a number of pipes. The interior is constructed with great art, and suited to many purposes, because of exceedingly delicate vertical tubes; furthermore, because of the hollow interior of the body, the upright part of which—if but moved a hair's breadth, is at once out of order, so that, when wind is blown into the body by means of bellows, a roaring dissonance of sounds is emitted. If, however, everything required for order and structure, is in its right place, the instrument has a sub-dued tone, which remains flawless, if the player observes the consonances correctly. Then, everything has been avoided that has caused the dissonant noise.

And what is more, Francesco played the lyre, limbuta, quinterna, rubeba, the pan-pipe, and every other instrument excellently. For everything that emits sweet sound he showed great zeal, vying with the instruments that are used with the mouth, in manifold ways. Adding to their sound that of the human voice, he has invented from both tone sources a third mixed art of music which brought joy to every one.

Filippo Villani on Francesco Landini in
"Liber de civitatis Florentiae famosis civibus".

THE RENAISSANCE

"Noblesse Oblige"

A courtier must also be a musician; he must be able to sing by sight, and must be familiar with various instruments. The loveliest and most artistic music can be performed by a string quartet; on the other hand, keyboard instruments are more perfect on account of the harmony of the consonances and the ease with which many pieces can be executed, filling the soul with the charm of music. The courtier should not pursue his musical pleasures in the presence of non-aristocrats, or of the masses. Let him cultivate his music in a small but congenial circle, particularly in the presence of ladies, the sight of whom, will make him more susceptible to the beauty of music.

Much more beautiful than just ordinary singing (more-part singing) is the song to the viol because all the loveliness is consigned to but one voice, and it is with greatest attention that the fine performance and the melody is listened to, because the ear is not engaged by more than this one and only voice. Besides this every little mistake is more noticeable, which is not the case when many sing together and one is helping the other. Most of all do I like to hear the Recitativo which lends to the text such beauty and effect and is simply unique accompanied by the viol.

Baldassare Castiglione in his
"Il Corteggiano"
Florence, 1528.

Advice to a Future Organist

INTABULATE the works of prominent men and continue to do so until you can easily play on all the keys, on the black as well as on the white, and in all the modes that are possible on the monochord. Although you should practice in all the modes, see that you become schooled in one that serves many purposes. And assign certain hours of the day, in which to play new ones; and others for playing those already tabulated, (so as not to forget them); and again other hours for practice of your hands.

> Juan Bermudo
> "Declaracion de instrumentos musicales", 1555.

A Man of the Renaissance Attacks "Gothic Music"

THE art of counterpoint has originated in olden times and among people (The Netherlanders) who were lacking in all culture and scholarship, and by their names alone proclaimed their barbarism (Obrecht, Okeghem, etc.).

All the arts declined because of the rage of the barbarians who overran Italy. In place of the beautiful, perfectly formed architecture of the old Romans, they introduced their barbaric Gothic art, until Filippo Brunelleschi instead of using the stupid German style, revived the old style of architecture, and Giotto as well resuscitated the lost old art of painting. Now music is experiencing a similar rebirth but it must be said, it is true, that we are somewhat late.

> G. B. Doni
> "De praestantia musicae veteris", 1647.

Aversion to the Rigid Polyphonic Forms

CAN you understand the peculiar obstinacy of the parallel and contrary fugues, that so often and so insistently are used in the contrapuntal forms, which therefore are called "Ricercari" and are a special field of instrumental music. They are mostly composed for four parts and without any relation to the text, for no other purpose than to have a wider scope to be more pleasing to the ear, by the various qualities of the tones, the chords, and the movement. The imitations of such a fugue, which is treated with so scrupulous a care, rests on nothing but the ambition of either the composer or the singer!

Vincenzo Galilei
Dialogo "Della musica antica et
della moderna"
Florence, 1581.

A Man of the Renaissance Prefers Ancient Music to "Modern"

LIKE all other arts and sciences, the antique music has perished, owing to the storms of war, and other unfortunate events, and so little light has been retained that much of its former excellence is held to be but a dream and a fable. Now, when the art of tones had been lost, one began to find rules and laws for the composition of singing with instruments, especially that of the organ; more particularly the joining of several arias together, as they are played on that instrument. Wherefore they borrowed those rules from the citharists and the organists.

This is quite in order when there is question only of flattering and gratifying the ear with chords. But it is deadly for sense and expression, for it only serves to make the song manifold and full-toned, which is not only sometimes but never in accordance with the intention of the poet or orator. There you find one singing the first syllable, and another the last;

they repeat words and syllables four to six times, one in heaven, the other on earth and — if there are more — in the abyss. They drag a single syllable through twenty and some times more notes, whereby they imitate at one time the twittering of the birds and, at another, the howling of dogs. And so the impudence of our time has made of music a frivolous courtesan. Therefore music of this kind will be scorned and despised by the understanding intelligent and highly admired by the unintelligent masses. Did not the divine Plato ordain that one play in unison and not polyphonically?

Completely absurd and ridiculous is the way with which they, according to their idea, do justice to the words of the poem: They depict in childish manner, i.e. by dotted and syncopated notes, the sound of sobbing. The crashing of the drums, the tone of the trumpet are what they imitate when describing a descent to Hades and the singers growl as though to scare little children. When they wish to say: "He soared to the stars," they screech as though suffering from a stomach ache. For words like "weeping, laughing, singing, screaming, noise, false illusion, hard chains, strict ties, rugged mountains, steep cliffs, cruel and beautiful one, etc." they have descriptive phrases. Had Isocrates or another great orator wished to pronounce any single word in a similar manner, the laughter and the angry displeasure of his listeners would have stopped him. In order to express truly and correctly the emotions of the soul, they do not even have to learn from great orators, they can learn it from any tragedy or comedy enacted by the actors. They should pay attention to the emphasis on the single word, whether the voice is to be high or low, the speech is to be slow or fast, and how the words are to be accented. They should carefully note how the prince speaks to the vassal, or with one who is petitioning him; how the angry, the hurrying one, the matron, the girl, the silly boy, how the courtesan, how the lover addresses his loved one in order to touch her heart; how the lamenting one, the screamer, the frightened one, the gay one, etc. behaves. For, even the animal has a voice with which to express pain, woe, or well-being.

> *Vincenzo Galilei*
> *"Dialogo della musica antica e*
> *della moderna" (1581).*

A Woman Composer of the Renaissance
(Laura Bovio of Bologna)

HOW many musicians have travelled from afar attracted by her reputation and her eminent qualities. Not only is she experienced in composition, but so accomplished on every instrument, and so inventive of rare fancies, and so wonderful in style, that she does not only conquer the heart but also makes the mind soar and one seems to be listening to the harmonies of angels.

Music — both instrumental and vocal — is practised in almost all the convents. In some of the convents the nuns sing so beautifully that their voices sound like heavenly music, and often the people of Milan go there in order to listen to it.

> *From the Preface to a Collection*
> *of Madrigals, 1583.*

Two Antagonistic Queens as Virginal Players

SIR James Melvil gives an account of a curious conversation he had with the Princess (Elizabeth), to whom he was sent on an embassy by Mary, Queen of Scots, in 1564. After Her Majesty had asked him how his Queen dressed? What the color of her hair was like? Whether that of hers was best?

Which of the two was fairest? And which of them was highest in stature?—she asked what kind of exercises she used. "I answered," says Melvil, "that when I received my dispatch, the Queen was lately come from the Highlands hunting; that when her more serious affairs permitted, she was taken up with the reading of history; that sometimes she recreated herself, playing upon the lute and virginal". Then Elizabeth asked, if she played well. I said: "Reasonably, for a Queen". The same day, after dinner, my Lord of Hunsden drew me up to a quiet gallery, that I may hear some music — but he said he must not avow it — and where I might hear the Queen play upon the virginal. After I had hearkened a while, I took the tapestry aside that hung before the door of the chamber, and seeing her head was toward the door, I entered within the chamber and stood a pretty space, hearing her play excellently well. But she left off immediately, as soon as she turned around and saw me. She appeared to be surprised to see me, and came forward, seeming to strike me with her hand; alleging she was not used to play before men, but, when she was solitary, to shun melancholy. She asked how I came there? I answered, as I was walking with Lord Hunsden, and we passed the chamber door, I heard such a melody as ravished me, whereby I was drawn in I knew not how; excusing my fault of homeliness as being brought up in the court of France, where such freedom was allowed; declaring myself willing to endure what kind of punishment Her Majesty should be pleased to inflict for so great an offense. Then she sat down low upon a cushion, and I upon my knees; but with her own hand she gave me a cushion to lay under my knee; which at first I refused, but she compelled me to take it. She inquired whether my Queen or she played best. In that I felt myself obliged to give her the praise.

"Sir James Melvil's Memoirs"
From Burney "A General History of Music", 1789.

Shakespeare's Praise of John Dowland
(1562 - 1626)

IF music and sweet poetry agree,
As they must need, the sister and the brother,
Then must the love be great, twixt thee and me,
Because I love the one, and thou the other.
Dowland to thee is dear, whose heavenly touch
Upon the lute doth ravish human sense;
Spenser to me, whose deep conceit is such,
As passing all conceit, needs no defense.
Thou lov'st to hear the sweet melodious sound
That Phoebus's lute, the Queen of Music makes,
And I, in deep delight am chiefly drowned,
When as himself to singing he betakes.
One god is god of both, as poets feign,
One might love both, and both in thee remain.

"Passionate Pilgrim"

Shakespeare on Music
I

FOR do but note a wild and wanton herd,
Or race of youthful and unhandled colts,
Fetching mad bounds, bellowing and neighing loud,
Which is the hot condition of their blood,
If they but hear perchance a trumpet sound,
Or any air of music touch their ears,
You shall perceive them make a mutual stand,
Their savage eyes turn'd to a modest gaze
By the sweet power of music; therefore the poet
Did feign that Orpheus drew trees, stones and floods;

41

Since nought so stockish, hard and full of rage,
But music for the time doth change his nature.
The man that hath no music in himself,
Nor is not moved with concord of sweet sounds,
Is fit for treasons, stratagems and spoils.
The motions of his spirit are dull as night
And his affections dark as Erebus.
Let no such man be trusted.

From "The Merchant of Venice".

II

Give me somme music. Now good morrow, friends.
Now, good Cesario, but that piece of song,
That old antique song we heard last night:
Methought it did relieve my passion much,
More than light airs and recollected terms
Of these most brisk and giddy paced times;
Come, but one verse.

From "Twelfth Night".

III

How oft, when thou my music playest,
Upon that blessed wood, whose motion sounds
With thy sweet fingers, when thou gently swayest
The wiry concord that mine ear confounds,
Do I envy those jacks, that nimble leap
To kiss the tender inward of thy hand
Whilst my poor lips, which should that harvest reap,
At the wood's boldness by thee blushing stand,
To be so tickled, they would change their state
And situation with those dancing chips —
O'er whom thy fingers walk with gentle gait —
Making dead wood more blest than living lips.
Since saucy jacks so happy are in this,
Give them thy fingers, me thy lips to kiss.

Sonnet to a Lady, playing the Virginal.

Giovanni Gabrieli Praises His Uncle Andrea

IF Andrea Gabrieli were not my uncle, I could, without fear assert that there have been few eminent painters and builders, and few tone masters and organists to equal him. I could praise his skill, his rare inventions, his new turns, his charming style of composing. I could recall the seriousness of art in his songs, but also their freshness and their loveliness. I could mention that his works so evidently manifest how unique he was in the invention of sounds, which express so perfectly the power of speech and thought. It was God's will to take him from this world to His Heavenly Joy, in the ripe, rich years of manhood, at a time when his mind was more alive than ever, and more rich in inventions of music. Many were the concerts, dialogues, and other compositions for voice and instruments, which he had carefully arranged for the use in high churches and academies, to present to you. Since I now wish to live as he lived and died, I dedicate these fruits of his art to you, Sir, and therewith fulfill his wish as well as satisfying my own.

From a letter of Giovanni Gabrieli to
Jacob Fugger in Augsburg, 1587.

THE BAROQUE PERIOD

Origin of The Opera

SOME kind of Cantilena, or melody, has been introduced in dramatic representations, at all times, either in the form of intermezzi (interludes), between the acts, or, occasionally, in the body and business of the piece. But it is still fresh in the memory of everyone, when the whole drama was first set to music, and sung from the beginning to the end; because anterior to the attempt of Emilio del Cavaliere, a Roman gentleman, extremely well versed in music, there seems to have been nothing of that kind undertaken that is worth mentioning. This composer published a drama at Rome in 1600, called "Dell'Anima e del Corpo". In the preface to which mention is made of a piece represented at Florence in 1588, at the nuptials of the Grand Duchess, in which were many fragments of his music; and where, likewise, after two years, was represented another drama set by him, called "Il Satiro".

It is necessary, however, to declare here, that those melodies are very different from such as are at present composed in what is commonly called "Recitativo" — being no other than arias full of contrivance, repetitions, echoes, etc., which are totally different from the true and genuine theatrical music, of which Signor Emilio could know nothing, for want of being acquainted with ancient authors and the usage of antiquity. It may therefore be said, that the first attempt at reviving theatrical music, after being lost for so many ages, was made at Florence, where so many noble arts have been recovered. This extraordinary event was brought about by the invention of recitatives which are now universally received, practiced, and preferred to the madrigal-style, in which the words are so utterly unintelligible.

The beginning of this century (1600), was the era of musical recitation on the public stage at Florence, though it had been used there in several private exhibitions before. There resided in that city, during these times, Signor Bardi de' Conti di Vernio, who was afterwards called to the service of Pope Clement VIII, by whom he was tenderly beloved, and made his Maestro di Camera. This most accomplished nobleman was particularly attached to the study of antiquity, and to the theory and practice of music, to which he had applied himself for many years so closely, that he became, for the time in which he lived, a correct and good composer. His house was the constant rendez-vous of all persons of genius, and a kind of flourishing academy where the young nobility often assembled to pass their leisure hours in laudable exercises and learned discourse: particularly on musical subjects, as it was the wish of all the company to recover that art of which the ancients related such wonders, as well as other notable inventions which had been ruined by the eruptions of barbarians.

During these discussions, it was universally allowed that, as modern music was extremely deficient in grace, and the expression of words,—it became necessary in order to obviate these objections, that some other species of Cantilena, or melody, should be tried by which the words should not be rendered unintelligible, nor the verse destroyed.

Vincenzo Galilei was at this time in some credit among musicians and, flattered with his reputation, pursued his musical studies with such diligence that, either by the help he received from others, or by the force of his own genius, he composed his work upon the abuse of modern music, which has since gone through two impressions. Animated by success, Galilei attempted new things, and assisted by Signor Giovanni, was the first to compose melodies for a single voice, having modulated that pathetic scene of Count Ugolino, written by Dante, which he sang himself very sweetly to the accompaniment of a viol. This essay certainly was very pleasing in general; however, there were some individuals who laughed at the attempt; notwithstanding which he set in the same style parts of the lamentations of Jeremiah, which were performed to a devout assembly.

At this time, Giulio Caccini Romano, a young, elegant and spirited singer, used to attend the meetings at the house of the Count di Vernio; and being seized with a strong passion for this kind of music, he studied it with great diligence; composing and singing to a single instrument, which was generally the theorbo, a large lute, played by Bardilla, who happened then to be at Florence. Caccini, therefore, in imitation of Galilei, but in a more beautiful and pleasing style, set many canzonets and sonnets, written by excellent poets, and not by such wretched scribblers as were usually employed before, and are still very frequently the favorites of musicians; so that he may be said to have been the first to see this error and to discover that the art of counterpoint will not alone complete the education of a musician, as is generally imagined; and he afterwards confessed, in a discourse prefixed to one of his works, that the conversations held at the Count del Vernio's were of more use to him than thirty years' study and exercise of his art. Here he likewise claims the merit of having first published songs for a single voice, which, indeed, had the greatest success. And it must be confessed, that we owe to him, in a great measure, the new and graceful manner of singing, which at that time spread itself all over Italy; for he composed a great number of airs which he taught to innumerable scholars, and among the rest to his daughter who became a famous singer and still continues very excellently in that capacity.

But not to defraud any one of his just praise, it is necessary to acknowledge in this place that Luca Marenzio, who flourished now at Rome, had brought the madrigal style to the highest degree of perfection, by the beautiful manner in which he made all the several parts of his compositions sing;

for before his time, if the harmony was full and masterly, nothing else was required.

In the recitative style, however, Caccini had a formidable rival in Jacopo Peri, a Florentine, who was not only a good composer but a famous singer, and performer on keyed instruments, having been taught by Christopher Malvezzi; and applying himself with great diligence and enthusiasm to this kind of singing, succeeded wonderfully and met with universal applause.

After the departure of Signor Bardi from Florence, Signor Jacopo Corsi became the patron of music and its professors, as well as of every other art and science, so that his house, during the remainder of his life, continued to be the retreat of the Muses and their votaries, of every country as well as of Tuscany. Ottavio Rinuccini was at this time united with him in the strictest bonds of friendship, which seldom is durable unless cemented by sympathetic affections; and being, as is well known, an excellent poet, whose works are to the last degree natural, full of grace, and pathòs, and, in a particular manner, calculated for music; as poetry and music are sister arts, he had an opportunity of cultivating both together, with equal success, and of communicating his discoveries and refinements to this illustrious assembly.

The first poem, set in this new way, and performed at the house of Signor Corsi, was "Dafne", a pastoral, written by Rinuccini, and set by Jacopo Peri and Caccini in a manner which charmed the whole city. Afterwards, other little fables and entire dramas were thus recited; but above all, the "Euridice" of Rinuccini, written and set to music for the royal nuptials of Maria de Medici's with the most Christian King Henry IV. The music of this drama, which was publicly produced at Florence, in the most splendid manner, was chiefly composed by Jacopo Peri, who performed a part in it himself, as in "Dafne" he had represented Apollo; the rest of the music was composed by Caccini, and the whole was exhibited in 1600,

50

in which year, and on the same occasion, was also performed the "Rape of Cephalus", in which the chief part was set by Caccini.

Great applause was likewise bestowed on "Ariadne", another dramatic production of Rinuccini, and clothed in suitable melody by Claudio Monteverde, at present Maestro di Capella to the Republic of Venice. He afterwards published the principal part of this production, which is "The Lamentation of Ariadne", and perhaps the most beautiful composition of this kind which our times have produced. Thus the original and true architects of this species of scenical music were Jacopo Corsi, and Ottavio Rinuccini, assisted by the three eminent artists above-mentioned, who had conferred great honor upon our city, as well as on the profession of music.

(In Charles Burney's Translation.)
G. B. Doni: "Della Musica Scenica", 1763.

Rebirth of the "Wagon of Thespis"

IN 1606, in Rome, at the performance of the opera "Carro di fideltà d'amore", by the Roman composer Paolo Quagliati, the stage, as in the days of Thespis, was a wagon, which carried the personnel, consisting of five singers and as many instruments, from street to street. A tremendous crowd followed the wagon and never grew tired of listening. Some assisted at the performance as often as five or six times; some even followed the wagon to its ten or twelve stopping places and never left it as long as it was in the streets.

Pietro della Valle:
"Discorso della Musica".

Dramatic Performance

*A scenic picture from Guarini's "Idropica", for which
Monteverdi set the prologue to music.*

(Mantua, June 2, 1608).

AFTER the cardinals, Princes and ambassadors were seated, the customary trumpet signal was given from the center
part of the stage. After the trumpets had sounded for the
third time, the great curtain suddenly opened. One saw clouds
that were constructed so artistically as to seem real. Beneath
them, waves were visible, surging back and forth, and from
them there gradually emerged the head of a woman. It was
Manto, — she who once founded Mantua. In slow measured
movements she arose and by this time the trumpets had ceased their playing. She reached a small island and, standing
there in the rushes, she sang to the accompaniment of instruments set up behind the scene, with such sweetness that
all her listeners were carried away.

> *Follino, Compendio delle sontuose feste fatte,
> anno MDCVIII, nella città di Mantova per le
> reali nozze del Serenissimo Principe D. Fran-
> cesco Gonzaga con la Serenissima Infanta Mar-
> gherita di Savoia.* (Mantua, 1608).

The Toccata

THIS style of music should not be subjected to ordinary
time any more than are the newer madrigals, in which the
time changes, and which are sung sometimes faster, sometimes slower, according to the sense of the words.

Toccatas of the day are rich in various kinds of passages, and manifold expressions, to which the measure should be adapted. The beginning must be played slowly in arpeggios, whereupon a faster measure can be taken at will. Understand me, reader, if you can. I do understand myself.

Girolamo Frescobaldi (1583-1643),
from a preface to a Collection of Toccatas.

Sonata and Canzona

"SONATA a sonando" (derived from sonare, i.e. sound) is thus called, because it is not executed by the human voice but by instruments, as are the canzones, of which very beautiful ones by Gabrieli and others (canzones and symphonies) can be found. But in my opinion there is this difference: the sonatas are set in a solemn and pompous manner and the canzones, having many black notes, are executed in rapid, gay and lively measure.

Michael Praetorius in "Syntagma Musicum"[1]

Coloraturas

MANY say that it is the bass that must be embellished, others again claim that it is the discant. It is my opinion that coloraturas should be added to all voices, but not always, only where it is suitable, each in its place, so that the coloratura is heard plainly and distinctly without allowing the composition to suffer. Only the vowels e or i should be colored, and never a, o, or u, nor should one do, as do some singers whose coloraturas sound gravely like the bleating of

[1] 1615-1620.

goats. Likewise, one should sing in an even voice, not allowing the voice to rise and fall, but emulate the style of the organ.

Herman Finkh
"Practica Musica", 1556.

The Latin Oratorio in Rome, 1639

THIS admirable enchanting music is only performed on the Fridays in Lent from three to six. The church is not quite so large as the Sainte Chapelle in Paris. In the back of the church there is a roomy choir with a very soft organ, agreeable to the singers. On both sides of the church, there are two small platforms for the most excellent instrument players. The singers began with a psalm in motet form, whereupon all the instruments played a magnificent symphony. Then the singers presented a story from the Old Testament, in the manner of a spiritual drama such as that of Susannah, Judith and Holophernes, David and Goliath. Each singer represented a character of history and pronounced his words with special emphasis. Thereupon one of the most famous preachers recited the exhortation, after the close of which the music of the Gospel of the day was recited, such as the story of the Samaritan, the woman of Canaan, of Mary Magdalen, of Lazarus, and that of the Agony of our Lord. The singers most admirably represented the various characters as described in the Gospel.

André Maugars: "Response faite à un curieux
sur le sentiment de la musique d'Italie".

Sacred Music in Rome, Anno 1639

AS regards instrumental music, this consisted of an organ, a harpsichord, a lyre, two or three violins, and as many lutes. At one time a viol, solely accompanied by the organ, was heard, later to be answered by another. Then all three played their different parts together after which all instruments joined in. Here a lute would variate on ten or twelve motives, of which each one was five or six bars long, and would do this in a thousand different ways, then again another would play the same, although deviating somewhat. In the antiphons, they executed excellent symphonies with one, two or three violins, and organ as well as a few lutes, in as much as they played certain airs in a dance rhythm, one instrument always answering the other.

André Maugars.

About the Origin of the Figured Bass

MANY were the reasons that caused me to set this type of concert. One of the most pronounced was the observation that, when a cantor wished to have three, two, or even one voice sing to the organ, he was obliged — realizing that there was a lack of compositions of this kind — to select one, two, or three voices from an existing five-, six-, seven-, or even eight-part motet. These parts were in closest connection with the others by means of imitations, inversions, and cadences, and also many other matters, which are in the nature of all such compositions. They were themselves, therefore, full of long and often repeated pauses, without proper cadences and without pleasing melody. They also showed very little melodious and tasteful development. In addition, there was the constant interruption of the words, which in certain parts were either entirely lacking, or were set together in a most inappropriate way. All this was bound to make this sort of song, incomplete, tiring, without charm,—yes, obnoxious to the listener, to say nothing of the inconvenience for the singers in the rendering of the song. I have long pondered over these difficulties, have tried to overcome these striking evils, and, thanks to God, I believe I have, by the composition of these my concerts, at last found the right means.

It is up to the organist to play the bass part and to use predominantly his left hand. If he desires to put the right hand into action as well, to ornament a cadenza, or any other embellishments, which are in place, he must do so in such a way, that the singing is not covered thereby, or that the singer is not confused by too rapid tone successions.

The middle parts can be executed on the organ with hands and feet. The singing voices, but not so much the accompaniment, are to beware of parallel fifths and octaves.

Lodovico Viadana
"Cento Concerti" (1602)

Monteverdi is Pretty Well Off

I DO not live like a rich man, but not like a poor one either. Above all, I am assured of an income until my death. My salary is paid regularly every two months; it is even sent into my house, if I hesitate to go and get it. In the Chapel, I am given full power to do as I please. It isn't even my duty to do the training, for that is the task of the Vice-Maestro. Beside all this, Venice is the most beautiful city in the world. If I am willing to exert myself, I can get additional 200 ducats to my fixed salary.

From a letter by Monteverdi,
September 10, 1627.

Monteverdi is Criticized by a Reactionary

Y OUR new rules are not very pleasing to the ear, and it could not be otherwise, since they infringe on the good old precepts, which are partly based on experience, the mother of all teaching, partly founded on a close observation of nature, and partly have been substantiated by the intellect. We must maintain that these new rules are distorted and unnatural, contrary to the essence of harmony, and alien to the purpose of the artist, which is to give pleasure. And the harshness of your discords stands out, unprepared and undisguised as though intended to agonize the ear. If this be not your intention, there is nothing left for you to do but to turn back to the ways of the old masters, because, following your present course, you will never attain your purpose, so long as concord and discord do not change their character, and their peculiarities towards each other. It is true, the old masters could not change discords into concords. The manner, however, in which they developed discords from concords and, on the other hand, dissolved discords into concords, caused their harshness to disappear. Yes, even to flatter the ear was thus made possible. But coming out abruptly, without any preparation, they cannot possibly have a good effect. How to use dissonances has been taught by Willaert, Cyprian de Rore, Palestrina, Merulo, Gabrieli, and Lasso. But what do these reformers care about that? They believe to have done enough, when they just hope to please the ear. The fools. Day and night, they endeavor to try out the effect of their phrases on their instruments crammed with dissonances. They do not realize that they are being fooled by their instruments,—they are satisfied to have produced a great noise of tones, a jumble of unrelated matter, and mountains of imperfections.

Artusi in "Della imperfettione della musica moderna" (1600-1603)

Monteverdi's "Stile Concitato"
("Tancredi e Clorinda")

THE principal emotions of mankind are three: anger, equanimity, prayer or humility. Of this we are assured by the great thinkers, and this is also confirmed by the nature of the human voice, with its high, low, and middle pitch. It is further corroborated in the art of tones, with its three-fold expression of soft, calm, and agitated. I weighed this carefully, and found in the works of past ages examples of the soft and calm, but not of the agitated manner, a form of expression Plato speaks about in his book on the "Republic", when he describes the tone and expression of a brave man, active in war-like pursuits and other activities of violence. Now I very well realize that our feelings are mostly stirred by contrasts, and that to arouse emotions of the heart and soul, is the aim of all good music. Boethius asserts: "The art of tones has been given us either to ennoble or to degrade the customs of a people." I therefore, with great zeal, endeavored to restore this manner of expression, and took into consideration words of all the great philosophers, that for war-like, violently agitated dances, a quick measure should be used; a slow measure however, for opposite conditions. I gave special attention to the continued quarter note: it seemed to me to correspond with the spondee when executed by an instrument. When, however, I split them into sixteenths ·and correlated them with an angry and contemptuous speech, this simple experiment proved to me that I had found what I was seeking, even though the pace of the speech could not keep up with the rapidity of the musical instrument. In order, however, to improve my experiment, I turned to the divine Tasso who, with supreme truth and aptitude, finds words to express any passion he wishes to depict. In his description of the battle of Clorinda with Tancred, I found what I needed. For here I could in music give expression to war-like action as well as to prayer, yes, even to death. In the year 1624, I presented for hearing my musical treatment of this narrative in the home of Geronimo Mocenigo, a noble gentleman, who held high posts in the illustrious Republic of Venice, and who is my special patron and protector. Present were most illustrious men of our noble Venice, and I received praise and applause. And since I had succeeded in producing an imitation of anger, I continued my research with still greater ardor, and created many sacred works and chamber music which not only did the artists praise by word of mouth, but which, because of their successful style, they copied in their own works, to my great joy and honor.

> *Monteverdi, in his preface to the*
> *"Madrigals", 1636.*

Viennese Choristers in the Sixteenth and Seventeenth Centuries

Vienna, 1612.

SINCE our "Kapellmeister" or others, are to give board and lodging to our Chapel Boy Singers, he shall receive for each boy, for food, for lodging, salt, light, laundry, mending expenses, barber, bath money, and similar items, the monthly sum of 4 florins 50 kreuzer, but the boys must, as is seemly, have as much food and drink as they need. On meat days three, and on fish days four good courses, and during the week three times roast, well kept and clean, and soup and meat should not be given for two, but for one course only, and meat and cabbage too, are to be counted as one course.

Then the drinking of wine shall be regulated: namely, each boy is to have with his meal one and a half pitcher of wine, but let it be such a wine, that will not make the boy sick, and for this he, the Kapellmeister is supposed to be responsible.

And also, the boys habitually should have a soup each morning, and later in the day some bread, which shall be served to them if they want it. Added to this, there is to be allowed one thaler monthly, making 14 Gulden a year, for six new shirts (40 kr. each) and for three pairs of pants (woolen in the winter, and leather in the summer); also two fustian jerkins (doublets), woolen in winter, the one for summer, however, without wool, together with price of making them at 6 florins each, and also a pair of shoes at 15 kr. for every month should be given to them. Paper, pen and ink, and other articles needed for writing should also be given, and 6 kr. a month be allowed for this expense.

Vienna, State Archives:
The Imperial Court Music Chapel in 1543-1612.

The "Clown" in the Baroque Opera

AND be the operas ever so fine,
Without Harlequin they'll never shine,
Nor ever will subsist;
For fools will ever want to see
Themselves in effigy.

Balthasar Feind, Hamburg, 17th Century.

Corelli in Naples

AT the time when Corelli enjoyed the highest reputation, his fame having reached the court of Naples, and excited a desire in the King[1] to hear him perform, he was invited by

[1] Presumably the Austrian Vice-King Martinitz.

order of His Majesty, to that capital. Corelli, with some reluctance, was at length prevailed on to accept the invitation; but, lest he should not be well accompanied, he took with him his own second violin and violoncello. At Naples he found Alessandro Scarlatti and several other masters who entreated him to play some of his concertos before the King. This he for some time declined, his whole band not being with him, and there being no time, he said, for rehearsal. At length, however, he consented, and in great trepidation performed the first of his concertos. His astonishment was great to find that the Neapolitan band executed his concertos almost as accurately at sight as did his own band, after repeated rehearsals, when they had almost got them by heart. "Si suona", he said to his second violin, "si suona a Napoli."

After this, being again admitted into His Majesty's presence, and asked to perform one of his sonatas, the King found one of the Adagios so long and dry, that, being tired, he quit the room to the great mortification of Corelli. Weeks later he was again desired to lead in the performance of a Masque composed by Scarlatti which was to be executed before the King. This he undertook, but from Scarlatti's little knowledge of the violin, the part was somewhat awkward and difficult: in one place it went up to F, and when they came to that passage, Corelli failed and was unable to execute it. He was all the more astonished to hear Petrillo, the Neapolitan leader, and the other violinists, perform that which had baffled his skill. A song succeeded this; it was a song in C minor, which Corelli led off in C major. "Ricomminciamo" said Scarlatti goodnaturedly. Still, Corelli persisted in the major key until Scarlatti felt obliged to call out to him and set him right. So mortified was poor Corelli with this disgrace and with the general bad figure he imagined he had made, here in Naples, that he stole back to Rome in silence.

It was soon after this that a hautbois player whose name the author could not recollect, acquired such applause in Rome, that Corelli, disgusted said he would never play again in public. All these mortifications and the success of Valentini whose concertos and performances — though infinitely inferior to those of Corelli — had become fashionable, threw him into such a state of melancholy and chagrin, as was thought — said Geminiani — to have hastened his death.

(Report of Francesco Geminiani (died 1762)
to Burney).
From Burney: "General History of Music"

A London Advertisement (1690)
"To all Lovers of the Best Sort of Musick"

Men say the times are strange. 'Tis true:
Cause many strange things hap to be.
Let it not then seem strange to you
That here one strange thing more you see.

THAT is, at Devereux-Court, next the Grecian coffee-house, at the Temple back-gate, there is a deaf person that teacheth musick to perfection; who by reason of his great age of 77 is come to town with his whole stock of rich musical furniture, v. instruments and books to put off (to whomsoever delights in such choise things) ; for he hath nothing of lighter vain, but all substantial, and solid musick. Some particulars do here follow.

1) There is a late invented organ which (for private use) excells all other fashioned organs whatever, and for which, substantial-artificial reasons will be given, and (for its beauty) it may become a nobleman's dining room.

2) There belongs to it a pair of fair large-sized, consort

62

viols, chiefly filled and suited for that, or consort use; and 'tis great pity they should be parted.

3) There is a Pedal Harpsicon (the absolute best sort of consort harpsicons that has been invented); there being in it more than 20 varieties, most of them to come in with the foot of the player, without the least hindrance of play (exceedingly pleasant), and

4) Is a single Harpsicon.

5) A new invented instrument, called a Dyphone, v. a double lute; it is both theorbo and French-lute compleat; and as easy to play upon as any other lute.

6) Several other Theorboes Lutes and Viols, very good.

7) Great store of choise collections of the works of the most famous composers, that have lived in these last hundred years, as Latin, English, Italian, and some French.

8) There is the publisher's own Musick's Monument; some few copies thereof he has still by him put off; it being a subscribed book, and not exposed to common sale. All these will be sold at very easy rates, for the reasons afore said; and because (indeed) he cannot stay in town longer than four months (exactly).

If any be desirous to partake of his experimental skill in this high-noble art, during his stay in town, he is ready to assist them; and (haply) they may obtain that from him, which they may not meet withal elsewhere. He teacheth these five things, v. the Theorbo, the French-Lute, and the Viol, in all their excellent ways and uses; as also composition, together with the knack of procuring invention to young composers, (the general and greatest difficulty they meet withal) this last thing not being attempted by any author (as he knows of) yet may be done; though some has been so wise (or otherwise) to contradict it.

Sed experientia docuit.

Any of these five things may be learned so understandingly, in this little time he stays (by such general rules as he gives, together with Musick's Monument, written principally to such purposes) as that any aptly inclined may (for the future) teach themselves without any other help.

Advertisement of Thomas Mace, Author of
"Musick's Monument" (1676).

Old German Droll Stories About Bad Habits

Hoffmeister: Since the gentlemen are telling droll stories about the habits of musicians, I will add my bit. I knew an organist, who, when he played, not only did so with mouth wide open, but so twisted and wriggled his body, that a woodcarver would surely have wanted to carve such a figure. For which reason he did not dare to play in the presence of a pregnant woman, for fear that she might, after seeing his horrible monkey-like contortions, give birth to some monstrosity, or might even have a miscarriage.

Demodocus: My dear Herr Hoffmeister, this reminds me of another true story, also about an organist with his mouth wide open, and this is the tale: At Corinth, there lived an excellent organist, who was often called upon to play at the home of the residing prince. After he had played there several times without asking for his pay, his wife at last grew impatient with him, for his faint-heartedness, and said: he had in all other respects a big mouth, and a wide open one, but when it came to opening it, when needed, there was nobody home. Other musicians always received their full pay, but he hardly ever got anything. If, for once he would open his mouth, he too might get something. The organist took no offense at this well-meant correction and accepted it patiently, and was determined to follow his wife's advice. So, when the prince once again was entertaining guests and he was called upon to play on the spinet,—noticing that the prince was in a good mood,—he opened his mouth as wide as he could, while playing, so that the prince, taking note of this, and thinking his behavior ludicrous and strange, sent a page to inquire what had happened to him and whether his mouth had become unhinged. The organist replied that he could not disclose the truth to any one, but to His Illustrious Highness himself. Whereupon the prince sent for him, and ordered him to give an explanation for his extraordinary "mouthal" gymnastics. The organist hereupon related, how his wife bitterly berated him for having so often come home without his gratuity and had advised him, if he were again called upon to play, to open his mouth, so as to get something. Well, he had done so now, and was hoping for some result. This pleased the prince and he ordered his secretary to bring fifty ducats "to close the organist's mouth." Which was done at once.

Euclides: When I was a boy, and still went to school, I knew an organist, who, when he played the figured bass, nodded his head at each note. This certainly was a ludicrous enough sight.

Hoffmeister: I saw a similar sight in Agrigentum, in Sicily, where a violinist shook his head at each note, which was particularly droll when he played fast.

Demodocus: I knew one, who, when he had to climb up on his violin, higher than the discant A, would snap at it, as a dog snaps at a fly buzzing around his head.

Euclides: These episodes all refer to organists, and we must not forget the cantors. I know one who cannot sing unless he holds his left hand to his cheek.

Hoffmeister: And I saw one at Syracuse, who had a handkerchief wound around his baton, to beat time, and appeared to be waving a flag.

Demodocus: As there are many whimsical fellows among all men, so among the cantorists. One of these used to delight us, for, whenever he wished to be effective, he went to a corner and shouted into it.

Euclides: If the gentlemen had seen the custodian at Portabella, they would undoubtedly have had even more to laugh at. Since, when he sang he tightly closed his eyes, opened his mouth so wide as to almost touch his ears, and got his face full of wrinkles. And when he looked into his song book, he would open his eyes wide, like a calf, then suddenly shut them tightly again, thus giving himself such a funny appearance that even one suffering from gout, would have to laugh.

Phrynis: These and other bad habits are ugly enough, but easier to bear, than when a musician, while thinking highly of consonances, in life combines them with dissonances of deceit, trickery, intrigue, envy, cringing, arrogance, debauchery, harlotry, and other vices.

Wolffgang Caspar Printz von Waldthurn
"Phrynidis Mytilinaei, or Satiric Composer's
3rd part" (1696)

Musica Terrestris et Coelestis

CHRONICLERS of history declare that there is a cave in England, under a mountain, and that on the top of that cave, there is a hole. Now, when the wind blows into this cavern and strikes it, a sound, resembling a cymbal, is heard, sweetly musical and keeping perfect time. When, in the forest the leaves are stirred by a sudden wind, it sounds as though birds were singing. Those who have travelled through Persia, relate that high up in the mountains, there are three hills, where in olden times the wise men were supposed to have lived. The first of these gives out thundering reverberations, resembling the howling of thousands of people, coming from the skies. When ar-

PLATE 1.—Chinese Zither and Lute

PLATE 2.—Feast of the Roses, British India

PLATE 3.—Aulos Player and Tympanon Playing Woman from Campana, "Opere Antiche in Plastica"

PLATE 4.—Ancient Roman Ballet, Marble Relief from the time of the Roman Empire found in a tomb of Via Appia [Two Dancers, Negresses, Swing Rattles]

rived at the center hill, there is still greater turmoil. But from the third, there arises a tumult, resembling the rejoicing at a victory gained. And now, turning from the great deep sea of tones and voices of a resounding nature, we reach a harbor where nothing remains for us, but to raise our eyes and voices heavenward, and with songs of praise give thanks to the Highest Leader, who allows us to sing so joyfully in praise of the works of His Hands. He has led me into the celestial choir of His never ending and immeasurable loveliness and has filled my heart and ear with a pleasing surging, so that little is wanting and I have forgotten the vain pleasures of life, the swarming wild cave holes, and the caverns of a transitory world, and will no longer listen to them. All we need is that our souls be drawn heavenward and become worthy, after this vain and decrepit life, to join in the sweet heavenly chorus, above which there is nothing higher. Which will happen if we serve God with fear and true love, unceasingly and ever conscious of the terrifying celestial trumpets and bugles, when it will be said: Arise ye dead and come to be judged. . . .

Athanasius Kircher: "Phonurgia", 1684.

Healing by Music

The Opinion of a "Baroque Man"

THE tarantula is a small venomous animal, a vermin, or an Apulian spider, filled to the brim with poison. He who is bitten by this spider can only be cured by music and dancing. Melancholic people or those who have been bitten by a tarantula, filled with an especially great amount of the poison, are cured by loud and sounding drums and tympani or other similar instruments rather than by more subtle ones. Since this fluid is very thick and tough and the physical system is regulated by dampness, great force from outside is required to break up the poison. Choleric and bilious people and those rich in blood, are more easily cured by cytharas, violins, lutes, harpsichords and other sweetly sounding instruments, because of their thin and more easily dissolved life stream.

For it is written and said, that this experiment has been made in the city of Andria, in the ducal palace, in the presence of one of our Patres and the entire Court: the Duchess herself, to spread this miracle of nature, had a search made for such a tarantula or spider and had it placed on a small vertical piece of wood and put into a dish filled with water, and then the cythara players were sent for. The spider, at first made no move at the sound of the cythara music, but as soon as an evenly proportioned certain tune was played, the little animal began to move its feet and to jump, and not only did it act as though about to dance, but actually did so, jumping according to the music. When the cytharist stopped playing, the spider at once stopped dancing. The players, being paid by the authorities and having orders to play for the miserably unhappy, inquired — in order to obtain a quicker and easier cure — just where the spider had been, and what the color of the spider was, which had injured the patient. Whereupon they would go to said place, where the tarantulas in great numbers were spinning their webs. When these jolly medici and players were heard with their instruments and music, and when they played all kinds of songs, one could, to one's great astonishment, see, how at times one kind, and then another of the spiders, would dance and jump, while the rest remained silent. When they saw the kind whose color had been designated by the patient, start to dance, they were sure they had found the right tone and melody with which to cure the patient. And they say that the sick person is infallibly helped when they play the right tone and melody.

Athanasius Kircher, "Phonurgia"

A Great Musician of the Baroque Period
Satirizing His Time
"Maestro" Caraffa — a Musical Quack —
Tries to Fool Honest Musicians

CARAFFA, a German with an Italian name, had been carrying instruments for various famous musicians in Italy. So, at home he tried to make the people believe that the spirit of the Lord was within him, doublefold, and that he had every reason to make himself known to the world. As he well knew that he had no prospects of a position either in Rome or Venice, where the best artists are living, he came to Germany, in the hope of making his fortune there. He arrived in a famous residential city. It was the custom there for musicians to gather once or twice a week, to improve themselves in their profession, and also to bring harmony to their souls,—of which people of this class are most greatly in need. He heard from the inn-keeper, on the day of his arrival, that the Court Chapel was to meet that very night, in a house on the market place. Caraffa, by messenger, sent them word that a foreign musician had arrived from Italy, who begged for the honor of appearing in their famous collegium as a humble listener. They told the messenger, to give their humblest respects to the foreign gentleman, and that they would be greatly honored by his visit. But they inquired of the messenger, before letting him depart, whether his master was a born Italian. He said he didn't know, but since he spoke in a very foreign manner, it would be logical to assume that he hadn't eaten his childhood pap in Germany. After the messenger had left, the two, whose turn it was to furnish the music for that evening, wanted to run back home, to fetch their finest sonatas and concertos, so as not to disgrace themselves before the foreigner. For they were of that

69

class, who consider a composer or any other musician who has not been in Italy, a booby.

Now we must admit that music, particularly as to style of performance, is to a high degree flourishing in Italy. But no one will deny that Italy has many a know-nothing, and Germany many a master. For the climate can not make such a difference. Take for instance, fruits. We get fruit from foreign countries, lemons, citrons and oranges, that is not as good as it is in Italy. . . .

As our two musicians had rushed down the stairs, and went to the door, meditating on which of their music pieces would be most suitable, they ran into the foreign musician, already arrived. What were they to do? They had, for courtesy sake, to stay and receive him, and lead him into the music-room. The guest had hardly entered, when all hands were outstretched to greet him, vying with one another to be the first to welcome him. And now arose a flood of compliments. He would gladly have been the first to pay his compliments, but the others believed that it was up to them to speak first, as courtesy demanded. So a man by the name of Zeidelbaer, the bass, addressed him as follows: "Highly esteemed Sir, we are highly honored, at having so famous a musician with us." Another, the tenor, named Nachtwaechter, (night-watchman), thought that he must express himself more artistically and declared: "We are highly grateful to Italy for dispensing with so worthy a son of her muses, and to allow him to have taken this long journey to Germany to visit our unworthy Collegium." At last, Caraffa too began his harangue: "Highly esteemed gentlemen, troppo, troppo. You praise me too much and raise me to the 'stelle'. I should beg your pardon for taking the liberty of coming here. But the gentlemen are too 'cortesi' to think this. They probably know that it is customary in Italy for an 'artefice' or 'musico' to visit another 'senza timore'. Gentlemen, do me the favor not to let me interrupt you in your musical 'delizie'. I desire only to be an appreciative listener".

These tirades were not only corrupt, but, because of his foreign pronunciation of the German words, ridiculous as well.

When they were through with all this, they begged him to do the Collegium the honor to play one of their lowly pieces with them. But since they were ignorant of which instrument he played, he had but to give the order and the part would be placed before him. Whereupon he retorted that he was a singer, it is true, but since they had no piece with Italian text, he would accompany their music on the harpsichord. Caraffa had noticed that in the sonata to be played the figured bass was very simply set. He therefore assumed that all the other parts were thus composed and that in the "continuo" (figured bass part) of the next movement, there would be no more difficulty than in this one. The concert masters, at first had been worried, lest they disgrace themselves before him; now it was for him to be afraid of being put to shame by the figured bass. However, as he always knew how to lie himself out of everything, he was not lacking in ingenuity now. "My dear signori", he began, "I am presumptuous enough to play the harpsichord in this piece although this instrument is my weakness. For what I lay most stress on is the composition. This has obliged me, to practice the harpsichord just enough to accompany my compositions when I wish to sing them. My playing therefore is but simple, because my first consideration has always been, that there be not too much bizarre stuff in the general bass playing, so that the voices and the instruments can be plainly heard."

Now, these words were not stupid. For it is indeed silly for an organist, when accompanying, to pour out his whole sack of mannerisms at once, and to come along with all sorts of phantastic whims and runs, where they are least suited. When, for instance, the singer wishes to express sorrow, he bangs out such noise and clamor, with his right hand, as if all joy had suddenly flown into his shoulder. Or, when the singer is executing coloraturas, not wanting his hands to be idle, he runs a race with the other fellow. Nor is it praiseworthy to play as though you had lead in your fingers, or to make the figured bass sound heavy, as if a chorale from Hermann Schein's hymn book was to be intoned.

However, we will now see what Caraffa did. Before going to the instrument, he took from his pocket two snuffboxes, offering a snuff to each member of the company; for he wished in his words, in his music and in his habits to have an Italian appearance. Then he went to the harpsichord, put a box on each side, took a snuff, and then proceeded to play a few chords as an introduction. He could not make a fool of himself doing that, for when these people hear or see a foreigner, they find everything he does or says better and finer than what an acquaintance or a native can do. The performance began, and Caraffa continued in his wily way. When a great number of figures showed over the notes, to be executed by the right hand, he would with his right hand, reach for the snuff-box to the right, to take a quick snuff. If, however, there were many notes in the bass part, he would grab the other box with his left hand. And in this manner he managed to skip over the difficult parts that scared him. And at other times, he would have to blow his nose. His musical colleagues soon noticed where he was cracked. But since he had always acted with great dexterity, and had, previously complained of his catarrh, they, to a certain extent still believed in him.

From Joh. Kuhnau's satirical novel
"The Musical Quack" (1700).

THE BAROQUE PERIOD

Tartini Dreams His "Devil Sonata" (1713)

HE is said to have dreamed that he had made a pact with the devil, who now, as his servitor in the beyond, was eager to fulfill all his wishes. He was moved by the desire to find out whether the devil was a good musician, and for this purpose he handed him his fiddle and asked him to play. What was his astonishment, when Satan played a sonata of such originality and beauty and executed it with such skill and spirit, that it surpassed anything he himself had ever done. His excitement was so great, that he listened breathlessly, and as a result of this ever-growing tension, he finally awakened. He immediately grabbed his violin, to repeat, now that he was awake, what he had heard in his dream. But to his great disappointment, he was unable to reproduce more than a few unsatisfactory reminiscences of what he had heard, which, however, seemed important enough to him, to call the work, that had originated under his hands: "The Devil's Sonata".

From E. Naumann: "Italian Tone Poets".

PRE-CLASSICAL TIME

A Theoretician of the Eighteenth Century
On the Overture

OF all musical compositions, performed by instruments, it is the overture, which has retained its precedence. Its real place is at the beginning of an opera, or some other play, but very often it is played before suites and other chamber music. We have the French to thank for its origin, and it is they who excel in the creating of that musical form.

The overture consists of two parts, the first of which is characterized by a spirited but elevated style; the other part has a brilliant theme, which may be a fugue or merely an imitation of one. Most composers combine the allegro with a grave movement, which form, however, does not seem to find many adherents. The Italians use the symphony before their operas and other dramatic performances, as well as before church music: in the case of the former, replacing the overture; in the latter, the sonatas.[1]

Joh. Mattheson, "Neu-Eroeffnetes Orchester"

---

1 Mattheson's statements seem somewhat confusing since the French overture consisted of a slow pathetic section followed by a fugato; which again was followed by another slow movement. The Italian overture (symphony) consisted of a spirited part followed by a slow section, and this one again was followed by another lively part.

Another Statement on the Overture

THIS theatrical symphony was originally taken over by the Italians from the intrada, a sort of instrumental piece, stemming from the trumpet music, and used as an introduction. It is characterized by a confusing clamor. As there was little melody in these compositions, the authors cleverly contrived to make the old symphonies easier and more tuneful, and to cleanse them of what was antiquated; but retained the liveliness and brisk character of the intrada — thus combining the two kinds of music. And from this combination derived the present form of the symphony.

Joh. Ad. Scheibe (1708-1776) *in his "Der critische Musicus"* (1737-1740).

What A Rationalist of the 18th Century Demanded From A Melody

WE can take no pleasure in anything, in which we have no part. From this, naturally, are drawn seven rules:

1) That there should be something in all melodies with which every one is familiar.

2) Everything forced, far-fetched, should be avoided.

3) Nature should be followed in most respects,—noise in some.

4) You should put higher art aside, or cover it well.

5) The French should be imitated more than the Italians.

6) The melody should have definite limits, easily accessible to everyone.

7) Brevity should be preferred to length.

Mattheson: "Der Vollkommene Kapellmeister" (1739)

The Most Frightful Animal of the Prussian Monarchy

AT a social gathering, mention was made of how the King, whom no one could please, took so much from Quantz, who, in his turn, treated others with such unbearable arrogance, and who, again, was tyrannized by his wife. Phil. Em. Bach, a long time silent, gave them a riddle to solve: To name the most fearful animal in the Prussian Monarchy. They·all tried but no one could solve the riddle. This most frightful beast of the Prussian Monarchy, yes, of all Europe, was not Herr Quantz, but was no other than Madame Quantz's pet-dog, for this animal was so frightful, that Madame herself was afraid of it, that Mme. Quantz put fear into the soul of Herr Quantz, and the greatest monarch of the world[1] was in awe of Quantz.

From the Review:
"Deutsche Musikkultur", 1936.

[1] Frederic the Great.

GLUCK — OPERA AND BALLET

PLATE 5.—King David Playing a String Instrument with Musicians and Dancers [Psalterium Aureum, St. Gall, Ninth Century]

PLATE 6.—Devices of the Jewish Temple on the Triumphal Arch of Titus, Rome

PLATE 7.—Roman Work-Song, Marble Relief, Villa Albani from Campana, "Opere Antiche in Plastica"

PLATE 8.—Heinrich Frauenlob with Minstrels [From the Heidelberg Min-
nesinger Manuscript, 14th Century]

Noverre, The Creator of the Tragic Ballet

A ballet is a picture, or rather a series of pictures, held together by an action. The stage is, so to say, the canvas upon which the creator of the ballet presents his ideas; the choice of music, the decors, the costumes, determine the colors; the ballet-master is the painter.

If the great passions belong to tragedy, they are therefore no less indispensable for this species of pantomime. Our art is, to a certain degree, subject to perspective; small details are lost by distance. Dance pictures demand strongly outlined traits, strong characters, daring mass effects, contrasts, and parallelisms. All its parts should be laid out on a grand scale, but with restraint and conviction. The theatre bans everything superfluous, and therefore anything enfeebling must be avoided; it allows only of just enough people on the stage, as are needed for the representation of the drama. There are, without doubt, many things which the pantomime cannot represent, but in the emotional sphere, there are degrees of expression, over and beyond words to describe. And it is here, that the dance triumphs; a step, a gesture, a mien, can suggest what never can be expressed by other means. The deeper the feeling, the less will we find words to express them.

My endeavors, my zeal, my efforts, have enabled me to deliver the dance from the state of boredom and lethargy into which it had fallen. I had the courage to combat firmly rooted prejudices, consequent on time and habit. I opened up new paths for the dance, and I trod them firmly. The convincing example given me, during my stay in London, by the immortal Garrick, fired my zeal. I left behind me the accepted style, and turned toward one which really answered the purpose of the dance, the heroic pantomime.

Admiring the tremendous amount of masterpieces, which poetry, painting and music have produced, I must regard the ballet as the youngest sister in this illustrious and venerable family, as being the outcome of genius and phantasy. These alone can give to it untold riches; here we find restraint, good taste and grace; beautiful proportions, power and charm of expression; this too is art of the proper division of space and grouping; here too are found the exact directions for gestures and movements of the figures according to the degree of agitation they are under, and the passions that govern them.

J. G. Noverre, "Lettres sur la Danse" 1760

Bouffonists and Anti-bouffonists
in Mortal Combat
(1754)

ABOUT a year ago, a band of Italian musicians, not unlike a certain people (gypsies) wandered all over Europe and finally arrived here. All of Paris was lured into their concerts and they had more brilliant successes than they dared hope for. This should not seem so extraordinary for a nation that carries the love of novelty to a sort of mania. At the arrival of these new Amphions (the opera troupe, with Pergolesi's "La Serva Padrona", from Naples) which crowds went to see, our own great masters, Lully, Campra, Destouches, — yes, even Rameau — seemed but pupils, even though hitherto we had greatly appreciated their merits and their superiority. We regarded them as people, good enough to keep boredom away, dishonored them by assigning to them the role of mere street minstrels. In short: our madness for the newcomers went so far as almost to cause riots.

A citizen by the name of Rousseau, whose curious way of thinking is well known to the world, is the author of a treatise, in which he tries to prove that the arts and sciences are infinitely more detrimental than useful to society. This treatise has received the prize of the Academy of Dijon, — proof of the calibre of thinking of our provincial academies. But to return to the latest work of this M. Rousseau, wherein, at the cost of French music, he idolizes foreign art, and which, because of its singular content, has had such large sales, that several editions had to be brought out in short succession, is called: "A letter on French Music". As this script was written in anything but moderate language, nothing but an uproar could result.

The famous foreign singer and castrato, Caffarelli, the head of this band from Naples, was dining with M. de la Poplinière[1] and a poet, named Ballot, a great admirer of Rameau. They began to dispute. The castrato drunk with the eulogium of the citizen of Geneva, loudly shouted, that — if the French people wanted to show good taste, they must begin by refusing their own music and adopting the style of his country. M. Ballot fought back, but with poor reasoning. Caffarelli responded, and since Ballot could counter but with luke-warm logic, he resorted to abuse. The Italian was not slow to respond. In short, these two people grew so angry that they would have strangled each other, had not the guests at the table interfered and separated them. But they vowed to meet at some other place. They did, and scuffled around in such a manner, that poor Ballot, who was not so good a fencer as Caffarelli, received a few stabs from which it is feared, he will not recover.

From a Paris Newspaper Report of 1754, recorded by Marpurg. (Historisch-Kritische Beitraege).

1) The famous tax collector and maecenas.

Dramatic Truth and the Cantilena
Open Letter of La Harpe to Gluck

Y OUR letter in the "Journal de Paris" has aroused in me a desire to meet you. What you say is true: the song, and particularly the Da Capo Aria are often not in the right place. We owe you gratitude for having led art — the charm of which has often led astray the great masters — back to a natural expression. Even Italy must do you this justice. Sensible people share your opinion: that interest is lost, if one yields oneself entirely to the cantilena; that it is ridiculous, and perhaps too common, to introduce pleasing arias in a strong situation, when an abandoned maiden sings a rondo, a romance or a bravour aria. Who would not admit, that, in such cases, this is an abuse? But that is not the question. The point is to know whether a well written, periodic aria (in spite of the ridiculousness ascribed to the period) can not be strong and expressive. I believe that a great many examples might refute this opinion. You, yourself have created arias, with all the warmth and beauty of melody. It is only necessary to know how to handle an aria, and when to use it. And, looked at from this point of view, you, as well as Italian masters, have given ample proof of this. If now—I do not know why,—the contrary is to be proved to us, have we not cause for indignation with those designing people, whose misplaced and uncomprehending enthusiasm manifests a partisanship, which might well be laid to the discredit of the whole nation, as concerning a matter of general importance?

How is it possible to make us believe, that passion is of a continuous and unequal quality and allows of no rest? We well know that the great emotions cannot be sharply defined, and cannot be always made to sound as well as your recitativi obligati, wherein you are unique and great; but if nature permits such effects to be the centre of interest, do you still believe that a well-ordered, well-executed, purposeful, well-ended aria cannot be incorporated into a situation, and that the charm of a beautiful song would not add to its dramatic expression?

Gluck Answers

SINCE I regard music not only as an art to please the ear, but as one of the greatest means of touching the heart, and arousing emotions, I have, consequent on this view, adopted a new method. I have occupied myself with the scene, have sought effective means of expression, and have pre-eminently aimed at coherence of the parts. I saw all the singers and a large number of music masters rise up against me, but all scholarly and cultured men of Germany and Italy, without exception, have made amends to me by their esteem and praise. Not so in France. For, although there be some well-informed and cultured men who compensate me for the loss of the good opinion of others, — there still are many, who have openly plotted against me. It would seem that, in spite of the gentlemen, who feel themselves happy when writing about matters foreign to them — judging from the applause given me by the audience — little attention will be paid to their point of view and to their phrases.

But what is your opinion of the attack made upon me by M. La Harpe? He is an amusing scholar. He speaks of music in a way designed to make every choir boy in Europe shrug his shoulders. Are you not going to say something to him, since you have heretofore defended me successfully?

From the "Journal de Paris", 1777.

Elysian Discussions on Gluck, Rameau, Lully and Orpheus

LULLY: Divine Orpheus, what chance brings you here?

Orpheus: I am not the famous Orpheus of Thrace, who was a musician, poet and law-maker all in one. Nor am I the illustrious Orpheus, whom your brother has introduced at court with such success. I have but the outer appearance of my ancestor, but I owe my talents to the German swan. It is because of my indebtedness to his art that I am here.

Rameau: The German swan, who may that be?

Orpheus: One of the most famous artists in Europe.

Rameau: And what is his name?

Orpheus: Christopher Gluck.

Rameau: The name has a somewhat rude sound.

Orpheus: What is in a name? Name and merit are two different matters. Genius belongs to all nations and the true wise man is a citizen of the whole world.

Lully: But in which country was this clever musician born?

Orpheus: In Germany. He lives in Vienna. A connoisseur of fine arts has lured him to France, and in Paris he has given full evidence of his power and insight. The most gracious queen of the world, Marie Antoinette, who combines personal charm with fine gifts of the intellect, who, with a glance wins all hearts, and whose generous soul knows how to value and to reward merit, has showered him with benevolence and graciousness in order to hold him.

Rameau: What is the name of the opera he has produced in Paris?

Orpheus: Iphigenie, by Racine.

Rameau: That to me seems impossible. A tragedy by Racine, set to music, must be insufferable, boring in the extreme

Orpheus: By no means. Art has assisted in making it interesting. A modern writer has eliminated the superfluous scenes and has condensed the action. The ingenious musician has imbued it with warmth and energy, and has increased the interest without diminishing the beauty. To put it in a few words: All but the ignorant favor this opera.

Lully: The man must have great ability, if only the ignorant and all the ignorant are against him.

Orpheus: I have the score with me, — judge for yourself, if so it pleases you.

Rameau: I am eager to see it.

Lully: So am I.

Orpheus: I leave it for you to judge.

Rameau: The overture is picturesque and beautiful; it must be very effective.

Lully: But what do I see? The man has put all his choruses into dramatic action. This is contrary to usage and against the rules of the theatre.

Orpheus: For my part,—let him. Genius is above rules. And besides, this was an antique custom.

Lully: But I maintain that he is wrong and that this new reform is ridiculous.

Orpheus: But it is still more ridiculous to set a crowd of people on the stage like statues, and this at a time when the action of the play demands much movement. Are they to stand there lifeless, when a festival is being celebrated, or a sacrifice is to be made? Let us look back to the origin of the chorus. I will prove to you how well the Greeks understood to give importance to the chorus on the stage.

Lully: Then the author of "Iphigenie" has re-introduced this custom only to imitate the ancients?

Orpheus: Not at all. But he has discovered that your choruses have no reality whatsoever.

Rameau: And is that his sole merit?

Orpheus: I lack the time to converse with you, Gentlemen, any longer, because I must find "Eurydice" (Opera by Gluck, performed in Paris in 1774). Read the score carefully and you will find how well the superiority of his genius and the power of his expression make him master of the scene. Farewell.

Lully: Tell me, dear Orpheus, before you leave us, what the world thinks of us, since the appearance of "Iphigenie"?

Orpheus: To be honest with you, because you want it so: all people of good taste say: there is too much art in M. Rameau's harmonies and too little in M. Lully's melodies. While the composer of "Iphigenie" has combined with your illustrious gifts, lively coloring, changes in turns and shadings, and truth of expression,—he has had, by the perfection of his art which is always true to nature, the good fortune of — surpassing you.

Arnauld, 1774.

Rousseau Explains the Art of Gluck to a Pupil

AS far as the passage is concerned which you say you had difficulty in understanding, yes, even in listening to it, I can well tell you the reason. It is, predominantly, that you can do nothing without me, and will, to some extent, always be inexperienced. But you have, at any rate, felt the beauty of the part referred to,—and that is something. But what there is about this music that you do not understand, I will try, as far as possible, to explain to you. The great master has known how to develop from the same harmony, nay, the same chord, two entirely opposed impressions in their full effect: namely the exquisitely tender song of Orpheus, and the horrible screams of the furies. The repetition of the "No", again and again, is one of the most sublime inventions I know of; I have heard it said that no one can refrain from trembling upon hearing this terrifying "No."

From Siegmeier:
"On Ritter Gluck and his Works", (1837).

A German Philosopher on Italian
and French Opera:
Lessing

THERE was a time when poetry and music combined formed one art. Their separation did not come about unnaturally: this I will not deny. Still less will I censure the practice of the one art without the other. But I can regret, that, because of the separation, no thought at all is given to the one time union, or if any thought is given to it, one art is always treated as subordinate to the other, and nothing is known of the effect common to both and in equal part. And we must also remember that there is but one such combination in which poetry is the assisting art, and that is the opera. A combination, however, where music is an assisting or secondary art, has so far not been dealt with. Perhaps an essential distinction could here be made between the French and the Italian opera: in the French opera, poetry is less assistant and, consequently, its music can not be so brilliant; in the Italian opera, on the other hand, everything is subordinated to the music. This can be seen from the librettos of Metastasio, from the unnecessary crowding of characters, and from the bad habit of closing every scene, even the most passionate, with an aria. The singer wants applause, when he leaves the stage, and he must therefore

91

have his cadenza. We should, in this respect, examine the best French operas, as against those of Metastasio.

Or did I wish to say that in the opera both combinations have received consideration? Namely, in the combination where poetry is the assisting art: in the aria, and in the one, where music is the subordinate art: in the recitativo? It would seem so. Only the question here would arise, whether this mixed combination, where alternately one art helps the other, would as a whole be natural.

Gotthold Ephraim Lessing:
From "Laokoon."

"Briefe Eines Aufmerksamen Reisenden
Die Musik Betreffend"
(1774 - 1776)

IN the "Herrmann's Schlacht", Gluck several times imitated the sound of horns, and the cries of the combatants behind their armors. Once he declared he would have to invent a new instrument, especially for this composition. It is difficult to give a clear idea of this music from Gluck's style of presentation. The war songs seem almost too declamatory, and are seldom melodious. It is a great pity that the artist did not write it down, for one could then have recognized the genius special to this great man, since he did not in any way bind himself to the demands made by the new stage or the singers, but instead freely followed his lofty genius, fervently imbued with the spirit of the great poet.

J. F. Reichardt on Gluck's composition of the
"Herrmann's Schlacht".

Gluck in Paris

From the colorful memoirs of a court painter

E ARL Christian, a friend of the French, but inimical to their music, had offered Gluck (who, at that time was in Paris to conduct one of his operas) residence in his palais,—an offer which Gluck most gratefully accepted. Gluck who had with him his wife, his (adopted) daughter, and a servant, moved into his quarters, and it was in this manner, that Gluck and I became close neighbors,—a door of his study leading into mine.

The rehearsals of his opera "Iphigenie" were already in progress, and they proved to be very stormy affairs. Gluck was in open warfare with his poet, Du Roullet, who was not always willing to sacrifice the verses of Racine to the wishes of the composer. The members of the orchestra, so he asserted, did not always play their instruments properly; the singers, male and female, according to Gluck, could neither sing nor recite. Their French pride, naturally was bitterly hurt by these outbreaks, coming as they did from a German master: they would have preferred an Italian yoke.

These rehearsals, which more or less bore the character of lectures or discourses, were a source of great worry to his wife, Mme. Gluck. His faithful companion endeavored to restrain his temper and his Germanic frankness at these instructions, called rehearsals. All the artists concerned were the idolized favorites of the Parisians, accustomed to storms of applause, and they, in all seriousness, considered themselves the greatest artists in the world. The Parisian public, naturally, took great interest in this matter and, as was to be expected, sided with Lully and Rameau, and seemed determined to acknowledge no taste but that which had so long been their delight.

Such was the state of affairs when Gluck and his family

93

moved into our palais. Gluck was so eager to join us that he didn't await the complete renovation of his apartments. We called for him and his family in the carriage of the Countess Forbach, who retained us all for dinner. Ravanel, in the meantime had fetched Gluck's clavier, the violins, the music and the ladies' effects from the "hotel garni", and had installed them in the new lodgings. It was not long after, that Gluck felt himself perfectly at home with us. He sat down at the instrument, took some music paper and began to compose and to sing,—without any voice to speak of, it is true,—but with a great deal of feeling.

And so I had, for the first time, seen the famous man of whom so much had been said — for, and against. Anyone meeting Gluck, wearing his round wig and his large overcoat, would never have taken him for a prominent person and a creative genius. He was a little above medium height, stocky, strong and muscular, without being stout; his head was round, his face ruddy, broad and pock-marked; the eyes were small and deeply set, but very bright and full of fire and expression. Being frank in manner, and easily excited, he could not conform to the conventional rules and customs of good society. A lover of truth, he called things by their name, and therefore, twenty times a day, offended the sensitive ears of the Parisians, used to flattery and insincere conversation, by a want of what was called politeness. Unappreciative of praise, except when coming from persons he esteemed, he desired to please connoisseurs only. He loved his wife, his daughter and his friends, even though he was not tender with them, nor was he in the habit of flattering any one. Without ever becoming intoxicated or spoiling his stomach, he was a hearty drinker and eater. He never denied being grasping and fond of money, and displayed a goodly portion of egotism, particularly at table, where he was wont to claim first right to the best morsel. His wife, a woman of simple but distinguished manners, loved her husband passionately, and managed to be his governess, even when she seemed to bow to his every will. Gluck himself had no children. His adopted daughter was his brother's child. She was then sixteen years of age, had a very good figure, blue eyes, a rather long face and a somewhat wide mouth, displaying resplendently white teeth. She was very well brought up, gay, charming, gifted and most intelligent, had a beautiful voice, and her taste and method, cultivated by her father and the famous Millico,[1] were those of a finished artist.

The rooms which Gluck occupied, had not yet been completely renovated. There were a number of men still at work, and one day, when we had a look at the unfinished room, we saw a young girl, on a ladder, papering the walls. As she stood high above us, and her skirt was rather short, we could not refrain from complimenting her on her beautiful legs. Parrying our jokes and comments, she bent her knee, so that her legs were covered, and, turning to Gluck, she said: "I have a favor to ask of you: a young poet, living in our house ardently desires to have the honor of working for you". "Very well", said Gluck, "send him to me to-morrow. I will test him and if his work pleases me, I will give him something to do".

The little working girl introduced her poet, who was none other than Moline. Under Gluck's direction, he immediately proceeded to transcribe the opera "Orpheus and Eurydice". This created renewed and dangerous enmity for Gluck, for, Marmontel, Sedaine, and other prominent poets, who had striven for the honor of serving the German composer, attacked him violently, because he preferred a young unknown poet to them. They called him a barbarian who was unable to appreciate the beauty of French verse. When Gluck heard of this, he merely laughed, saying: "The composer of an opera has no use for chiseled verses, to which the listener can pay

---

[1] Giuseppe Millico (1730-1802), composer and famous castrato, whom Gluck considered one of the greatest soprani of his day.

but little attention. The poet must create for him beautiful ideas, and, as the circumstances require, strong, interesting, tender, or gruesome situations. It is the function of the musician to give them adequate expression, by appealing to the imagination of the hearer, moving and impressing him with harmonious sounds derived from nature. You can see that so difficult a task can not be endangered by the moods of the poet, who only thinks of his rhyme and his verse, without considering whether or not they are suited to the music. So let these phrase-makers say what they want! I do not require their help and am very well satisfied with the poet of the little working girl, who does what I tell him to do".

Gluck daily attended the rehearsals from 9 o'clock in the morning until noon. When, bathed in perspiration, from his exertions, he came home with his wife, Mme. Gluck removed his wig, rubbed his head with warm towels, and changed his attire,—all of which he submitted to, without a word. Exhausted as he was, he began to talk at table only.

Mme. Gluck confided to me her worry and anxiety, at the daily rehearsals, where her husband's intractability and the lack of good will on the part of the musicians and artists might lead to a conflict, having most unpleasant consequences. "If you were to attend these rehearsals with me, and could keep within the bounds of French courtesy my husband's violent temper, and if you could mitigate the animosity of the musicians and the singers, I should be most grateful to you". The overture and two thirds of the opera had already proceeded quite successfully, even though the composer had found fault with a thousand details, and had demanded twenty and more da capos. When it came to the last third, however, he tore around like a madman: now the violins were at fault, then the wind instruments had failed to give proper expression to his ideas! While conducting he would suddenly break off, singing the part with the desired expression; then again, after continuing for a while, he would stop them, screaming at the top of his lungs: "This isn't worth a devil's mite"! I, mentally, at times saw the violins and other instruments flying at his head. Being acquainted with the first violinist, the concert-master, M. Canevas, I induced him to calm the hot-heads, by explaining to them, that Gluck, being a foreigner, in his eagerness, was not always conscious of the weight of his words, but that he was far from wishing to insult them; that he had the success of the opera close at heart, and desired nothing better than that they share the honors with him. Realizing, that what Gluck wanted, was right, he did succeed in soothing the musicians. When it came to the singers, how-ever,—that was another matter. Mlle. Arnould, for instance, complained that her part in "Iphigenie" was merely a spoken one, and that she wished to sing great arias. "In order to sing great arias, one must know how to sing", replied Gluck, "and that is what made me write music suited to you and your capabilities. Try to speak well: that is all I ask of you, and consider well that screaming is not singing!" "Very well", responded the famous singer, who was amazed as much as offended upon hearing this truth, "since you think so little of me, you will not be surprised to hear that I no longer feel any responsibility for the success of your opera, and that I am not at all concerned about sharing your fame".

"If you really mean that, Mademoiselle", retorted Gluck, "please repeat your remark. I have already found a substitute for you". So she was obliged to yield to this German Orpheus, for, with all her wit, she was unable to extricate herself from this embarrassing situation. She had to follow his instructions like a good pupil, and make the best of a bad bargain.

The rehearsals now were being attended by the public in general. The opinions on Gluck's work differed greatly, and the "pillars of the National Grand Opera" feared for the fame of their idols, Lully and Rameau, which they saw dimmed by this Teutonic innovator. The public, being blind, or rather deaf, might force them, to the detriment of the good taste, inherited from their ancestors, to accept the new ideas. They raged against "Iphigenie", spoke contemptuously of the opera, and instigated all sorts of schemes and intrigues against Gluck, in the social circles. Lovers of music, wishing to form their own judgment, streamed to the rehearsals, and took sides for and against it, with an ardor, that led one to feel the nation's salvation to be at stake. Gluck, however, was so taken up with his work, that he paid no attention to all this fracas. Not so the artists, who resented being called down by a "musicien allemand", and treated like school-children. The Abbé Arnaud and many other scholars, on the other hand, were ardent partisans of Gluck. The public at large, eagerly awaited the first presentation of a work, that had caused such a stir and so much heated controversy. But all this strife, instigated by the followers of Lully and Rameau, missed its aim, and merely served to hasten the revolution in music.

Gluck was not pleased but showed no concern over the fate of his opera. His renown in Germany and Italy was firmly established. In France, music was still in its swaddling clothes, and therefore he didn't consider recognition in that country of too great value. His hopes of success did not run high, but he expressed no opinion. One day, at dinner, a young Savoyard brought him a letter. He opened it, and, as was his custom, glanced at the signature first. To my great astonishment, he seemed moved and delighted. "At last", he exclaimed, "a praise that truly flatters me! So all my work was not in vain, after all. Read this and read it aloud."

And this was the letter: "Dear Chevalier: I have just come from a rehearsal of your opera "Iphigenie". You have made actual, what, hitherto I have deemed impossible. Kindly accept my sincerest congratulation and my very devoted greetings.

J. J. Rousseau."

Paris, April 17th, 1774.

98

GLUCK — OPERA AND BALLET

The opera was at last produced on April 19th, with the most sumptuous settings imaginable, with the text by Du Roullet, who had followed the verses of Racine as closely as the composer permitted. Tickets had been bought up by speculators, who sold them in the streets and in the cafes for three and four times more than their price. The opera house was filled to capacity. I was in a box with Gluck and his family. My heart beat for the composer, but he himself was free of the nervousness which usually overcomes authors on similar occasions.

Mlle. Arnould played the title role with all the charm at her disposal, and with all the finesse of her art, which she, already highly gifted by nature, had acquired by diligent study. She even sang with taste and accuracy the arias and recitatives within the range of her voice, and received lively and repeated applause, which even the rumblings of Gluck's opponents could not stifle. Larrivée sang "Agamemnon" with sufficient expression, but his acting was wanting in dignity. Le Gros was a somewhat awkward Achilles. It was impossible for me to recognize the Homeric hero. Neither his figure nor his countenance were in the least heroic. His voice was fine but he screamed at the top of his lungs, and comported himself like a lunatic. The beautiful Mme Duplant sang the part of Klytemnestra somewhat faultily. In spite of all these defects, which only a keen critic would detect, this first performance was greeted with applause and was carried to its close, which Gluck's adversaries had endeavored to prevent with all possible means and intrigues. The Earl congratulated Gluck, and before leaving for Versailles, he said: "Have a clean copy made of your score and have it suitably bound to be presented to the monarch. I myself will introduce you to the King as soon as you have it ready."

The second performance was lauded to the skies. The success was an undoubted one and the cabale was broken. "Iphigenie" was placed on the repertory, and for twenty

times or more, was received with undisputed and ever growing approbation. And so a new era in music had begun. In
order to make quite sure, Gluck desired that a performance
of "Castor and Pollux" by Rameau be given. I went to the
performance with Gluck and his family: the house was half
empty.

The score, in the meantime, had been carefully copied and
bound in light blue silk, and the Earl now took Gluck, who
had arrayed himself in a richly gold-embroidered coat, to be
presented to the King. The latter, who, as a rule, when introduced to distinguished foreigners, contented himself, when
passing through the gallery, on his way to mass, with stopping a moment, to honor the guest with a nod of his head,
had deigned this time — surrounded by his entire court, —
to address Gluck, and accepted with pleasure the score, con-
gratulating him on his success. All the spectators, amazed at
this reception, wondered who this extra-ordinary man could be.
After his return, Mme. Forbach invited him to a dinner, at
which the Earl was present. Gluck attacked his belated meal
with great appetite, without once alluding to his reception in
Versailles. The Earl, somewhat perplexed at this continued
silence, finally asked him. "Were you not pleased with the
King's reception?" "Yes, Your Highness", he retorted, "I well
realized that His Majesty very rarely addresses persons to
whom he is introduced, and I should have felt flattered. However, if I write another opera in Paris I should prefer to dedicate it to a "general collector of taxes" because he may give
me ducats instead of compliments".

This retort caused consternation among the guests and
the Earl was displeased and quickly changed the subject.

I by no means approved of Gluck's remark. Since, however, I knew him so well, I did not quite agree with the
gentlemen present. He was a child of nature and a greater
philosopher than he may have thought himself. The renown
coming from the masses, and potentates, meant nothing to

him. Incense never went to his head. All meaningless praise coming from any one whom he did not credit with sound judgment,—any difference of state resting on a whim of the great, or on great wealth, had no weight with him. But never have I heard him utter anything derogatory or malicious about even an adversary. He was, very chary of praise, however, flattered no one, and wished to shine on his own merit only.

A man of this calibre was bound to love independence and must find means, even in his own private life of assuring it. He therefore loved money for this reason only: Without being stingy, he regarded it as a symbol of liberation from the fetters of slavery, from the subjugation to social customs, from the ennui of long waits in ante-chambers,—in short, from humiliating situations as a result of poverty.

Gluck was now busy in his study, arranging the French text for the opera "Orpheus", which originally had been written in Italian. He had to change some bars of his score. This generally happened after the good Moline had failed to find the right words for the music. It was then, that the Chevalier would rage against the poverty of the French language, and announce to me, that he would rather write two German operas than one in this thankless language.

The rehearsals for "Orpheus" were less agitated than those of "Iphigenie", because the musicians had realized what the composer wanted, and the singers, in the ban of his domineering personality, feared him.

The first scene, where Orpheus, overcome with grief, rises, and during the glorious intoning of the dirge for Eurydice by the chorus, breaks out into the despairing cry: "Eurydice!", was being rehearsed. Gluck was not satisfied with Le Gros. He made him repeat his cry over and over again because there was too much singing in it. At last he addressed him impatiently: "Monsieur, you are incomprehensible. You always scream when you should sing, but when you are sup-

101

posed to scream, you cannot do it. Cease to think of either the music or the chorus, but just scream painfully, as though your leg was being sawed off, and when you can do that, then only do you depict this pain as morally justified and coming from the heart. . . . ." Le Gros now complied perfectly with the composer's intentions. This isolated scream, which, as something outside of music, disrupts the sweet harmony of the chorus, achieved best results and touched the soul of even the most insensitive. Only a man of superior genius could feel and express with such consummate artistry the charm of what is so close to nature.

In the later rehearsals of "Orpheus" there were renewed scenes of a stormy nature. Gluck demanded of the dancers, executing the ballet of the Furies and Demons, that, while endeavoring to hinder Orpheus from descending into Hades, they call their simple "No!" into Orpheus' song, in varied shades of wild fury. They refused to comply with this unheard-of innovation, violating every sacred statute of the Academy of Music. Gluck was a painter of tones. With his gift for the picturesque, he foresaw the tremendous effect of this changing "No!" of the dancers,—first hoarsely uttered with demoniac fury, then gradually diminishing, as the divine singer and his lyre, moved the underworld forces to compassion with his overpowering grief.

There was a great struggle, for and against. Gluck was adamant, and finally the dancers screamed their "No!" waving about their serpents and dancing light-footedly, gracefully and with great art, around the son of Apollo. This scene, which in the end gave pleasure even to the performers, proved marvelously impressive. The raucous, pitiless calls heard from time to time above the sweet and harmonious sounds of the Orpheus music, seemed to render his pleading song to the lyre all the more moving and sorrowful.

One of my friends desired to have one of Goethe's poems

put to music by Gluck.[1] When I mentioned it to the latter, he refused point blank. A little later, when I again approached him with this plea, he declared angrily: "I told you once before that I was too busy. I have to compose two operas a year for Paris, and am under obligations to Vienna, and what is more, I don't write music like other people, who carry motifs around in their wallets, to which they write any kind of music and manage to write an opera in a very short time without much effort. That is not my way! It is the words which inspire me with motifs and songs. I try to reproduce nature and to paint in tones, whereby I often sweat blood and water. . . . I have already refused Marmontel, Sedaine, and other clever versifiers, and therefore beg you to leave me in peace."

From the Memoirs of Johann Christoph von Mannlich,
Berlin, 1910.

Further Reports on Gluck

MADAME Forbach, one fine day, drove us all to the Bois de Boulogne, for afternoon refreshment. While there, a distinguished group of ladies and gentlemen, on horseback, rode by. Gluck recognized the Dauphine and immediately arose. The Princess who happened to be gazing our way, joyously called out: "Why, there is Gluck!" She turned her horse around and came up to us. After shaking hands with her compatriot, bowing to Mme. Gluck, she conversed with both of them about the success of "Iphigenie", about Vienna, and particularly about her brother Joseph. She was beautiful and looked like an angel. The brilliant court surrounding her, ready to obey her every wish, gave her the appearance of a queen. A number of curious spectators had gathered around

[1] It was Johanna Fahlmer, court-painter, a friend of Goethe's who desired to bring Goethe and Gluck in closer connection. When Gluck's niece died in Vienna in April 1776, he asked Klopstock and Wieland to write a Cantata on her death. Wieland answered that only Klopstock and Goethe were able to do this. Then Gluck approached Goethe who at that time refused.

us, and to the right and to the left of me, I heard people exclaim: "Lord, what a glorious Queen we are going to have, and how beautiful and charming she is!" She again shook hands with Gluck, bowed a gracious farewell to all of us and galloped away. The old man was deeply moved. His eyes were full of tears and he could not find enough words in praise of the immortal Maria Theresia and her illustrious family. On many occasions I have observed the strong and loyal affection of the Austrians for their illustrious reigning house: a fact, which, without doubt, speaks well for both parties.

Marie Antoinette, Gluck's former pupil, in 1773 had invited the master to Paris, to conduct his opera. Another happy surprise awaited him that day. We had returned shortly before dark, and, to fill in the time before supper, Mlle. Gluck sang for me my favorite song "Ich bin ein Teutsches Maedchen" ("I am a German Girl"), and some Italian songs, which I accompanied with the violin. Our concert was interrupted by Gluck who was indignant at not yet getting his supper. Hardly had we unfolded our napkins, when a man, a stranger to me, dashed into the room, threw his arms around Gluck's neck, and almost strangled him in his embrace. He wept and laughed, saying from time to time: "I have you again! You are mine again!" He released the master only to embrace Mme. and Mlle. Gluck with the same ardor. They too had uttered a scream of joy at sight of this man, and the father, especially seemed to be delighted to see him.

The mellifluous voice of the newcomer, and everything I had been told about Gluck's favorite pupil, led me to recognize in him, Signor Millico, a "finished singer",—as he had so often been called by Gluck. He had heard in London that Gluck had died of an acute indigestion. "Just think of my grief! I had a mass read at once in the chapel of the Foreign Ambassadors. And I dropped all my obligations. A few days later, I heard that the news of your death was a mistake, that your opera had been lauded to the skies, and that you were working on your "Orpheus". I then had but one desire, and that was to see you again. I ordered horses, got into my carriage, and post-haste, I drove day and night, and here I am, in your arms!" Gluck was silent but deeply overcome by this token of a true and tender friendship. "I cancelled all my engagements and told my agents and friends that urgent affairs, impossible of postponement, were taking me to Paris, but gave them my word of honor, not to sing here in Paris."

Millico was treated like a child of the family and always spoke of "Papa and Mama Gluck". He had his guitar and harp brought to Gluck's residence. Musicales were arranged, at which duets sung by Millico and Mlle. Gluck aroused our greatest enthusiasm. Soon our little concerts were becoming well-known and many a one tried in vain to get admission, because Millico, true to his promise, refused his permission.

The weather was fine and the evenings mild, so that we were accustomed to go walking on the boulevards adjoining our garden. Millico taking his mandolin, conceived the idea of following the custom of Italian strollers through the streets. He played on his mandolin and sang duets with Mlle. Gluck. Soon after the first measures, carriages stopped, windows were opened, people ran from the cafés into the street, and strollers from all sides gathered around us. When the crowd became too great and threatened to crush us, Millico would give his partner a hint at which they would suddenly stop in the midst of their song. This drove away the crowd. After all had gone, they would resume their duet where they had left off, and again we became surrounded by many. These musical promenades in the Roman fashion so delighted Papa Gluck that he always accompanied us.

Dispute over the Arts
Music and Painting

AT a gathering of prominent men Gluck was asked to give his ideas on music. He attributed to music a supremely high importance. Vernet and I were of the opposite opinion and were the advocates of painting. Also the opinions of the others differed and the dispute ran high. Gluck, irritated at our obstinacy, cried out: "You and your painting! Everything you create remains forever in the same position. You are able to hold but one single moment;—the before and after,—are not within your reach. I have seen the famous pictures in the Vatican, and they are exactly the same as they were centuries ago." Then he opened his mouth wide and imitated the expression and posture of Heliodor: "But it remains unchangeably glorious and admirable, while music is subject to the very frequent changes of method and fashion. Because it is less stable than painting, you have indeed the advantage of gradually preparing our souls for certain definite moods and impressions in the field of music, but, on the other hand, music without words tells us but indistinctly and never clearly what it wants from us." Caillot then gave a rather drastic example. He proceeded to sing the song

"Je ne sais à quoi me resoudre,
Je ne sais où porter mes pas,
Ce malheur est un coup de foudre,
Pour moi, pire que le trepas"

from the opera "Le Roi et le Fermier", that song in which Richard sings of despair and grief at the loss of his beloved one. Caillot sang the song with all the charm and expression that only he could put into it, he, the famous singer and actor. We were all carried away. "But", asked Gluck, "Just what do you wish to prove?" "You will see", Caillot replied. And

106

now he began to describe all the agony and symptoms of a man befallen by an acute attack of colic in the street, seeking a place in which to hide. "Let us see, whether this same music won't apply to the feelings and actions of this man." Saying this, he got into the position and put on the mien of such a person while he started to sing the same song. Uproarious laughter naturally greeted him and prevented him from finishing. Even Gluck had to admit laughingly, that there was a limitation to music as well as to other arts which could not be passed with impunity.

Orpheus Rehearsal

EVERY morning now, I accompanied the family Gluck to the rehearsals of "Orpheus". The demons finally yelled their "Non" with great delight and precison; Le Gros sang his moving plea to the guardian of the underworld: "laissez-moi vous toucher par mes larmes" with beautiful voice. On August 2nd, 1774, the première of the opera took place and notwithstanding the virulent attacks of the Lully and Rameau adherents, it was a great success. The touching agonized wails with which Orpheus, pathetically and realistically, interrupts the moving sweet melodies of the weeping nymphs over Eurydice's grave; the chorus of the dancing demons, in contrast to Orpheus' melodious weeping; the "Non" as the supremely artistic expression of their increasing and gradually diminishing rage;— all this found enthusiastic response in the audience and forced even his opponents who were not so fond of this truly dramatic style, to the confession that never before had they listened to music which had made so deep and lasting an impression on them.

Gluck's Young Days

MADAME Gluck one day had arranged a picnic at St. Cloud. There were all kinds of provisions and some very good Rhine wine. Papa Gluck ate and drank well and was enjoying himself to the full. "I have always, during my long life, yearned for the fourteen days of absolute liberty I enjoyed in my younger days. I shall never forget them", he told us. Then he began to relate: "My father was a forester in a small Bohemian town and he wanted me to become his successor. But in my home land, music was practised by young and old, even in the tiniest villages: by youth in the schools, by older people in the church choruses. I was passionately fond of this art and made rapid progress. I played several instruments and my teacher gave me extra lessons in his leisure hours. All my thoughts and desires were of music alone and forestry interested me not at all. This angered my father, who claimed that music alone would never afford me a living. I therefore practised at night, but this disturbed the household and my father hid all my instruments. In my musical enthusiasm, all that was left for me, was to take a "Maultrommel" (Jew's harp,) and practise on it. I soon mastered it. But my greatest bliss was to take part in the church-chorus. I implored my father to let me study in Vienna. His obstinacy drove me to despair. One fine day, with a few groschen in my pocket, I secretly left my home and decided to get to Vienna on foot. On the way, my playing of the trump so delighted the peasants that they willingly gave me food and lodging. On Sundays and holidays I played this or that instrument in the churches and was regarded as quite a virtuoso. As a rule, the priest then would board and lodge me for a few days. I felt free and independent and wandered along merrily. The last priest with whom I stopped, gave me a letter to friends in Vienna, but he advised me that there were thousands of virtuosi like myself in Vienna and that, even with my talent, but without money, I would die of hunger. I told him who I was and whence I came. He was greatly interested and communicated with my father. He succeeded in over-ruling his objections so that he, my father, finally promised me financial aid. I had lost my glorious independence, it is true, and the boundless delights of a vagabond life, but I could, without hindrance, indulge in my great passion, music, from morning until night. And so I became what I now am, but ever and anon, I look back on those two weeks spent with my trump, and I long to relive them."

Joy and youthful fire illumined the countenance of the sixty year old, when he evoked these memories. "If only I could, my years and my career not withstanding, revive those days!"

We all listened silently. I suggested that we form a company of strolling comedians under assumed names, wandering from place to place and producing Italian operas. Gluck enthusiastically accepted the idea and began immediately to distribute the roles. "My daughter and Millico will sing the main parts and I will play the piano. My wife can go around collecting the money from door to door. Fontenet and you will play the violin, and you also will look after the settings. A basso and a grazioso are lacking, but we can pick them up at the various towns."

Gluck looked forward with great glee to this comical tournée, and would have been glad to start it at once. "There will always be a sum for the town poor, and the politicians and honoraries will be at loggerheads and will shake their heads at this strange company of strolling players. They will consider it beneath their dignity to visit this burlesque affair, and the hall will at first be empty. But soon the curious will come running and before long, the houses will be crowded. The fashionable beaux will court you", he turned to his daughter, "conquests and offers of marriage will follow, which we will laugh at over our meals. And having grown tired of one place, we can go on to the next. But since we do not desire to make more than our costs, we will, after the last performance, invite our honored audience to dine with us."

Dear good Papa Gluck was in despair that his obligations in Paris would hinder him from carrying out these beautiful plans at once, and that he would have to wait until the following summer before realizing his lovely dreams.

Mannlich's "Memoirs."

BACH AND HANDEL

Bach is Reproved in Arnstadt for Prolonged Absence and Improper Playing

Actum, February 21, 1706.

THE Organist in the New Church, Bach, is interrogated as to where he has lately been for so long and from whom he obtained leave to go.

Ille: He has been to Luebeck in order to comprehend one thing and another about his art, but had asked leave beforehand from the Superintendent.

Dominus Superintendens: He had asked for only four weeks, but had stayed about four times as long.

Ille: Hoped that the organ playing had been so taken care of by the one he had engaged for the purpose that no complaint could be entered on that account.

Nos: Reprove him for having hitherto made many curious variations in the chorale, and mingled many strange tones in it, and for the fact that the Congregation has been confused by it. In the future, if he wishes to introduce a tonus peregrinus, he was to hold it out, and not to turn too quickly to something else, or, as had hitherto been his habit, even play a tonus contrarius. In addition, it was quite disagreeable that hitherto no concerted music had been performed (concerted music for voices and instruments), for which he was responsible, because he did not wish to get along with the students; accordingly he was to declare himself as to whether he was willing to play for figured music as well as chorales sung by the students. For a Capellmeister could not be engaged just for his sake. If he did not wish to do so, he should but state the fact categorice so that other arrangements could be made and someone engaged who would.

Ille: If he were provided with a competent conductor (Director) he would perform well enough.

Resolvitur: He is to declare himself within eight days.

> *Excerpts from the Proceedings of the*
> *Arnstadt Consistory.*

The Certificate of Bach's Appointment in Muehlhausen

WE, the sworn Burgomasters of Muehlhausen, Free City of the Holy Empire, and Members of the Council of the Parish of St. Blasius', herewith make known that, as the post of organist there is open, having become vacant through the decease of our late friend and colleague, Mr. Johan Georg Ahle, we have called hither, in order to fill the said post, Mr. Johann Sebastian Bach of the Third Church at Arnstadt, and have engaged him as our organist in the said Church of St. Blasius, on condition that he be loyal and true above all to the Magistrate of this town, not alone defend our common city from all harm but also work for its best interests, show himself willing in the execution of the duties required of him and be available at all times, particularly attend to his service faithfully and industriously on Sundays, Feast Days, and other Holy Days, keep the organ entrusted to him at least in good condition, call the attention of those serving at any time as the appointed supervisors to any defects found in it and industriously watch over its repairs and music; be zealous in observing all the requirements of a decent and respectable life, also avoid unseemly society and suspicious company; and just as the said Mr. Bach has obliged himself

114

by a handshake to show his agreement with all the foregoing and to conduct himself accordingly, so we have promised to give him, as his yearly salary:

85 gulden in money and the following emoluments in kind:

54 bushels of grain,

2 cords of wool, 1 beech and 1 oak or aspen,

6 times threescore fagots delivered to the door instead of acreage,

and having accordingly had the present certificate of appointment executed, with the seal of the Chancellery affixed.

(L.S.) Parishioners of Muehlhausen
Imperial Free City of the Holy Empire.

Done the 15th of June, 1707.

From "The Bach Reader"
edited by Hans T. David and Arthur Mendel.

Bach Requests His Dismissal in Muehlhausen

"TO the Everywhere Honored and Most Highly Esteemed Parishioners of the Church of St. Blasius

A Humble Memorial

Your Magnificence, Honored and Noble Sirs, Honored and Learned Sirs, Honored and Wise Sirs, Most Gracious Patroni and Gentlemen![1]

The manner in which Your Magnificence and my Most Respected Patrons most graciously engaged my humble self for the post of organist of the Church of St. Blasius when it became vacant a year ago, and Your Graciousness in permitting me to enjoy a better living, I must ever acknowledge with obedient thanks. Even though I should always have liked to

---

1 According to Spitta, the various forms of salutation refer, in succession to the Burgomaster, the Town Councilors, (the school officials and others) learned persons, and finally the ordinary burghers.

work toward the goal, namely, a well-regulated church music, to the Glory of God and in conformance with your wishes, and would, according to my small means, have helped out as much as possible with the church music that is growing up in almost every township, and often better than the harmony that is fashioned here, and therefore have acquired from far and wide, not without cost, a good store of the choicest church compositions, just as I have also fulfilled my duty in delivering the project for remedying the faults of the organ and should gladly have discharged every other duty of my office — yet it has not been possible to accomplish all this without hindrance, and there are, at present, hardly any signs that in the future a change may take place (although it would rejoice the souls belonging to this very Church); to which I should humbly add that, however simple my manner of living — I can live but poorly — considering the house rent and other most necessary expenses.

Now, God has brought it to pass that an unexpected change should offer itself to me, in which I see the possibility of a more adequate living and the achievement of my goal of a well-regulated church music without further vexation, since I have received the gracious admission of His Serene Highness of Saxe-Weimar into his Court Capelle and Chamber Music.

Accordingly, I have felt I must bring my intention in this matter with obedient respect, to the notice of my Most Gracious Patrons, and at the same time beg them to content themselves for the time being with the modest services I have rendered to the Church and to furnish me at the earliest moment with a gracious dismissal. If I can contribute anything further to the service of Your Honor's Church I will do so more in deed than in words, remaining forever,

Honored Sir, Most Gracious Patrons, and Gentlemen, Your Honor's most obedient servant

Joh. Seb. Bach

Muehlhausen, June 25, Anno 1708.

The Dismissal Is Granted

Excerpt from the Proceedings of the Parish Meeting

of St. Blasius' Church

Actum, June 26, 1708

Dom. Cons. Dr. Meckbach: The organist Bach had received a call to Weimar and had accepted the same, and had accordingly made written request for his dismissal.

He submitted: Since he could not be made to stay, consent must doubtless be given to his dismissal, but in notifying him it should be suggested that he help to bring to completion the project that had been undertaken.

From Hans T. David and Arthur Mendel
"The Bach Reader"

J. S. Bach Appointed Thomas Cantor

Excerpt from the Records of the Thomas-Schule

May 5, 1723

THEN appeared Mr. Johann Sebastian Bach, hitherto Capellmeister at the Court of the Prince of Anhalt-Cöthen, in the Council Chamber, and after he had taken his place behind the chairs, Dominus Consul Regens Dr. Lange stated that various candidates had presented themselves for service as Cantor of the School of St. Thomas; but since he had been considered the most capable for the post, he had been unanimously elected, and he should be introduced by the Superintendent here, and the same should be given him as the deceased Mr. Kuhnau had had.

Ille: Expressed his most obedient thanks for the fact that he had been thought of, and promised his full loyalty and industry.

117

Further: At the instructions of the Honorable and Learned Council, the Honorable Superintendent Dr. Deyling was notified by me that the quondam Anhalt capellmeister at Cöthen, Mr. Johann Sebastian Bach, had been unanimously elected to have the goodness to attend to everything in connection with the post of Cantor at the Thomas-Schule here, of which fact it had been thought necessary to notify him so that he might have the goodness to attend to everything in connection with the Presentation, and so forth.

Ille: Expressed his thanks for the said notification, and he would not fail to attend to the Presentation and whatever was necessary.

Further: I likewise notified the Honorable Pastor of the Thomas-Kirche, Licentiate Weise, of the fact of the election of Mr. J. S. Bach as Cantor of the Thomas-Schule; he expressed his most obedient thanks for the notification, and invoked God's blessing upon the choice.

Bach's Final Undertaking

Whereas the Honorable and Most Wise Council of this Town of Leipzig have engaged me as Cantor of the Thomas-Schule and have desired an undertaking from me in respect to the following points, to wit:

(1) That I shall set the boys a shining example of an honest, retiring manner of life, serve the School industriously, and instruct the boys conscientiously;

(2) Bring the music in both the principal Churches of this town into good estate, to the best of my ability;

(3) Show to the Honorable and Most Wise Council all proper respect and obedience, and protect and further everywhere as best I may its honor and reputation; likewise if a gentleman of the Council desires the boys for a musical oc-

casion unhesitatingly provide him with the same, but otherwise never permit them to go out of town to funerals or weddings without the previous knowledge and consent of the Burgomaster and Honorable Directors of the School currently in office;

(4) Give due obedience to the Honorable Inspectors and Directors of the School in each and every instruction which the same shall issue in the name of the Honorable and Most Wise Council;

(5) Not take any boys into the School who have not already laid a foundation in music, or are not at least suited to being instructed therein, nor do the same without the previous knowledge and consent of the Honorable Inspectors and Directors;

(6) So that the Churches may not have to be put to unnecessary expense, faithfully instruct the boys not only in vocal but also in instrumental music;

(7) In order to preserve the good order in the Churches, so arrange the music that it shall not last too long, and shall be of such a nature as not to make an operatic impression, but rather incite the listeners to devotion;

(8) Provide the New Church with good scholars;

(9) Treat the boys in a friendly manner and with caution, but, in case they do not wish to obey, chastise them with moderation or report them to the proper place;

(10) Faithfully attend to the instruction in the School and whatever else it befits me to do;

(11) And if I cannot undertake this myself, arrange that it be done by some other capable person without expense to the Honorable and Most Wise Council or to the School;

(12) Not go out of town without the permission of the Honorable Burgomaster currently in office;

(13) Always so far as possible walk with the boys at funerals, as is customary;

(14) And shall not accept or wish to accept any office in the University without the consent of the Honorable and Learned Council;

(15) Now therefore I do hereby undertake and bind myself faithfully to observe all of the said requirements, and on the pain of losing my post not to act contrary to them, in witness whereof I have set my hand and seal to this agreement.

Johann Sebastian Bach

Done in Leipzig, May 5, 1723.

From: Hans T. David and Arthur Mendel
"The Bach Reader".

J. S. Bach Complains About the University of Leipzig

TO His Most Serene Highness, The Most Mighty Prince And Lord, Frederick Augustus, King of Poland, . . . My Most Gracious King, Elector, And Master . . .

Your Most Serene Highness, Most Mighty King And Elector, Most Gracious Master!

May Your Royal Majesty and Serene Electoral Highness most graciously deign to permit it to be pointed out, with most humble obedience, how the Directorship of Music of the Old and New Divine Service at A Worshipful University at Leipzig, with the compensation and incidental fees of the same, has always been connected with the Cantorate of St. Thomas's here, even during the life of my predecessor, but during the vacancy which followed the death of the latter it was given to the organist of St. Nicholas's, Goerner, and on my entering upon my new post the directorship of the so-called Old Service was again left to me, but the compensation therefor was later withdrawn and given with the directorship of the New Service to the above-mentioned organist of St. Nicholas's; and although I have duly addressed myself to A Worshipful University, and made application that the old arrangement should be left intact, yet the best I have been able to obtain is an offer of half the salary, 12 gulden.

Whereas, however, Most Gracious King and Elector, A Worshipful University has expressly required that I furnish the music for the Old Service, and has accepted me for it, and I have until now performed this office; whereas the salary that has been attached to the directorship of the New Service was never previously connected with the latter but specifically with the Old Service, just as the direction of the New Service at its inception was connected with the Old Service; and whereas, while I did not wish to dispute the directorship of the New Service with the organist of St. Nicholas's, yet the withdrawal of the salary, which, in fact, always belonged to the Old Service even before the New was instituted, is deeply disturbing and slighting to me: and whereas Church Patroni are not in the habit of changing the disposition of the regular compensation ear-marked and provided for a servant of the Church, either by withdrawing it entirely or by decreasing it, in spite of which I have had to perform my office in respect to the above-mentioned Old Service for over two years already without compensation — accordingly my most obedient prayer and entreaty goes forth to Your Royal Majesty and Serene Electoral Highness that Your Majesty may issue most gracious commands that A Worshipful University at Leipzig shall leave the arrangement as it was formerly, and grant me the directorship of the New Service in addition to the directorship of the Old, and particularly the full compensation for the Old Service and the incidental fees accruing from both. For this Most High and Royal Favor, I shall remain all my life long

Your Royal Majesty's and Your Serene Electoral Highness's most humble and obedient servant

Johann Sebastian Bach

Leipzig, September 14, 1725

Bach: *Bombastic and Baroque*

THIS great man would be the admired of all nations, if he had more compliance, and if the beauty of his pieces were not dimmed by too much art, the bombastic and muddled manner of his style depriving them of the natural element. Because he judges by his own fingers, his pieces are exceedingly difficult to play, since he expects his singers and instrumentalists, with their voices and instruments, to achieve exactly what he does on the clavier. All ornamentations, all the little flourishes, that this method (the figured bass) calls for, he expresses in real notes, and this deprives his pieces, not only of harmonious beauty, but renders his songs quite unintelligible as well. In short, he represents in music what Herr von Lohenstein stands for in poetry.

Scheibe in his Review, "Der Critische Musicus."

The Glorification of God:
The Aim of the Figured Bass

THE figured bass is the perfect fundament of all music. It is to be played with both hands, in such a manner, that the left hand plays the prescribed notes, the right hand, however,

122

executes the con- and dissonances, so that a pleasing harmony will result, to the Honor of God, and the soothing delight of the spirit. As in all music, the be all and the end all, the sole aim of the figured bass should be, to the Glory of God and for a recreation of the soul. Where this is not taken into consideration, nothing results but a devilish whining and droning.

From Bach's
"Thorough Instruction
in the Figured Bass."

Bach — A New Orpheus

Johann Mathias Gessner, Rector of the Thomas Schule at Leipzig on his Colleague.

YOU would deem all this of minor importance, were you to arise from the dead, and could see Bach, as he plays the piano or organ, and races over the keys, here with both hands,— there with rapid feet, and all alone, evolves a series of quite different, yet co-related tones . . . I repeat,—if you could but see this one man, achieving what a multitude of your antique cithara players, and a thousand flutists together could not do. He, not only makes one melody sing, but works them all together into one; out of thirty or forty musicians he manages to control,—this one by a glance, that one by treading the measure, a third, with threatening finger; he indicates to each the tone,—to one in a higher, to another in a lower, to a third in the middle range; holding them all together, and although having the most difficult task of all, he detects at once, the slightest dissonance, and this amid the greatest clamor of the collaborators; at the slightest divergence, he immediately restores stability. Rhythm is the very essence of his being, and with his acute ear, he grasps all the harmonies, and, within the limited compass of his own voice, causes all the voices to come out clearly and distinctly. I am, generally speaking a great admirer of the methods of antiquity, but I believe that

123

my friend Bach, or any who may be likened to him, combines within himself many men like Orpheus, and twenty singers like Arion.

Bach Plays in Dresden

ON December 1, 1736, the famous Capellmeister to the Prince of Saxe-Weissenfels and Director Musices at Leipzig, Mr. Johann Sebastian Bach, made himself heard from 2 to 4 o'clock on the new organ (according to the "Dresdener Handschrift" this instrument, built by Gottfried Silbermann, had 35 sounding stops for the three keyboards and 8—ranging from 32-foot to 4-foot and including a mixture for the pedal) in the Frauenkirche, in the presence of the Russian Ambassador, Von Keyserlingk, and many Persons of Rank, also a large attendance of other persons and artists, with particular admiration, wherefore also His Royal Majesty most graciously named the same, because of his great ability in composing, to be His Majesty's Composer.

From the "Dresdener Nachrichten". ("Bach Reader.")

Bach Visits Frederick The Great

"The Musical Offering"

WE hear from Potsdam that last Sunday (May 7) the famous Capellmeister from Leipzig, Mr. Bach, arrived with the intention of hearing the excellent Royal Music at that place. In the evening, at about the time when the regular chamber music in the Royal apartments usually begins, His Majesty was informed that Capellmeister Bach had arrived at Potsdam and was waiting in His Majesty's antechamber for His Majesty's most gracious permission to listen to the music. His August Self immediately gave orders that Bach be admitted, and went, at his entrance, to the so-called "forte and piano", condescending also to play, in person and without any preparation, a theme to be executed by Capellmeister Bach in a fugue. This was done so happily by the aforementioned Capellmeister that not only His Majesty was pleased to show his satisfaction thereat, but also all those present were seized with astonishment. Mr. Bach has found the subject propounded to him so exceedingly beautiful that he intends to set it down on paper in a regular fugue and have it engraved on copper. On Monday, the famous man was heard on the organ in the Church of the Holy Ghost at Potsdam and earned great acclaim from the auditors attending in great number. In the evening, His Majesty charged him again with the execution of a fugue, in six parts, which he accomplished just as skillfully as on the previous occasion, to the pleasure of His Majesty and to the general admiration.

Report in the "Spener'sche Zeitung",
Berlin, May 11, 1747.

Bach's Eyes Operated Upon
The Surgeon's Report

I HAVE seen a vast variety of singular animals, as dromedaries, camels, etc., and particularly at Leipsic, where a celebrated master of music, who had already arrived to his 88th year (?) received his sight by my hands; it is with this very man that the famous Handel was first educated, and with whom I once thought to have had the same success, having all circumstances in his favor, motions of the pupil, light, etc.,

125

MUSICAL DOCUMENTS

but, upon drawing the curtain, we found the bottom defective, from a paralytic disorder.

From "The History of the Travels and
Adventures of the Chevalier Taylor,
Opthalmiater" . . . written by himself, 1761.

Bach's Death

LAST Tuesday, that is, the 28th instant, the famous musician, Mr. Johann Sebastian Bach, Royal Polish and Electoral Saxon Court Composer, Capellmeister of the Princely Court of Saxe-Weissenfels and of Anhalt-Cöthen, Director Chori Musici and Cantor of the Thomas-Schule here, in the 66th year of his age, from the unhappy consequences of the very unsuccessful eye operation by a well-known English oculist. The loss of this uncommonly able man is uncommonly mourned by all true connoisseurs of music.

From the "Spener'sche Zeitung",
August 3, 1750.

Handel Discusses Solmisation and Greek Modes in a Letter to Mattheson

"Sir:

The letter I have just received from you obliges me to answer you more fully than I have previously done on the two points in question. I do not hesitate to assert that my opinion is in general conformity with that which you have so well expounded and proved in your book on Solmisation and the Greek Modes. The question, it seems to me, reduces itself to this: whether one ought to prefer a method which is easy and one of the most perfect; or one which is full of great

126

difficulties, capable not only of disgusting music students, but also causing them to waste valuable time, which could be far better used in exploring art and cultivating the natural gifts? Not that I would say that one can find absolutely no use in Solmisation; but since one can acquire the same knowledge in far less time by the method which is so successfully used at present, I do not see why one should not choose the road which leads us more easily and in less time to the object desired.

As to the Greek Modes, I find, Sir, that you have said all that can be said on them. A knowledge of them is doubtless necessary to those who wish to practise and perform ancient music composed in these modes: but since we are now freed from the limitations of ancient music, I do not see of what use the Greek Modes can be in modern music. These, Sir, are my sentiments, and I should be glad if you would let me know whether they respond to what you expect from me.

With regard to the second point, you can judge for yourself that it requires a good deal of research, which I am unable to give owing to my many pressing engagements. When I am a little less occupied, I will think over the more important epochs in the course of my profession, in order that you may see the esteem with which I have the honor to be, Sir,

Your very Humble and Obedient Servant,

G. F. Handel."

London, Feb. 21, 1719.

From Mattheson: "Das Neu Eroeffnete Orchester".

Handel — The Great Bear

HE was called "The Great Bear". For he was like a giant, broad, fat, thick, with large hands and feet, huge arms and thighs. His hands were so fat that the bones were lost in the flesh, and formed dimples. He came along, on his crooked

legs, with lumbering swaying gait, very upright, his head bent
back, under a large white perruque, the curls of which fell
in large ringlets over his shoulders. His long face resembled
that of a horse — later in life a steer, — and was drowned
in fat, with double cheeks, three-fold chin, a broad large
straight nose, and red, off-standing ears. He looked straight
at people, a mischievous gleam in his eye, a mocking twist
to his lips. His mien was imposing, and jovial at the same
time,—at times somewhat dark and sour. "But when he
smiled", says Burney, "it was the sun, emerging from a dark
cloud". His face then suddenly radiated intelligence, wit, and
good humor.

From Romain Rolland: "Life of Handel".

Report on Handel's "Watermusic"

ON Wednesday evening at about 8, the King took water
at Whitehall in an open barge, wherein were also the Duchess
of Bolton, the Duchess of Newcastle, the Countess of Godol-
phin, Madam Kilmanseck, and the Earl of Orkney, and went
up the river towards Chelsea. Many other barges with persons
of quality attended, and so great a number of boats, that the
whole river in a manner was covered: a city company's barge
was employed for the musick, where were fifty instruments
of all sorts, who play'd all the way from Lambeth (while
the barges drove with the tide, without rowing, as far as
Chelsea), the finest symphonies, composed express for this
occasion, by Mr. Handel: which His Majesty liked so well,
that he caused it to be played over three times in going and
returning. At eleven, His Majesty went ashore at Chelsea,
where a supper was prepared, and then there was another very
fine consort of musick which lasted till 2: after which His

Majesty came again into his barge, and returned the same way, the musick continuing to play till he landed".

From the "Daily Courant" of July 19, 1717

"Tweedledum and Tweedledee"

"Some say compared to Bononcini
That Mynheer Handel's but a ninny:
Others aver, that to him, Handel
Is scarcely fit to hold a candle;
Strange all this difference should be
'Twixt Tweedledum and Tweedledee."

John Byron ridiculing the quarrel between Handel and Bononcini. ("Spectator", 1721).

A London Satyre of 1727

Making Fun of the Opera Stars

"Cuzzoni can no longer charm,
Faustina now does all alarm;
And we must buy her pipe so clear
With hundreds, twenty-five a year.
And if a brace of powder'd coxcombs meet
They kiss and slabber in the open street:
They talk not of our Army or our Fleet;
But of the warble of Cuzzoni sweet,
Of the delicious pipe of Senesino
And of the squalling trill of Harlequino;
With better voice, and fifty times her skill,
Poor Robinson is always treated ill:
But, such is the good nature of the town
'Tis now the mode to cry the English down.

129

They care not, whether credit or fall,
The opera with them is all in all.
They'll talk of tickets rising to a guinea,
Of pensions, duchesses, and Bononcini
Of a new eunuch in Bernardi's place,
And of Cuzzoni's conquest or disgrace".

From Chrysander: "Georg Fr. Handel".

Two Letters and a Bouquet
Handel to Teleman

I WAS just about to start from the Hague for London when your very agreeable letter was given me by Mr. Passerini. I just had the time to hear his wife sing. Your protection and recommendation sufficed to excite my curiosity, and I must show her my great approbation, for I was soon convinced of her rare merit. They are going to Scotland to fulfill some engagements for concerts for a season of six months. There she could perfect herself in the English language, and then (since they have the intention to stay for a while in London) I shall not fail to render them any service they need from me.

I was very touched by your polite remarks full of friendship. Your obliging manners and your reputation have made a great impression on. my heart and on my mind, and I shall always reciprocate your kindness. Rest assured that you will always find in me sincerity and true esteem.

I thank you for the beautiful work "du système d'intervalles" which you have kindly sent me, it is worthy of your occupation and of your knowledge.

I congratulate you on your perfect state of health which you are enjoying at a fairly advanced age and I wish you with

BACH AND HANDEL

all my heart the continuation of all sorts of prosperity for
several years to come. If your passion for exotic plants could
prolong your days and sustain the vivacity that is natural to
you, I offer myself with great pleasure to contribute to it in
some manner. I therefore make you a present, and I send you
(by the enclosed address) a case of flowers; I am told by
the connoisseurs of plants that they are choice flowers and of
a charming rarity; if what they say is true, you will have the
best plants in all England, the season being still proper for
having flowers. You will be the best judge of them, I await
your decision hereon. Meanwhile don't let me wait too long
a time for your agreeable reply to this, for I am with the
greatest friendship . . . .

G. F. Handel

From Erich H. Müller:
"The Letters and Writings of G. F. Handel".

HAYDN, MOZART

The Duties of a "Kapellmeister"
at a Princely Court
Joseph Haydn in Eisenstadt

IN the "Convention und Verhaltungsnorma" of May 1st, 1764, we read that "Haydn entered into the service of Prince Esterhazy as Vice-Kapellmeister, while the former Kapellmeister, Gregorius Werner, although old and sickly, and no longer able to perform his duties, is still retained as Ober-kapellmeister, in view of his diligent and faithful services, and Joseph Haydn seemingly takes the position of his subordinate." Together with the admonitions, customary at that time, namely, that he behave as a self-respecting officer of a princely court, his duties are set down in the "Convention und Verhaltungsnorma": "He is expected to produce at once any composition called for; he is not to mention the name of said composition to any one, or to have it copied, nor is he permitted to compose anything for any one else without special permission." According to Paragraph 5, he is to present himself daily, in the fore- and afternoon, in the antechamber to await his orders. Furthermore it is his duty to see that the musicians arrive promptly and to note down the late-comers or the absentees. And as a matter of course, he is under obligation to see that the singers and the orchestra rehearse assiduously, and to keep the orchestra in good trim, so as to retain its high standard, which would be to his credit and would commend him to future princely favor. It is up to him to smoothe out all difficulties among the musicians; and he, as well as they, must appear "in uniform", neatly attired, with white stockings, and white linen, and with the hair either in

135

braids or in bags, but always in the same fashion. For this he would receive annually 400 Gulden Rhenish, and besides, either the right to the officer's table or half a Gulden daily for his meals.

From the "Convention und Verhaltungsnorma"
for the Esterhazy Orchestra.

"The Seven Words of Christ on the Cross"

ABOUT fifteen years ago, I was requested by a canon of Cadix, to compose instrumental music to the Seven Words of Christ on the Cross. It was customary in Cadix, at that time, to present an oratorio in the main church during Lent. The following preparations must have greatly added to its impressiveness. The walls, windows, and pillars of the church were covered with black cloth, and only one lamp hanging in the center, relieved the darkness of the edifice. At noon, all doors were closed and the music began. After a reasonable prelude, the Bishop stepped into the pulpit, and, after uttering one of the Seven Words of Christ on the Cross, he delivered a meditation on this word. When he had ended, he stepped down from the pulpit, and knelt before the altar. During this silent prayer the music played. The Bishop mounted and left the pulpit a second and a third time, and did so seven times, and after each close of the speech, the orchestra again tuned in.

My composition was to conform to this representation. The task of composing seven successive adagios each of which was to last about ten minutes, was not an easy one, for there was always the danger of tiring the hearers, and I soon found that I could not limit myself to the time prescribed.

The music was originally without text, and was presented in this form. It was only later that I was advised to add the text, so that the oratorio "The Seven Words of Christ on the Cross" is now to appear for the first time at Breitkopf & Haertel, in Leipzig, as a complete, and, as far as the music is concerned, entirely new work. The favor with which this work has been received by intelligent connoisseurs, gives me hope that it will not fail to please the general public as well. Vienna, March, 1801.

> *Joseph Haydn's preface to the*
> *edition of Breitkopf & Haertel.*

Haydn and Dittersdorf Fooling Tavern Fiddlers

HAYDN and Dittersdorf were, at one time, strolling through the streets of Vienna, when they heard minuets by Haydn, played very badly in a beer-house.

"We must play a joke on these fellows", they said to each other. They entered and ordered drinks. After having listened to the music for a while, Haydn finally asked: "By whom is this music?" They gave him his own name. "O, what atrocious stuff", he said. Whereat the musicians grew so enraged, that had Haydn not taken precipitous flight, one of them, would have thrown his violin at his head.

> *From G. A. Griesinger*
> *"Biographische Notizen ueber Joseph Haydn",*
> *(1810).*

Conversation Between Joseph II and Dittersdorf

Emperor: Have you heard Mozart play?
Dittersdorf: As often as three times.
Emperor: And how did you like him?
Dittersdorf: As much as every lover of music must like him.

Emperor: And have you heard Clementi?

Dittersdorf: I have heard him too.

Emperor: Some prefer him to Mozart. What do you think?

Dittersdorf: In Clementi's playing, art alone predominates; Mozart, however, plays with both art and taste.

Emperor: That is what I too have said. What do you think of Mozart's compositions?

Dittersdorf: He is undoubtedly one of the greatest and most original geniuses, and I have, up to the present time, known of no composer possessed of such an astonishing richness of ideas. My only wish is that he be not extravagant with it. He does not let his listeners get their breath, for hardly does he give us a beautiful thought to meditate on when lo, there is another, more delightful one to supplant it. And this goes on and on, so that, at the end, it is impossible to retain all these beautiful fancies.

Emperor: In his theatrical pieces, he has but one fault, of which the singers complain, that his orchestral accompaniment often deadens the singing.

Dittersdorf: That would surprise me: It is possible to employ both harmony and instrumental accompaniment without detriment to the cantilena.

Emperor: This gift you possess in a masterly degree. And what do you think of Haydn's compositions?

Dittersdorf: I have heard none of his theatrical compositions.

Emperor: You have not missed much. He does just as Mozart does. What do you think of his chamber music?

Dittersdorf: That it is creating a sensation the world over and rightly so.

Emperor: Doesn't he trifle too much at times?

Dittersdorf: He has the gift of trifling without however demeaning his art.

Emperor: Mozart, then, could be compared to Klopstock, and Haydn to Gellert?

Dittersdorf: That is what I would say.
Emperor: Next Saturday I shall hear your "Doctor and Apothecary".[1] I ordered its repetition. I will appear at the theatre in person and will see you there. In the meantime, Farewell.

> *From the Autobiography of*
> *Ditters von Dittersdorf.*

[1] The most popular operetta of the time.

About Haydn's Intention to write an "American Symphony"
The Master's Attitude Toward Program Music

I.

HAYDN began his work by weaving out some sort of a program or story on which to base his music, and which served to inflame his imagination.

So he once imagined the story of a friend, who, a father of several children, and with little wealth to speak of, embarked for America, prompted by a desire to acquire riches. The chief events of this voyage form the subject of one of Haydn's symphonies.

It begins with the embarkation. The wind over the seas is favorable, and swells the sails; the ship leaves the port, while from the shore are heard the laments of the family and the good wishes of friends. The ship glides through the waves safely and lands him on foreign, unknown soil. Barbaric music is heard, dances and singing form the middle part of the symphony.

Enriched and loaded with exchanged wares, the traveler again lifts anchor, and sets sail for home. The wind at first is favorable, and in the symphony we repeatedly hear the first motif. But presently the sea grows rougher, the sky becomes lowering, and a terrific gale breaks out. The tones and chords of the music are turned topsy-turvy; confusion reigns. Through the moans of the voyagers, the roar of the sea, the howling of the storm, the melody is carried from the chromatic to the pathetic. Dominant and diminished chords, modulations in half-tone intervals, depict the terror and fear of the unhappy ones. Gradually the elements calm down, a gentle wind is rustling,—the bringers of peace and quiet. The friend reaches his haven, the anchor is lowered amidst the evvivas, blessings and wonder of the sons and friends, and a curious crowd. The symphony ends in joy and happiness.

II.

It is easy to see how many ideas the master could draw from such a subject and how it could stir his imagination. I cannot recall which symphony had this subject for basis. I only know that he mentioned it several times as the subject of one of the symphonies,[1] and had notes on the matter but they have been lost. Maestro (Wenzel) Pichel mentioned it frequently.

In another symphony the good Haydn made use of an imaginary dialogue between Jesus and the unrepentant sinner, symbolizing the parable of the Prodigal Son. And the other symphonies all originated in this manner. Without betraying the reason, Haydn gave certain names to his symphonies, which, if not familiar with the connection seem irrational and ludicrous. Some bear titles as: "the Beautiful Circassian", "Roxalane", "The Greek Helena", "The Solitary", "The Enamored Schoolmaster", "The Persian", "The Poltroon", "The Queen", — all names referring to some story on which the composer has based his musical works.

From Giuseppe Carpani, "Le Haydine", 1812.

[1] Haydn may have had the intention to write this symphony.

Dr. Mus. Joseph Haydn

IN June, 1791, Haydn received the doctorate of Oxford. Again it was Burney who procured for him this rare distinction. He induced him to take the necessary steps, travelled with him to Oxford, and was untiring in his efforts to procure for the esteemed master the honor of the title of Doctor of Oxford.

The granting of this distinction was attended with a solemn ritual. Haydn was attired in a white mantle, the sleeves of which were lined with red silk; the dainty little hat was of silk; and thus arrayed he sat down in the doctor's chair. The music began and Elisabeth Mara sang. Haydn was requested to perform some of his own music. He stepped up to the organ, but before seating himself, he lifted the mantle from his breast, waved it with both hands, and — in a loud voice — called out: "I thank you". The assembled audience delightedly answered: "You speak English very well."

According to Dies, Haydn told him that he felt very droll in this garb, and what was worse, he had to show himself in the streets, in this masquerade, for three days. "However, I owe much, if not everything to this honor received, for I made the acquaintance of the highest people and had access to the best houses, because of it."

From August Reissmann "Joseph Haydn."

Burney's High Esteem for Haydn

WITH the equally and yet more popularly celebrated Haydn, Dr. Burney was in correspondence many years, before that noble and truly creative composer visited England; and almost enthusiastic was the admiration with which the musical historian opened upon the subject and the matchless merits of that sublime genius, in the fourth volume of the "History of Music".

"I am now", he says, "happily arrived at that part of my narrative where it is necessary to speak of Haydn, the incomparable Haydn, from whose productions I have received more pleasure late in life when tired of most other music, then I ever enjoyed in the most ignorant and rapturous part of my youth, when everything was new, and the disposition to be pleased was undiminished by criticism or satiety."

From "Memoirs of Dr. Burney"
(Edited by his daughter,
Mme. Frances Burney-d'Arblay)

Haydn Pleads for Mozart

IT would be audacious of me to take up my work in Prague side by side with so great a man as Mozart. No one can stand up beside him. And if I could imbue the mind and soul of every music lover, — and particularly of those on high, — with the same great musical understanding and the profound feeling, I have for his inimitable works, the nations would vie with one another for the possession of so precious a gem. Let Prague keep the rare man, and let it reward him, for, without this, the history of a striving genius is a sad one, and gives little encouragement and incentive for further striving to posterity. So many promising spirits are dejected for the want of it. I am indignant that this one and only man has not been engaged by some royal or imperial court. Pardon me for this digression, but I love the dear man so much.

From a letter of Haydn (Dec. 1787)
to the Prague music lover Rott,
(Nettl: "Mozart in Bohemia").

Haydn Becomes A Mason in Vienna

HAYDN was received on the 11th of February (1785) in the Lodge "Zur wahren Eintracht" after he had been elected by ballot, on the 24th of January. In the minutes it is stated: "The candidates, Bros. Hallberg and Joseph Haydn were balloted 'all clear' and after the usual felicitations the 28th of January was set for their admittance." On the 28th of January, Mozart was present to greet his friend and master, now as "Brother". The initiation, however, did not take place, since the records show that Haydn was prevented from coming. Accordingly, in the 353rd meeting "the candidate Joseph Haydn was relieved of the payment of fees and his initiation was set for the 11th of February." In the meeting of the 11th of February there was presented for admittance: "the candidate Joseph Haydn, Matthew's son, age 51 years, born May 1, religion Catholic, middle class origin, born in Rohrau, position Kapellmeister to Prince Esterhazy".

Haydn had been admitted to the Lodge "Zur wahren Eintracht". Again Born had presided. But Haydn seems to have attended the Lodge only once, although in a letter dated February 2, to Count Apponyi, another member of the Lodge he wrote from Esterhaz: "Just yesterday I received a note from my future sponsor, Herr von Weber, that they awaited me last Friday with great longing, to conduct my admittance, which I look forward to with impatience. Since, however, through the carelessness of our Hussars I did not receive the invitation at the proper time, they have postponed the ceremony until next Friday, the 11th of February. Oh, that today were Friday, that I might live through the indescribable happiness of being in a circle of such worthy men!"

(*Paul Nettl "Mozart and Freemasonry."*)

A Touching Scene With Old Haydn
Johann F. Reichardt Sees Haydn and Beethoven and Enjoys "Iphigenie" and "Don Giovanni"

IT has given me much pleasure to have heard Gluck's "Iphigenie" sung by the marvelous Milder.[1] It was produced at the Burgtheater a few days ago. The limited decorations and scenic effects of the theatre were detrimental to the performance as a whole. But I enjoyed the beautiful voice of the artist in all its fullness and richness, and was genuinely charmed by it. It is without exception the most beautiful, the fullest, the purest voice I have heard anywhere — in England, Germany, France and Italy. The singer's appearance too, and her acting were great and noble. In her declamation and in the execution of the recitativi, her striving for perfect distinctness and intelligibility, however, caused too many long syllables. She lacked the fire and spirit of our good Schick[2]—as several Berliners sitting near me who probably had been greatly impressed by the far more brilliant performance in Berlin—justly remarked. For my part, on the whole, I much preferred Milder, because of her magnificent, soft and pure voice and her heroic appearance. Her presentation is a truly tragic one, without affectations, opera tricks and steps, and distortions of throat and body.

As to the ballet, which, even though not equaling the more brilliant, characteristic and superabundant ballet of the Paris Opera, had a far better artistic arrangement and grander execution than can be found in the Berlin performance. Nor has the Italian Opera had, as yet, anything to equal it.

I have been anxiously waiting for a free and quiet mo-

[1] Pauline Anna Milder-Hauptmann (1785-1838), famous Prima Donna whose powerful voice caused Haydn to tell her: "Darling, you have a voice as big as a house".
[2] Another famous singer of that time.

144

Fraulein Kurzbeck, whom he loves
with paternal affection, and Frau von Pereira, who — as for
everything great and beautiful is full of enthusiasm for him
— led me to the master. We drove almost a full hour through
the little alleys and by-paths of a distant suburb. There we
found the wonderful old man in a small but very pretty cot-
tage belonging to him. He was seated in a small room, at a
table with a green cover, attired in a simple but very clean
grey suit, with white buttons, wearing a carefully curled and
powdered wig. He sat stiffly, almost rigidly, with both hands
on the table, not unlike a wax figure. Mlle. Kurzbeck explained
to him that she wished to introduce me. I was a little worried
lest he might not know my name, or in his state of apathy
would not remember it, and was struck — and I can truly
say ashamed — when the old master opened wide his bright
eyes and said: "Reichardt, a real man; where is he?" I had
just entered and, with outstretched arms, he called across the
table: "My dear Reichardt, come here, I must press you to my
heart!" And then he kissed me and cordially shook hands
with me. He stroked my cheek three or four times with his
thin hands and remarked to the others: "How happy I am
to see that an artist has such a kind and honest face." I sat
down next to him, and held his hand in mine. He gazed at me
a while, deeply moved, and then said: "Still young and fresh.
Ah, I have used my mind too much, and am a child again",
and he wept bitter tears. The ladies, in order to spare him,
wanted to leave but the dear old man said: "No, no, let me
go on, it does me good. These are tears of joy over that man
here, who will fare better than I did." I could find no words
of gratitude, could only kiss his hand most feelingly.

When after a full hour we did finally leave him, he held
me back, holding my hand tightly, and begged me, kissing me
over and over again, to come to see him at least once a week.

I also visited and interviewed Beethoven. They pay so

145

little attention to him here, that no one knew where he lived. To question him, was not difficult, after I found him at last in a large, desolate and lonely residence. He was at first as gloomy as his house, but soon brightened and seemed as pleased to see me as I was to see him. He told me about matters that I needed to know, and he did it in a hearty and frank manner. He is a vigorous nature, outwardly cyclopean, but warm, kind and cordial.

At the large and beautiful "Theater an der Wien", formerly Schikaneder's, I enjoyed a performance of the one and only "Don Giovanni". I heard Mlle. Milder sing Elvira again most beautifully. She also acted very well. You can imagine how great an artist she must be if she could please me so well in this part and in all her others. Yes, I will even state — had Herr Fischer been here to play and to sing the Don Giovanni as wonderfully as he does for us — that I never had heard that opera so perfectly presented. The orchestra was better than I have ever heard it, and I have never before seen such fine settings. The last scene showed the inferno, into which Don Giovanni is cast. What pleased me most was that he was not driven by devils, nor grabbed, but gradually surrounded and hemmed in, in an ever smaller circle and thus forced toward the infernal abyss, to fall into it at last.

> *From Johann F. Reichardt's*
> *"Letters from Vienna"*
> *(Dated November 30, 1808).*

A French Encyclopedist is Amazed by Young Mozart

WE have just now seen the two charming children of Herr Mozart, Kapellmeister to the Prince-Bishop of Salzburg, who during their stay in Paris, in 1764, had so great a success. Their

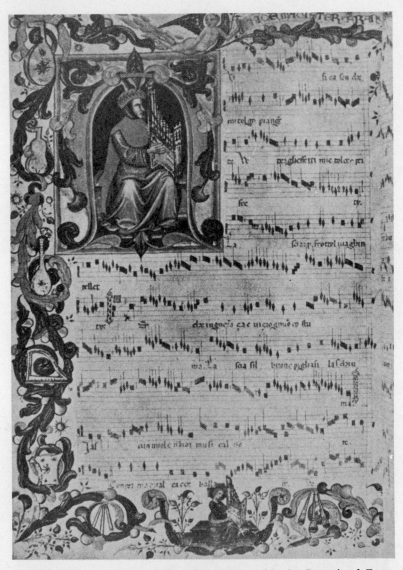

PLATE 9.—From the Squarcialupi Manuscript with the Portrait of Francesco Landino [Biblioteca Laurenziana, Florence]

PLATE 10.—Claudio Montiverdi [From the portrait reproduced in the "Fiori Poetici" (1644), in the Possession of the Biblioteca Ambrosiana in Milan]

PLATE 11.—Frontispiece of Athanasius Kircher's Phonurgia—1673.

ATHANASII KIRCHERI
E SOC. JESU.

PHONURGIA
NOVA
SIVE

.Conjugium Mechanico-phyſicum

ARTIS & NATVRÆ

PARANYMPHA PHONOSOPHIA
Concinnatum;

quà

UNIVERSA SONORUM NATURA, PROPRIETAS, VIRES
effectuúmq, prodigioſorum Cauſæ, novâ & multiplici experimentorum exhibitione enu-
cleantur; Inſtrumentorum Acuſticorum, Machinarúmq, ad Naturæ prototypon
adaptandarum, tum ad ſonos ad remotiſſima ſpatia propagandos, tum in abditis domo-
rum receſſibus per occultioris ingenii machinamenta clam palámve ſermo-
cinandi modus & ratio traditur, tum denique in Bellorum tumul-
tibus ſingularis hujuſmodi Organorum Uſus, & praxis
per novam Phonologiam deſcribitur.

CAMPIDONÆ
Per Rudolphum Dreherr.   Anno M. DC. LXXIII.

PLATE 12.—Title Page of Athanasius Kircher's Phonurgia—1673.

father has been in England eighteen months, and six months
in Holland, and has of late brought them back here, on their
way to Salzburg. All over, where these children have visited,
there has been but one opinion, and they have astonished all
connoisseurs. Mademoiselle Mozart, now thirteen years old,
by the way, grown very pretty, has the most brilliant and beautiful way of playing the piano, and her brother alone can
steal the applause from her. And this curious boy is now nine
years old. He has grown hardly at all, but he has made wonderful progress in music. As early as two years ago he has
composed and edited sonatas; and since then, he has had
six sonatas printed for the Queen of England; six for the
Princess of Nassau-Weilburg; he has composed Symphonies
for a large orchestra, that have been performed and were acclaimed with great praise. He has even written several Italian
arias, and I am not giving up hope, that he will have written
an opera for some Italian theatre before he is twelve years old.
He heard Manzuoli in London all winter long, and has made
such good use of this, that he, although his voice is very small,
sings with both feeling and taste. But the most unbelievable
of all is his profound knowledge of harmony and its intricate
ways, so that the Prince of Brunswick, truest judge in these
matters, has said that many a superior Kapellmeister would
die without ever having learned what this nine year old
boy already knows. We have seen him for an hour and a
half under the impact storm of musicians from whose brows
the perspiration ran down in streams, and who had all the
trouble in the world, to withdraw, creditably, from this struggle with a boy who left the battle field without the least sign
of fatigue. I have seen him confuse and bring to silence organists who considered themselves most proficient. In London
(J. Chr.) Bach took him between his knees, and both played
alternately on the same piano, uninterruptedly for two hours,
in the presence of the King and the Queen. Here he has stood
the same test under Raupach, a clever musician, who has been

in St. Petersburg for a long while, and who improvises in a very superior manner. There would be a great deal more to tell about this unique phenomenon. And, by the way, he is one of the most charming creatures that you want to see: everything he says and does is full of life and soul, combined with the natural charm and loveliness of his youth. By his gaiety he even removes the fear that one may have, that so ripe a fruit might fall before its full maturity. If these children live, they will not stay in Salzburg. Soon the sovereigns will quarrel over possessing them. The father (Leopold Mozart) is not only a fine musician, but he is also a man of good sense and intelligence, and never yet have I seen a man of his profession combine such capacity for earning money with talent.

> *Friedrich Melchior Grimm, from his*
> *"Correspondence littéraire" (1764).*

The Baron's Admiration for the Child Prodigy
Wolfgang Amadeus

NOT only is it easy for the child to execute with the utmost exactitude the most difficult pieces — and that with hands so small that they scarcely can span a sixth — yes, it is incredible to hear him improvise for hours with greatest enthusiasm and an exuberance of charming fancies giving vent to his genius. He has such skill on the keyboard, that, if you cover it with a cloth, he still will continue to play with the same celerity and exactitude. It is but a small matter for him to decipher anything you would place before him, and he writes and composes with marvelous ease, without using the piano to garble his chords.

> *From "Correspondence Littéraire", Paris 1764.*

Mozart Made A Mason

"PROPOSED: Kapellmeister Mozart. — Our past Secr. Br. Hoffman forgot to register this member proposed by the Hon. Master . . . He has been proposed four weeks ago at the hon. district . . . and we should like, therefore, in the coming week, to take steps for his admittance, if the Hon. Brothers . . . have no objections."

From Paul Nettl's
"Mozart and Freemasonry".

Mozart and the Rock of Gibraltar

FROM a poem by Michael Denis: "Gibraltar" which Mozart had in mind to set to music and of which sketches are preserved.

"The thunder rolls at thy feet, o Calpe,
Yet thy aged brow looks fearless on worlds beneath.
Behold: a cloud arising from the western wave!
Rising, it spreads, portentous, as it moves.
It shivers in the wind, Calpe,
A cloud of sails! The wings of aid.
How awful streams Britannia's flag,
Flag of thy trusty guardian,
It streams, o Calpe, but night hangs over it."

Mozart, in a letter to his father (December 28, 1782) wrote about his work on the hymn "Gibraltar" as follows:

"I have before me a very difficult task, a bardic hymn about "Gibraltar" by Denis, but this is a secret, since a young lady wants to honor Denis with it. The ode is noble, beautiful — everything that one can wish — only too exaggerated and bombastic for my sensitive ears. But what

149

can you expect? The golden mean, truth in all things, is no longer known or cherished."

Paul Nettl.
(*N. Y. Times, Nov. 1940*).

Mozart to a Friend

MY opera "Don Giovanni" was performed on October 29th at Prague, and was a great success. It had its fourth performance last night, and that was for my benefit. I wish my good friends could be here with me but one night to share in my joy.

Isn't it true, that you are becoming more and more convinced of the justice of my lecture to you? Is not there a great difference, immeasurably wide, between a fickle, whimsical love, and the bliss which a true and reasonable union can procure?

To Baron von Jacquin in Vienna.
(*Prague, November 4, 1787*). (*Extract*)

Mozart In Financial Troubles

SINCE I cannot find true friends, I am obliged to raise money from usurers. But because it takes time to hunt for and find, among this most unchristian class of human beings, the most Christian ones, I am, at the present time, so denuded, that I must beg you, dearest friend, to help me out with the most necessary. If you could but know how all this distresses and worries me; it has prevented me all this time from finishing my quartets. I have two pupils now, and I should like to have eight. Please spread the fact that I am giving lessons.

From a letter to Puchberg, May 17th, 1790.

Lorenzo Da Ponte in New York Writes the Stories of
"Figaro" and "Don Giovanni"

IT wasn't long before several composers came to me for librettos, but at that time, there were only two deserving of my respect: Martini, at that time favorite composer of Emperor Joseph (II.), and Mozart whom I had the occasion to meet at the home of Baron Wetzlar,[1] his great friend and admirer. Wolfgang Mozart, although endowed with talents surpassing those of any composer of past, present, and future, had not been able as yet, owing to the intrigues of his enemies, to utilize his divine genius here in Vienna. He had remained in the dark, as a precious gem, hidden in the depths of the earth, must hide its glowing brilliance and worth. It is with pride and satisfaction that I can reflect on the fact, that it was to a large degree thanks to my perseverance and firmness that Europe and the world now possess the superior, excellent vocal compositions of this marvelous genius. The injustice and the envy of the journalists, the newspaper reporters, and still more the biographers of Mozart, denied the credit for all this to an Italian, but all Vienna and all who have known him and me in Germany, Bohemia and Saxony, his family and — more than all others — Baron Wetzlar, under whose roof emanated the first spark of that noble flame, will bear testimony to the truth of my assertions.

And, gracious Baron, of whose friendly consideration I recently received new proof, you, who love and revere this divine man so deeply, and who also have a part in his fame, please acknowledge me, before your age, should these memoirs ever fall into your hands (I shall see to it that they do) and do me the justice which two prejudiced Germans have

1 Baron Raymund Wetzlar was a Jewish banker, friend and protector of Mozart in whose home the great composer lived for some time.

tried to withhold from me: see to it that in public news-papers some truthloving writer may proclaim what the malevol-ence of others has covered up. Then will a beam of light, be it ever so small, fall on the honored memory of your friend Da Ponte.

After the great success of "Burbero", I went to Mozart, told him what had happened to me with Casti, Rosenberg and the Emperor, and asked him whether he would care to put into music a drama of mine. "That I would gladly do", he answered, "but I do not know whether I will get the per-mission to perform it". "Let that", I answered, "be my care." And so I went about happily, thinking of the plays I was to write for my two good friends, Mozart and Martini. The immeasurable genius of the former, I realized, de-manded a subject wide, manifold and lofty. When I was at one time conversing with him on the subject, he spoke to me of making an opera text of the Beaumarchais comedy "Le Mariage de Figaro". I approved entirely of the idea, and promised to do it; but there were great difficulties to overcome.

Not so long ago, the Emperor had forbidden the "Deut-sche Theatergesellschaft" to perform that comedy, which, he said, was too liberal for a well-bred audience: how would it be with an opera text? Baron Wetzlar, with great generosity, offered to pay me a good price for the opera, and, should it prove impossible to have it given in Vienna, to have it per-formed in London or Paris. Yet I refused his offer and pro-posed to write the text and the music secretly, awaiting a favorable opportunity to present it to the theatre directors and to the Emperor. I would use the utmost discretion in pre-senting it. Martini was the only one to hear my beautiful secret, and, because of his great esteem for Mozart, he agreed with me, not to write to the latter until the "Figaro" had been finished.

So I went to work on it while he wrote the music. It was

all ready in six weeks. Mozart's good luck would have it that there was a scarcity of scores at the theatre. At the first suitable opportunity, without telling any one about it, I took the "Figaro", to hand it, in person, to the Emperor. What did he say? "You know that Mozart, so superior in the field of instrumental music, has written but one opera, and that not an important one to be sure." "I too," I replied, "had it not been for Your Majesty, would have written but one drama in Vienna". "That is right", the Emperor said, "but I have forbidden this "Mariage de Figaro" to be played by the German troupe". "Yes", I answered, "but since I have written an opera and not a comedy, I have had to suppress many scenes, and have had to condense still more, and I have done this to those scenes that might offend the delicacy of feeling and the decorum of a theatre which is Your Majesty's. As far as the music is concerned, I think it is a work of great and wonderful beauty". "Very well, if that is the case, I shall depend on your taste for the music, and on your intelligence for the decorum. Let the copyist have the score."

I ran to see Mozart, but had not yet finished giving him the good news when a messenger from the Emperor arrived, bringing him a note which ordered him to appear at the palace at once. He obeyed the imperial order. The Emperor had him play some of the parts which pleased him extremely, and, — without exaggerating — of which not one aroused his displeasure. He had, in musical matters, exquisite taste, and, be it said, in all the fine arts as well. The great success which the work has had the world over, proves clearly that he was not wrong in his judgment. To learn that the Emperor found delight in Mozart's new composition, did, however, not please the other Viennese composers and Count Rosenberg who no more liked Mozart than did Casti. . .

We were, therefore, Mozart as well as I, not without a justified fear that we might again have to suffer from

153

the cabals of these, our not too good friends. They were not able to do much against us, but they did what they could. A certain (Francesco) Bussani, inspector of scenery and wardrobe, who was proficient in all professions except that of an honorable man, ran to Count Rosenberg when he heard that I had inserted a ballet into "Figaro", and told him in tones of astonishment and disapproval: "Your Excellency, the poet has introduced a ballet into his opera!" The Count immediately sent for me, and now began the grim little dialogue here following: "So Signore Poeta has introduced a ballet into his opera, is that right?" "Yes, Your Excellency." "Perhaps Signore Poeta is ignorant of the fact that the Emperor does not wish to see ballets in his theatre?" "No, Your Excellency". "Well, I am now telling you so, and furthermore I declare that you will have to suppress the ballet". Bussani repeatedly said this "Signore Poeta" and he said it in a tone really implying "Sir Jackass" or something similar. But my "Your Excellency" also had the required flavor! So, I answered again: "No, Your Excellency." "Do you have the libretto with you?" "Yes, Your Excellency". "Where is the ballet?" "Here, Your Excellency." "And this is how that is done"—saying which, he tore out two pages of the drama, threw them into the fire and, with a courtly air, returned the book, with the words: "You see, Signore Poeta, that I can do anything I please".

I, at once repaired to see Mozart who, at hearing this bad news, was in despair. He wanted to see the Count at once, to rate Bussani, to run to the Emperor, and to withdraw his score. I had great pain to soothe him. Finally I begged him to give me just two days and to let me go ahead.

The dress rehearsal of the opera was to take place that same day. I went, in person, to the Emperor, in order to report this to him, and he promised to be there promptly. And, indeed, he did appear and with him half the nobility of Vienna. The Abbate Casti too came with him. The first act was received with general applause. At the close, there is a pantomimic scene between Susanna and the Count (Count Almaviva), during which the orchestra plays and the dance goes on. But when his almighty excellency, Rosenberg, tore out this scene, he had failed to realize one thing, namely, that this mute by-play of Susanna and the Count would, without the orchestra part that he had destroyed, give the impression of a marionette stage.

"What does that mean?" said the Emperor to Casti, who was sitting right behind him. "We must ask the poet", the Abbate answered, maliciously. So I was sent for at once but instead of answering the question put to me, I just presented my manuscript in which I had restored the scene. The Emperor read it and asked me why the dance that he saw in notation there, had been omitted? My silence led him to realize that there had been a little swindle somewhere. He turned to Count Rosenberg and questioned him on the matter. Rosenberg murmured that the dance had been omitted because there was no ballet personnel at the theatre. "Are there none in the other theatres?" the monarch asked. He was told there were some. "Very well, then raise as many as Da Ponte requires."

In less than half an hour the ballet personnel had been brought together. At the end of the second act, the suppressed scene was repeated and this time the Emperor called out: "Now, that is good." This further evidence of the Emperor's favor doubled the hatred and desire for revenge in the soul of my powerful persecutor. . .

In the meantime Mozart's opera was performed, which, putting to shame all doubters, all other composers, Count Rosenberg and Casti, and a hundred other devils — was generally well received and was judged to be (by the Emperor himself and by other true connoisseurs) something lofty and almost divine.

I now felt that the time had come to bring into flow my poetic vein, which seemed completely dried out. The opportunity soon offered. The three superior masters: Martini, Mozart and Salieri, applied to me for librettos. I loved and valued all three of them, and hoped from all three compensation for the past failures, and an increase of my small theatrical renown. I meditated whether it wouldn't be possible to satisfy all three and to write three operas at once. Salieri was not asking me for an original drama. In Paris he had written "Tarare". He wished to change it to an opera in the Italian style, and asked me for such a transposition. Mozart and Martini left the choice entirely to me. I chose "Don Giovanni" for Mozart, which subject pleased him immensely. For Martini I chose "The Tree of Diana". When I had found these three subjects, I went to the Emperor informing him of my intention to produce the three operas at once. "You won't succeed", said the Emperor. "Perhaps not," I replied, "but I am going to try. I shall write and think for Mozart at night, while reading Dante's "Inferno"; in the morning for Martini, with my imagination dwelling on Petrarca; and in the evening for Salieri, with my "Tasso" at hand."

I found my metaphor a very beautiful one and, arrived at home, immediately got to work. I went to my writing desk and sat down for twelve unbroken hours, a bottle of Tokay wine to my right, an ink-well in the middle, and a box of Sevilla tobacco to my left. A beautiful sixteen year old girl whom I should have loved as my daughter only—but—, lived in the same house with me, with her mother. She took care of the household and had permission to enter my room when I rang (which I very often did)—(particularly when my inspiration began to cool off). She used to bring a biscuit or a cup of coffee for me, and her beautiful ever-smiling face seemed made for bringing poetic inspiration and witty ideas. I continued, for two months, to work twelve hours a day with few interruptions, and during all this time she remained in the adjoining room, either with a book in her hand, or with a needle and embroidery, to be ready, at the ringing of the bell,

156

to come to me. She would then sit beside me, without moving, without opening her mouth, gazing at me firmly and smiling very alluringly. At times she sighed and seemed inclined to grieve. This child was my Calliope for those three operas, and for all the verses I wrote in the following six years. At first, I permitted frequent visits, but later I had to see less of her, so as not to lose too much time in making love, of which art she had complete mastery. In the meantime, I wrote, on the first day, between the Tokay, the Sevilla tobacco, the coffee, the bell and the youthful muse, the first two scenes of "Don Giovanni", two of the "Tree of Diana" and more than half the first act of "Tarare", the name of which I had changed to "Axur". The next morning I brought these scenes to the three composers who could hardly trust their eyes. In sixty-eight days, however, the first two operas were completely finished; and the third, by two-thirds. "The Tree of Diana" was the first of the operas to be performed.

The first performance had not yet taken place, when I was obliged to go to Prague, where Mozart's "Don Giovanni" was to have its première. The occasion was the arrival of the Duchess of Toscana. I stayed in Prague for a week to coach the actors who were to take part, but hardly had I stepped on the stage, when I was recalled to Vienna to hear that "Axur" was to be staged at once. This time the occasion being the wedding of the Archduke Franz. The Emperor himself had ordered me back, thus I had no chance to witness the performance of "Don Giovanni" in Prague, but Mozart notified me at once of its wonderful success, and Guardassoni (the Prague opera director) wrote to me: "Viva Da Ponte, viva Mozart. Performers as well as directors must count themselves fortunate. As long as they are alive, there will be no more thought of failures." The Emperor sent for me and graciously overwhelmed me with words of praise, made me a present of a hundred Zechines, and told me that he ardently desired to see "Don Giovanni".

Mozart returned and gave the score to the copyist at once, telling him to hurry on with it as the Emperor was obliged to leave soon. The performance took place and—dare I say it?—"Don Giovanni" was *not* a success! Every one except Mozart thought that something was missing. We made changes, added arias — and yet "Don Giovanni" was no success. And what did the Emperor say? "The opera is divine", he said, "perhaps even more beautiful than "Figaro", but it is not food for the teeth of my Viennese". I told Mozart what the Emperor had said, but he retorted coolly: "Allright, give them time to chew". He was not mistaken. I saw to it that his wishes that the opera be frequently given, were carried out. And really — the applause increased with each performance, and gradually the Viennese with the bad teeth, got the taste, learned to recognize its beauty and counted "Don Giovanni" among the finest works ever performed on the stage.

I tried to persuade Mozart to go to London with me. But he had recently, as a compensation for his divine operas, received an annuity for life, and was busy writing a German opera "The Magic Flute" from which he expected great fame. He demanded six months to think it over, and, I, in the meantime, underwent all kinds of changes, which forced my life into quite a different channel.

From Lorenzo Da Ponte's "Memoirs".

158

BEETHOVEN

Beethoven's Appearance

(As told by a close friend)

BEETHOVEN'S height was about 5 feet 4 inches. His body was stodgy, of firm bone structure and strong muscles; his head was unusually large, with long bristly hair, almost entirely gray, and usually neglected and hanging around his head, giving him a somewhat savage appearance, particularly when his beard had reached abnormal length, which was often the case. His forehead was high and broad; his brown eyes were small, and—when he laughed—almost entirely hidden in his head; on the other hand they would, at times, appear excessively large, rolling and flashing, with pupils turned upward. Sometimes, when an idea took possession of him, they would become immovable and he would stare before him. Beethoven's entire appearance would then undergo a striking change, take on an inspired and imposing aspect, and the small figure — corresponding to the stature of his soul — would seem to rise to gigantic height. These moments of inspiration occasionally came to him in the gayest company and in the street, when he excited the attention of all passers-by. What was going on within him was expressed only by his glowing eyes and face;—he never gesticulated either with his hands or with his head, except when he had an orchestra before him. His mouth was well formed, and his lips were regular; his nose was broad. His smile illumined his countenance, and gave it a surpassingly kind and sweet expression, which was particularly encouraging to strangers. His laughter was loud and ringing, and distorted somewhat the spiritualized and strongly marked face: the big head began to swell, the face grew still broader, and very often resembled a grinning mask. It was a good thing that this effect passed quickly. His chin had a dimple, and two longish dents on either side, lending a rather peculiar appearance to the whole. His skin was of a yellowish coloring, which however disappeared in the summer, when on his long wanderings in the open air it would take on a brownish-reddish tint, covering his full red cheeks like a varnish.

A dress coat of fine blue cloth (the favored color in those days) with metal buttons, became him excellently. Such a one, and another of green cloth, were never missing from his wardrobe. In summer, he was always seen wearing white pantalons, shoes, and white stockings (the fashion at that time). Vest and tie were always white and immaculate, no matter what the season. In addition to this attire, imagine a light gait and an upright carriage — these ever characterizing the master — and — you have before you, Beethoven's personality.

From Anton Schindler's
"Biographie von Ludwig van Beethoven"
(1840)

The Lord of the Keys

IN the year 1798, while I was studying law, Beethoven, the giant among the piano-players, came to Prague. He gave a well-attended concert in the "Konvikt Saal", in which he played his C major Concerto op. 15, the Adagio and graceful Rondo from the Sonata in A major, op. 2, and then, as a finale, closed with free improvisations on a theme given to him by Countess Schlick, from Mozart's "Titus": "Ah, tu fosti il primo oggetto". Beethoven's grandiose playing and the daring representation of his improvisations, stirred me in quite a curious way—yes, I felt myself so bowed down, that for

PLATE 13.—Printz, "Phrynis Mitylenaeus or the Satirical Composer"

PLATE 14.—Arcangelo Corelli.

IOANNES MATTHESON
Celsitudinis Imperialis Magni Russiæ Principi
Supremi Holsatiæ Ducis
Legationum Consiliarius.
æt.
nat. Hamburg d. 28 Sept. A. 1681.

PLATE 15.—Portrait of Johann Mattheson [Engraving after Wahll by Haid]

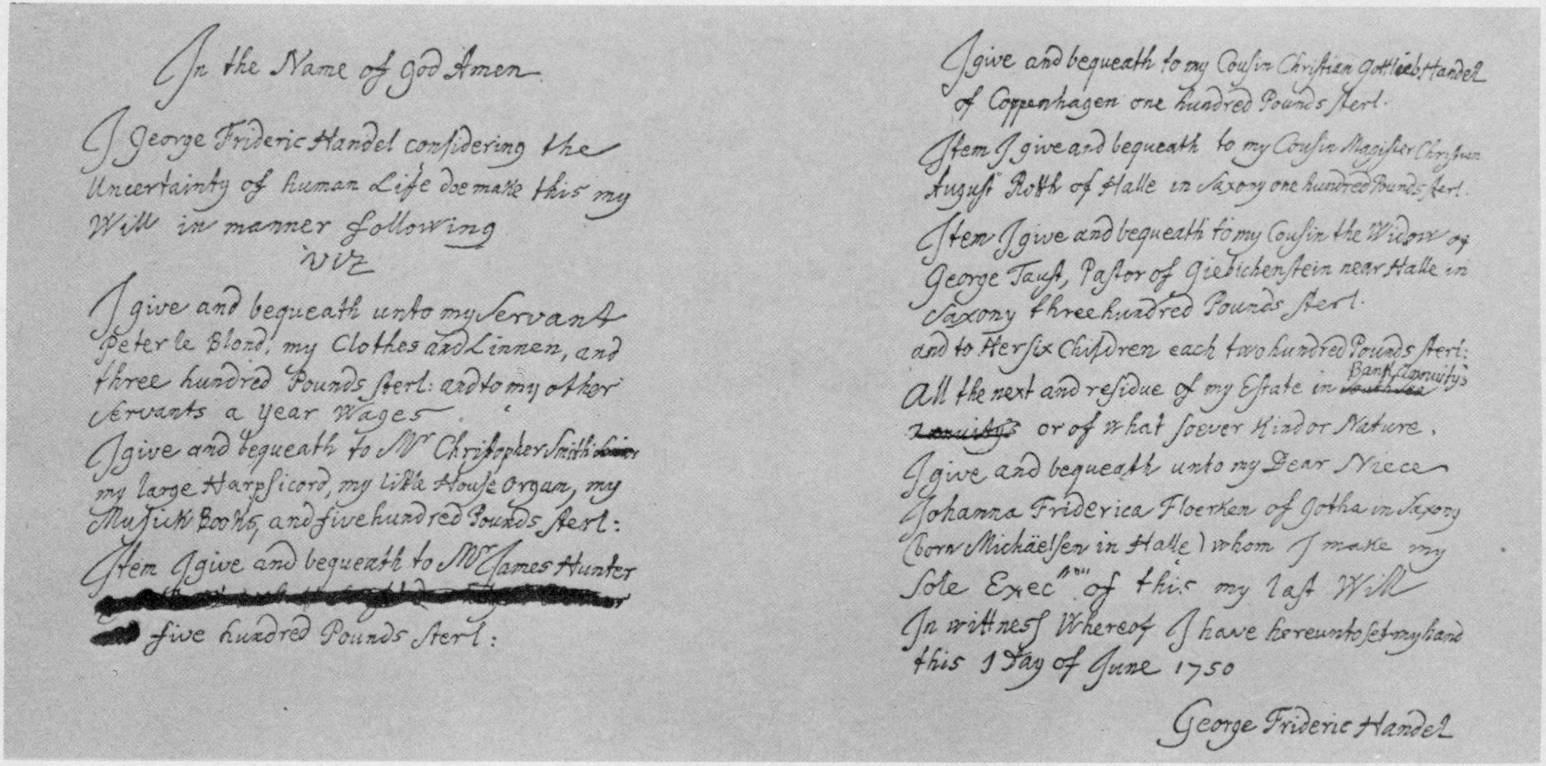

PLATE 16.—George Frederic Handel's Last Will dated June 1st, 1750

days I did not touch a piano, and it was only my unconquerable love of music, and later a sensible reasoning, that brought me to resume my pilgrimages to the piano, as of old, and with increased industriousness. I heard Beethoven in his second concert, but neither his playing nor his compositions made the same overwhelming impression on me. This time he played the Concerto in Bb major, which he had composed in Prague. Then I heard him for a third time at the home of Graf Clary, where besides the graceful Rondo of the A major Sonata, he improvised on the theme "Ah, vous dirai-je, Maman." This time I could with calmness follow Beethoven's artistic achievement: I did admire his vigorous brilliant playing, but I did not feel as bowed down as before,—I did not fail to notice his sudden daring breaks from one motif to another, whereby the organized union, a gradual development of ideas seemed lost. These flaws often weaken his greatest works, that he has so happily conceived. At times the unprepared listener is violently thrown out of a blissful mood. The original and out-of-the-ordinary seemed to be his main object in composition. This is corroborated by an answer he gave to a lady, when asked whether he often visited Mozart's operas: he did not know them, nor did he like to listen to music of other composers because he did not wish to sacrifice his own originality.

Beethoven left Prague, and I am happy I heard the Master of piano-playing in his own creations.

Wenzel Johann Tomaschek (1774-1850).
("Libussa" IV)

Beethoven Takes Leave of Life
The Heiligenstadt Testament

To my brothers Karl and Johann Beethoven:

O, my fellowmen, you who have thought and called me inimical, stubborn and misanthropic, how you wronged me! You do not know the causes underlying these charges. My mind and my heart, from childhood on were kindly disposed, and I longed to perform great deeds. But consider, that, for the past six years, an unhappy lot, an incurable ailment has befallen me, which has been worsened by ignorant physicians. Cheated of the hope of improvement from year to year, I was finally forced to accept the possibility of a lingering malady, which it might take years to cure, or worse still, which might prove to be incurable. Born with a fiery, vivacious temperament, and having a bent for social recreations, I was obliged, early in life, to retire from the world and to live a lonely life. When, at times, I tried to rise above this, how bitter, how sad was the experience, due to my poor hearing. And yet, I found it impossible to say to people: "Speak louder, shout, for I am deaf". How could I admit the weakness of a sense, that, in me, should be keener than in most,—a sense, that at one time I possessed in full perfection,—a perfection such as few in my profession have ever enjoyed. I could never do that. Therefore forgive me for withdrawing from you all, when I so gladly would have mingled with you. My misfortune is doubly hard to bear, because I know that I shall be misunderstood. For me there is to be no relaxation in human society, cultural conversation, exchange of views. Almost all alone I can approach human society only as far as the barest necessities demand. I am condemned to live like one banished. Whenever I approach a social gathering, a hot dread fills me, lest my condition be noticed.

And it was thus, that I have spent these last six weeks in the country. Following the orders of my physician—orders which only too well met with my present disposition—I am as sparing as possible of my hearing, but, at times, a longing for social intercourse has driven me to disregard his instructions. But how humiliating, when, someone, standing beside me, heard the playing of a flute, from afar, and I heard nothing; or when a shepherd was heard singing, and I heard him not. Such experiences almost drove me to desperation and I was on the brink of taking my life.

Art alone hindered me. It seemed inconceivable that I should leave this world, without having produced all that I felt I must. And so I go on, leading this miserable life, — a truly miserable one, with a body so irritable, that upon the slightest occasion, a sudden change can throw me from the best condition into the worst one.

Patience — that is the name of her who must be my guide, and I have made my choice. I hope my resolve to persevere will last, until it pleases the relentless Parcae to break off the thread. Perhaps I shall succeed, perhaps not. I am resigned. To become a philosopher at the age of twenty-six, is not so easy, and harder for the artist than for another.

O. God, Thou art looking down on me, Thou knowest, Thou canst see into my inmost being, Thou knowest that the love of humanity and the desire to do good ever actuate me. And, O, you human beings who read this, think how you have wronged me, and if there be among you one as unhappy as I am, let him console himself with the thought that he is not alone, that there is another like him, who, in spite of all natural obstacles has striven to keep his place in the ranks of worthy artists and men.

You, my brothers Karl and (Johann), if after my death Professor Schmidt should be still alive, please beg him, in my name, to give a description of my illness, and of the story of my malady, and, please, add these to the pages here, so that the world may become reconciled to me as much as possible. And at the same time I declare you both the heirs to my small fortune. Divide it justly, be friends, and help each other. What you may have done to hurt me, has long since been forgiven, as you know. I thank you, my brother Karl. in particular, for the devotion shown me these latter days. I wish you a life, better and less sorrowful than mine. Recommend virtue to your children: Virtue alone, not money brings happiness. I am speaking from experience. It was virtue that uplifted me in my misery, and it is because of virtue and my art, that I did not end my life by suicide. Farewell, and love one another.

And I thank all my friends, in particular Prince Lichnowsky, and Professor Schmidt. I should like you (my brothers) to take charge of Lichnowsky's instruments. But let there be no quarrel among you because of them. As soon as they can serve a useful purpose, sell them. How happy it would make me, if even from my grave, I could be of use.

And now it is done. I hasten toward death with joy. Should it come, before I have had time enough to devote to the unfoldment of all my powers, I might deem it too soon, despite my hard lot, and I might wish for it to come later. But even so, — should not the thought of being free from infinite suffering be a cause for gratification? Therefore, Death, come when Thou wilt: I shall meet Thee with fortitude.

Farewell, and do not forget me altogether after my death. I have earned this, for I have tried all my life to make you happy. So be it!

Heiligenstadt, October 6, 1802.

Ludwig van Beethoven.

Bettina Brentano, One of the Most Colorful Women of Her Age

Dear, dear Bettina:

I have already received two letters from you and I see from your letters to Toni, how often and how — only too favorably you are thinking of me. I carried your first letter around with me all summer long, and it has often given me joy. Even though I do not write to you very often, and you don't see me at all, believe me, in thoughts, I write you a thousand times.

What you think of the "riffraff" in Berlin, I would know, even if I had read nothing you have written. Talk, tattle about art, but no action. The best description of this is found in Schiller's "Die Fluesse", where the Spree speaks.*

You are going to marry, dear Bettina, or have already married, and I have not even seen you before. May all the happiness that marriage can give be yours and your husband's!

What shall I tell you about myself? "Have pity on my fate", I call out with Johanna. If I can save a few more years of life, I will be grateful, even for that, to the All-embracing, to the Highest.

When you write to Goethe, find all the words you can to express my deepest admiration and esteem for him. I am just about to write to him myself, about "Egmont" which I have put to music, and, be it said, only for love of his poems, that give me so much joy. But how can one thank a great poet, — the most precious gem of a nation, enough?

No more today, my dear Bettina. I have come from a bacchanal at 4 o'clock this morning, where I laughed a great deal, only to weep all the more today. Exuberant joy, very often drives me back into myself. — Many thanks to Clemens for his accommodating spirit. As far as the Cantata is concerned, the subject is not of enough interest for us here; it may be a different matter in Berlin.[1] As for affection, the sister has such a large portion of it, that not much remains for her brother — does that serve him?

And now, farewell, my dear, dear Bettina. I kiss your brow, and impress upon it, as though with a seal, all my thoughts of you. Write soon and often to your friend

Beethoven.

To Bettina von Brentano, Vienna, Feb. 10, 1811.

* In this poem the Spree impersonates a bragging person. Beethoven here ridicules the boasting and arrogant Berliners.

[1] It was a Cantata, written by Clemens von Brentano (Bettina's brother) on the death of Queen Luise of Prussia, composed by Reichardt.

Dedication of the Egmont-Music to Goethe

Your Excellency:

A pressing matter, inasmuch as a friend of mine is suddenly leaving (he admires you as I do), gives me but a moment's time to thank you for all the years that I have known you. You have been known to me since my childhood.

Bettina Brentano has assured me that you will receive me kindly, yes, even as a friend. But how could I believe in such a reception, since I can approach you only with greatest deference, with an unspeakable feeling for your great glorious creations. You will in a short time receive the music for "Egmont" from Leipzig, (Breitkopf & Haertel) that wonderful "Egmont" which I have put to music as warmly as I thought of and felt with you. I should very much wish to hear your opinion of it, for even a censure could be but profitable to my art, and would be as gladly accepted as the greatest praise.

Your Excellency's great admirer
Ludwig van Beethoven

April 12, 1811.

Goethe's Answer

Your kind letter, my most honored Sir, forwarded to me by Herr Oliva, has been received by me with the greatest pleasure. I thank you from my heart for the sentiments therein expressed, and I can assure you that I most sincerely return them, for I have never heard any of your works, performed by clever artists or amateurs, without wishing that I might hear you in person playing the piano, and take delight in your extraordinary talent.

Dear Bettina Brentano is surely deserving the sympathy you have shown her. She speaks rapturously of you and with the deepest affection, and counts the hours spent with you among the happiest of her life.

I shall probably find the music of "Egmont", dedicated to me, when I get home, and am already grateful for it, for I have heard it spoken of in the highest terms. I intend to have it performed at our theatre, to my play, this winter, and I am looking forward to a great enjoyment both for myself and the many admirers you have here. But most of all do I hope to have understood Herr Oliva rightly when he gave us hope that you intend to pay us a visit in Weimar. May it occur at a time, when not only the court, but all the music lovers will be assembled there. You would surely get a reception worthy of your merits and sentiments. But no one would be more interested than I, who, wishing you all the happiness in life, commend myself to your gracious remembrance, and thank you most sincerely for all the good come to me through you.

Goethe, Karlsbad, June 25, 1811.

To the Immortal Beloved . . .

Teplitz, July 6, 1812, in the morning.

My angel, my all, my ego!

Only a few words with a pencil (yours!). My apartment won't be ready until tomorrow. What a miserable waste of time!

Why this deep grief when necessity speaks? Can our love subsist, except by sacrifices, by not asking for everything? Can you change the fact that you are not wholly mine — I not wholly yours? O, Lord, gaze at beautiful nature, and resign yourself to what must be. Love demands everything and rightly so; and thus it is for me with you, and for you with me. Only you so easily forget that I must live for both you and me. If we were wholly united, you would feel the pain as little as I do.

My journey was terrible and I did not arrive before 4

169

o'clock yesterday morning. There were not horses enough and therefore, another route had to be taken, but what an awful road! At the station before the last, I was warned not to travel at night, I was warned of a forest we had to pass, — but that only tempted me the more. However, I was wrong. The coach broke down on a dirt road! Had it not been for the four postillons I had, I would have been left, lying on the way. Esterhazy, on his way here, had the same experience with eight horses that I had with four. But, on the other hand, I got pleasure even out of that, as is usual after I have overcome trouble.

Now quickly from the outer to the inner. We will probably see each other soon. I cannot, today, tell you about the observations I have made on my life these few days. Were our hearts ever united I would probably not have had to make them. My heart is overflowing with thoughts that I want to tell you. O, I think there are moments when language means nothing.

Be happy! Remain my true, my only love, as I am yours. As for the rest — what is to be for you and me — is in the hands of the Gods.

Your true
Ludwig.

Monday evening, July 6th.

You are suffering, dearest being — (only now do I realize that letters must be posted early in the morning, and that Thursday and Monday are the only days for mail to Karlsbad). You are suffering . . . Ah, where I am, you are with me; and in talking to you, I am talking to myself. Do what you can, so that I can live with you. What a life ! ! ! ! like this ! ! ! ! without you, annoyed by the kindness of people here and there, which I neither deserve nor want to deserve. Humility of man to man pains me. And when I consider myself in connection with the universe, what am I, and what is

He, whom they call the Greatest? And yet it is herein that lies the divine in man. I weep when I realize that only on Saturday you will get first news of me. No matter how much you love me, I love you more . . . But never hide anything from me, don't . . .

Good night! As one of the patients here, I must go to bed. O God, so near! so far! Is it not an edifice of heaven, our love? And as firm too, as the fortress of heaven . . .

Good Morning, July 7th.

Even in bed, my thoughts rush to you, my immortal beloved; at times they are happy, then again sad, waiting for fate to fulfill our wishes. I can live, either altogether with you or not at all. Yes, I am determined to wander afar until I can fly into your arms, and make myself quite at home with you, and can send my soul, imbued with you, into the realms of spirits. Yes, thus it must be. You will be resigned, all the more so, since you know how true I am to you. Never will another possess my heart, never, never! O, God, why must one leave what one loves so much! And yet my life in Vienna, as it now is, is but a poor one, and your love makes me the happiest as well as the most unhappy of men. At this period of my life I would need uniformity, a certain regularity: can this exist, our relations being what they are?

My angel, I hear that the post leaves every day; so I shall have to close, for you must get this letter at once. Be calm. Only by a calm revision of our being, can we attain our purpose to live together. Be calm! Love me!

Today, yesterday, what a tearful longing for you, you, you, my life, my all! ! Farewell. O! continue to love me! Never misunderstand the truest heart of your

beloved Ludwig.

Eternally yours.
Eternally mine.
Eternally we.

A Cheerful Letter About Two Friends Striding Through Life Together Without Seeing Each Other:

Vienna, April 8, 1815

IT is surely not permissible to be on friendly terms with any one as I am with you and yet to live so inimically without seeing each other. . . "Tout à vous", you wrote. "O, you braggart", I thought. No, no, that seems too bad. I would rather feel like thanking you nine-thousand times for your endeavors in my behalf, and yet I want to scold you twenty-thousand times that you left as quickly as you came. So all is illusion, is it? Friendship, empire, kingdom? — all but a mist that any gust of wind can dissipate, can change?

I may go to Teplitz, but it is not yet sure. I could, on that occasion, give the people of Prague something to listen to. What do you think about it, if you care to "think about me" at all? Since the affair of Lobkowitz has come to an end now, the "finis" is there — not without a "fi" (fooey) indeed.

Baron Pasqualati will probably visit you soon; he has had a great deal of trouble with me. Yes, o yes, it is quite easy to say what is right, but most difficult to get righteousness from others, correct?

How could I serve you with my art? Tell me, do you want me to sing about the monologue of a banished king, or the perjury of an usurper? Or rather about the two friends living side by side, who never see each other?[1]

Hoping to hear from you soon, as it may be easier to get close to one another when you are far away than if you were here. . . .

---

[1] Prof. Arnold Schering quoted these lines in his book "Beethoven und die Dichtung" and made it part of his theory that most of Beethoven's instrumental works are programmatic music.

I am your most devoted, your most respectful friend
Ludwig van Beethoven.

(*Letter to Johann Kanka in Prague*).

From Beethoven's Note Books (1812, 1813)

RESIGNATION, heartfelt resignation to one's fate. Only this can bring you the needed fortitude for service. O, bitter struggle!

Do everything, do your utmost, to work out what is necessary for the long journey. You must seek everything,—the fulfillment of your most divine desire—but you must seize it by observing the same steadfast way of thinking.

You can not be just one human being,—not for yourself, not for your own sake, only for that of others. There is no happiness for you, except for what is in yourself and in your art. O, God, give me the strength to conquer myself. Nothing must be allowed to hinder me from living my life.

Learn to be silent, O friend; silver resembles talking, but to know when to be silent at the right time, is pure gold.[1]

And should the clouds rain streams of life,
Never will the willow-tree bear dates!
Do not waste your time with bad people:
Common reeds will never yield sugar.
Can you forge a good sword with soft clay?
Does the wolf, fostered by man,
Ever change his nature?
Is it not the same rain,
That here, on salty soil, makes grow both thorns and
    thistles,
And flowers in the garden?

---

[1] Herder's words were composed by Beethoven who dedicated this canon to the English pianist Charles Neate, Jan. 16, 1816.

So do not waste seed and precious care:
To render evil for good, and good for evil, is one
      and the same.[1]

May 15, 1813.

See, thus is man. Therefore, when one has fallen, let another weep, but not dare to judge.

May 16, 1813.

Life resembles the vibration of the tones—
And man is like the lute:
When it falls to the ground
The pure tone is lost.
And it can not again recover.
Can only give displeasure,
Must not with others sound together,
Lest it brings discord,
Instead of unison to the ear,
In the pure, harmonious chorus.

May 17, 1813.

Are you asking why the stars
Rise and then descend?
Here only what is, is clear.
The 'why' will be revealed
When the dead rise again . . . [2]

God is immaterial. He is therefore beyond conception. As He is invisible, He can not have a form; but from the manifestation of His works we must conclude that He is eternal, omnipotent and omnipresent. Whatever is free from desire and greed, is the Mighty One. He alone. There is none greater than He. Brahma: His Spirit is bound up in itself. He, the Almighty, is present in every part of space. His omniscience is of His own comprehension and His comprehension includes every other. Of all all-comprehending qualities, omniscience is the greatest: there is no threefold being for it,—

---

[1] Herder's "Verschwendete Muehe."
[2] From Muellner's tragedy "Die Schuld."

it is independent of all. O, God, Thou art the true, the ever-blessing unchangeable light of all time and space. Thy wisdom recognizes thousands of laws, and yet, Thou ever acteth freely and to Thine glory. Thou standeth for everything that we revere: all glory and worship to Thee. Thou alone art the All Blessed One (Bhagavan)—Thou, the essence of all laws, the image of all wisdom, present to all the world, Thou, who bearest within thyself all things.[1]

Goethe's Opinion On Beethoven

I MADE Beethoven's acquaintance at Teplitz and was astounded at his talent. But I am sorry to say that his is an untamed personality. He is not far from wrong in finding the world detestable, but he does not, therefore, make it any the more enjoyable either for himself or for others. He must be excused however, and is greatly to be pitied for the loss of his hearing, which loss probably is more detrimental to the social than to the musical part of his being. Since he is of a naturally laconic disposition, this defect will make him still more so.

From a letter to Karl Friedrich Zelter
(Karlsbad, September 2, 1812).

A Humble Letter: Beethoven to Goethe

Your Excellency:

Ever living, as in the years of my youth, in your immortal, never-aging works, and never forgetting the happy hours lived in your presence, it so happens, that I must recall myself to you. I hope you have received "Meeresstille und Glueckliche Fahrt", put to music by me, and dedicated to

---

[1] Excerpts from an unknown text on Hindu philosophy.

Your Excellency. This work seemed to me, because of the contrast of its parts, well suited to expression in music. How happy I would be to learn whether I have succeeded in bringing my harmonies in concord with yours. Instruction from you, which I would regard as the truth, would be most welcome to me, for I love truth above everything, and never will it be said of me: "Veritas odium parit". It is very possible that others of your unparalleled poems, among them "Rastlose Liebe" will appear, put to music by me. How I would appreciate a general comment from you on my setting to music of your poems!

Now, Your Excellency, I have to make a petition. I have written a Mass, which I do not wish to publish just yet, preferring to have it produced at the most prominent courts. The gratuity is only fifty ducats. I have, therefore, addressed myself in this matter to the Weimar Embassy, which has accepted the petition, and promised to forward it to His Highness. The Mass is also to be performed as an Oratorio, and everybody knows that the various societies are very much in need of something of that order. I would beg of Your Excellency to call the attention of His Highness to my plea so that His Highness may subscribe to my petition. The Grandducal Embassy advised me that it would be to my advantage, if the Grandduke were to favor it beforehand. Although I have written very often, I have never received an answer.

You must know, I am no longer alone. For the past six years I have been father to the son of my deceased brother, a promising youth, sixteen years of age, in possession of scientific knowledge, and quite at home in the rich shafts of Greekdom. But in this country everything is very costly, and with youths who are studying, there is not only the present to be considered, there is the future as well, and much as I have hitherto looked only upward, I must now cast my gaze downward. My salary amounts to nothing. My illness, for the last years, has prevented me from going on artistic tours, and, doing anything else that would procure a livelihood. Should I ever again acquire my full health, I could surely expect better things.

Your Excellency, however, must not think that I dedicated "Meeresstille und Glueckliche Fahrt" to you, in order to insure your intervention, now asked for. The dedication was devised as early as May 1822, when I had no thought of making the Mass known in this manner; that only occurred to me a few weeks ago. The admiration, love and esteem I have felt for the one and only Goethe has been with me since my earliest youth. It is difficult to put anything like this into words, particularly by such a blunderer as I am, who has had but one thought, and that was to make music. But a curious feeling urges me again and again to tell you how much I live in, and by your writings. I know, you will not fail to intercede for an artist, who has known how difficult it is to gain a mere subsistence, and whom necessity now forces, to work for and create for another.

What is good, is ever obvious to us, and therefore I trust Your Excellency will not refuse my request. A few words from you would overwhelm me with supreme joy.

With the most heartfelt, unlimited esteem your devoted

Beethoven.

Vienna, Feb. 8, 1823.

Beethoven Did Not Dislike Pretty Women

ONE evening, when I came to Baden for my lesson, I found a beautiful lady with him, sitting on the sofa. As it seemed to me that I was in the way, I proceeded to leave at once, but Beethoven called me back and said: "Play a while". He and the lady were sitting behind me. I had played for quite a while, when the master suddenly called: "Ries, play something sentimental". And shortly thereafter he said: "Something melancholy". And then: "Something passionate".

Beethoven never visited me more often than when I was living in the house of a tailor, where there were three beautiful but irreproachable daughters. This also explains an allusion at the close of a letter, of July 24th, 1804, where he said: "Don't do too much tailoring, and remember me to the most beautiful of all the beautiful. And—send me half a dozen sewing needles."

From "Biographische Notizen ueber
Ludwig van Beethoven" by Dr. F. G. Wegeler
and Ferdinand Ries, 1838.

Nil Humani . . .
Critical Remarks of a Czech Composer
(1814)

ON the morning of October 10th, my brother and I visited Beethoven. The poor man's hearing was particularly bad that day, and we had to scream rather than to talk in order to be understood at all. The reception room was furnished with anything but grandeur, and the disorder reigning therein was as great as that in his hair. I found an upright piano-forte, and, on its stand, the text of a Cantata: "Der Glorreiche Augenblick" by Weissenbach. On the piano, there lay a pencil with which he had sketched his work. Side by side with this I found, on a small piece of paper, all sorts of ideas, without the least connection, jotted down: the most heterogeneous details thrown together, just as they have come into his mind. However, this was the material of the new Cantata.

His conversation was just as haphazard as was this motley of musical details. As is usual with the deaf, he carried on the conversation in a very loud voice, always stroking his ear with one hand as though seeking the weakened power of hearing.

Some parts of this conversation, which for me were without a meaning, I shall herewith report, omitting certain names the mention of which seems to me without importance.

I: Herr van Beethoven, you will pardon me for disturbing you. I am Tomaschek of Prague, Compositeur of Count Bouquoy. I am taking the liberty of visiting you, in company of my brother.

Beethoven: I am very pleased to make your acquaintance, and you are not disturbing me in the least.

I: Dr. R. (Dr. Josef Reger, lawyer) wishes to be remembered to you.

Beethoven: How is he? It is a long time since I have heard from him.

I: He would like to know how you have progressed with your law-suit.

Beethoven: There are so many formalities that little progress is made.

I: I hear, that you have composed a Requiem.

Beethoven: I wanted to write a Requiem as soon as this business was over. Why should I write before this affair is settled?

Now he began to tell me all about it. And here too, he spoke without coherence, more rhapsodically. Finally the conversation changed to other matters.

I: Herr van Beethoven seems to be very industrious.

Beethoven: Must I not? What would become of my fame?

I: Does my pupil Worzischek often come to see you?

Beethoven: He was here several times, but I did not hear him. Not long ago he brought me some of his compositions, which, for a young fellow like him, are well done. (Beethoven was alluding to the twelve rhapsodies for the piano-forte, which, dedicated to me, later appeared in print).

I: I suppose you seldom go out?

Beethoven: Hardly anywhere.

I: Tonight there is a première of Seyfried's opera; I have no desire to listen to such music.

Beethoven: Lord, there must be composers like that. What otherwise would the masses do?

I: I was also told that a young foreign artist has arrived here, who is said to be an extraordinary piano player.

Beethoven: Yes, I too have heard of him, but I have not heard him play. Lord, just let him stay here three months, and then we will hear what the Viennese think of his playing. I know how everything new takes here!

I: I don't suppose you have met him?

Beethoven: I did meet him at the performance of the "Schlacht" ("Battle of Vittoria"), at which occasion several of the local composers played some instrument. The big drum was assigned to that young man. Hahaha! And I was not at all satisfied with him: He did not strike it correctly, and always came in too late, so that I had to give him a good calling down. Hahaha! That angered him. There is nothing to him. He hasn't the courage to strike at the right time. (G. Meyerbeer).

This observation made both my brother and myself laugh heartily. Refusing Beethoven's invitation to stay for a meal, we left him, with the promise to visit him again before my departure.

November 24th.

I visited Beethoven again, for I had a great longing to see him before leaving Vienna. I was announced by his servant and admitted at once. If, on the occasion of my first visit, his apartment had been untidy, it was all the more so this time; for in the middle room I met two copyists, who were writing down, in great haste, his before mentioned, and now finished Cantata. In the second room, parts of scores, which were probably being corrected by Umlauf (to whom he introduced me) were lying all over the place, on tables, chairs, etc. Herr

180

Umlauf seemed to be of a happy disposition, for he was neither cold nor warm at our first meeting. The mutual impression we made on each other remained;—but he went and I stayed. Beethoven received me very cordially but seemed more deaf than ever before and I had to exert all my power to make myself understood. I will reproduce the dialogue here:

I: I have come to see you once more before my departure.

Beethoven: I thought you had already left Vienna. Have you been here all this time?

I: Yes, with the exception of a few excursions to Aspern and Wagram. You have been well?

Beethoven: O, as ever, I had much annoyance; it is hardly possible to continue living here.

I: I see you are very busy with your academy,—I should not like to disturb you in your work.

Beethoven: Not in the least, I am glad to see you. There are, believe me, annoyances and corrections without end, connected with an academy.

I: I just read a notice that you have postponed it. Is that right?

Beethoven: Everything was copied wrong. I was to have a rehearsal on the day of the performance, and that is why I was obliged to postpone the academy.

I: I wonder whether there is anything more troublesome or unpleasant than the preparations for an academy.

Beethoven: You may be right there. Stupidity prevents all progress. And last but not least: all the money it costs. It is inexcusable how art is now handled. I have to give one third of the proceeds to the theatre management, and a fifth to the prison. The devil take it all! When the event is over, I am going to inquire whether the art of tones is a free art or not. Believe me, there is nothing doing with art these days.—How long are you going to stay in Vienna?

I: I intend to leave on Monday.

Beethoven: Then I must give you a ticket for my academy. I thanked him and begged him not to bother. He, however, went into the other room, but returned immediately with the words that his servant, who had charge of the tickets, was not at home. I was to give him my address, and he would send me the ticket. Since he insisted, I put down my address, and we continued our conversation, as follows:

I: Did you see Meyerbeer's opera?

Beethoven: No, I understand it is very bad. I had to think of you: you were right when you said, that his composition would not be a success. I spoke to some of the opera singers, after the performance, in the "Weinstube" where they generally meet. I told them flatly: "There you distinguished yourselves once again! What asses you made of yourselves! You ought to be ashamed of yourselves not to know better, not to understand, not to be able to judge, and to make such a hubbub over this opera. Is it right to live to see old and good singers, so wanting in judgment? I should like to talk it over with you, but you do not understand me. . . ."

I: I was there. It began with Hallelujah, and ended with a Requiem. . . .

Beethoven: Hahaha! And it is just like that with his playing. I have often been asked whether I had heard him play. I said: "No". But judging from what my friends, who have some knowledge in the matter, told me, I could assume, that while he had skill, he, on the whole, was a very superficial person.

I: I was told he played at Mr.——'s home, before his departure for Paris, but that he was little liked.

Beethoven: Hahaha! What did I tell you? I know all about that. Just let him stay here half a year, and you will hear what they say about his playing. All that does not mean a thing. It has always been well known that the greatest piano players have also been the greatest composers, but

—how did they play? Not like the piano players of today, who merely run up and down the key-board, with drilled passages: putsch, putsch, putsch,—what does that signify? Nothing. The true piano virtuosi, when they played,—that was something coherent, something unified, something whole! It would—when written down—immediately have been recognized as a well thought-out piece of work. That is what piano-playing means. All the rest means nothing.

I: I think, it is ridiculous that Fuss, who himself has a very limited knowledge of piano playing has declared Meyerbeer to be the greatest of all piano players.

Beethoven: He has no idea of instrumental music. He is a miserable creature. I would tell him so to his face. He, at one time, praised a composition from which the ears of jackasses and goats peeped out all over. I had to laugh heartily at his ignorance. He does know something about singing and he should have left it at that. Of composition he knows bloody little.

I: I am taking with me a very poor opinion of Fuss!

Beethoven: As I said before, outside of singing he knows nothing.

I: I understand that Moscheles is creating quite a sensation here.

Beethoven: O Lord! He plays well, nicely, nicely. Outside of that, he is a — he will come to nothing. Those people have their social relations, where they often go and where they are praised, and praised again, and then it is all over with their art. I tell you, he will never get anywhere. I have been rash in my opinions and thus have made enemies; now I judge no one for the simple reason that I do not wish to harm any one. And I finally think: if the work is really good, it will stand — in spite of all attacks and envy; but if it is not solid and not firm, it will fall apart,—sustain it, and hold it up as much as you will!

I: That is also my philosophy.

Beethoven had in the meantime dressed, and prepared for going out. I left him. He wished me a pleasant journey, and asked me, should I stay longer in Vienna, to come to see him again.

But more interesting still for me was the 28th, which brought me to the great "Redoutensaal", at eleven o'clock in the morning, when the rehearsal of Beethoven's academy took place. I met Spohr and the Regierungsrat Sonnleithner, and I stayed with them until the end of the rehearsal. The vivacious mentality and brilliant wit of the latter formed a delightful contrast to Spohr's calm and equanimity.

The Symphony in A major to which I could not warm up, was rehearsed, and then followed the new Cantata, which undeniably showed Beethoven's genius, but the declamation and the organic tonal arrangement! ! ! ! The solution of this musical problem was, I repeat, entirely outside the limits of his genius. The colossal voice of Mme. Milder was heard even in the remotest corner of the hall; but, as a contrast, the violin solo sounded faint, although clearly and nicely performed by Herr Mayseder. Beethoven had miscalculated mightily when he intended a violin solo for so big a hall. The Cantata did not take. Its defects are such as could not be hidden either by genius or by renown. The academy closed with the "Schlacht von Vittoria", over which the greater part of the audience was beside itself, but which affected me painfully, inasmuch as I found a Beethoven to whom providence had allotted the highest throne, in the realm of music, among the crassest of materialists. It is true, I have been told that he himself designated the work as a piece of stupidity, and he cared for it only so far, as he therewith wished to win over the Viennese totally. I, however, believe, that he has won over the Viennese gradually, by his glorious compositions, and not by the "Schlacht".

When the orchestra was almost drowned by the noise of the drums' rattling and pounding, and when I put into words my disapproval of the uproarious applause, Herr von Sonnleithner, made a sarcastic remark. The academy was performed under the direction of Umlauf; Beethoven stood next to him, and beat time with him; but, owing to his deafness, he did it most incorrectly, which fact, however, caused no disturbance, for the orchestra followed Umlauf alone. Quite benumbed from the cataract, I was glad to get out into the fresh air.

Johann Wenzel Tomaschek
in his autobiographic sketch in the
Prague Year-Book "Libussa."

Beethoven and Zelter Oversleep a Meeting
(Karl Friedrich Zelter to Goethe)

Vienna, July 29th, 1819.

BEETHÒVEN, whom I so desired to see once more in this life, lives somewhere in the country, and no one knows where. I was willing to write to him, but I am told he is quite unapproachable, because he is almost entirely deaf. Perhaps it is better we remain as we are, since it might make me cross to find him cross.

July 30th.

As regards to music, they are quite conceited here, and that in the face of Italy considering herself to be "the only church to bring salvation". But they are truly cultured here. They stand for almost anything, but hold on to the best only.

185

They like to hear a mediocre opera if it is well produced, but they favor an excellent work even if it is not so well cast. Beethoven is praised to the sky because he really takes great pains and because (although! ! !) he is alive. Haydn is the one who offers them national humor. He is like a pure spring, which allows of no other stream. He lives in their midst because he springs from them. Every day they seem to be about to forget him, but every day he again lives in them.

Baden, August 16th.

Beethoven has moved to the country and no one knows where to. He has written from Baden to one of his lady friends, but he is not in Baden. They say he is inexpressibly maussade. Some even say he is a fool. How easily this is said! God forgive us all our sins! Also, the poor fellow is known to be completely deaf. . . . Don't I know from my own experience how it feels to watch my fingers playing which—woe to me, poor devil — are getting useless, one by one. . . .

Not long ago, Beethoven went into a restaurant; he sits down at a table, deep in thought, and after an hour calls the waiter: "'What do I owe?" "But Your Honor has not eaten anything. What do you want me to bring?" "O, bring what you will, but leave me alone."

The Archduke Rudolf is said to be his patron and to give him 150 Gulden yearly. With that he must get along, as do here all the children of the muses. They are kept like cats: he who does not know how to catch mice, can not save anything. And yet they are all as round and happy as weasels.

Vienna, September 14th.

The day before yesterday I wanted to visit Beethoven in Moedling. He was just on his way to Vienna, and so we met on the road, got out of the car and embraced each other most heartily. The unhappy man is really as good as deaf and I could hardly hold back my tears. . . . But I continued on to

186

Moedling, and he to Vienna! It was like a joke which tickled me not a little and I must tell it to you:

I had with me the music publisher Steiner, and since on the road it seemed rather impossible to converse with a deaf man, we arranged to meet with Beethoven in Vienna, at Steiner's music store, at four o'clock in the afternoon. So, after we had our meal in Moedling, we immediately proceeded to go back to Vienna. Filled with food like a badger, and tired as a dog, I lay down and overslept, forgetting about everything. When, in the evening, I went to the theatre, I saw Beethoven from afar. I was thunderstruck. The same happened to him upon seeing me — yet this was not the place to communicate with a deaf man. And this is the point of the joke:

In spite of the manifold blame cast on Beethoven — whether deserved or not — he has a reputation for integrity such as only very excellent people enjoy. Steiner, returning that afternoon from Moedling to Vienna, had immediately published the fact that Beethoven, in person, was to appear in his store, at four o'clock. He had asked some half a hundred guests to his narrow place which could hold about six or eight, with the result that both the store and the street were overflowing with more than fifty highly cultured people, who stood around, waiting in vain.

The real truth of the matter was only divulged to me the following day when I received a note from Beethoven, excusing himself for not having come to Steiner's store, because — he had overslept. . . .

The "Missa Solemnis" Angers
Beethoven's Neighbors

THE many hours that I have spent with the master when he was creating this great work, will ever be memorable to me. And the fugue in the Credo recalls even funny incidents.

This is the movement in the Mass where he felt himself most human, for it was by the sweat of his brow, that bar by bar, he beat time with his hands and feet, before bringing the notes on paper.

On one such occasion, his landlord gave him notice, because other parties in the house were complaining that they had no peace, night or day, because of Beethoven's pounding and stamping. And they declared he was crazy and an idiot. And he did, in truth, seem possessed at that time, the summer of 1819, and particularly when he was writing this fugue and the Benedictus.

From Schindler's Beethoven Biography.

Competition of Two Great Pianists

BEETHOVEN had already created a sensation with several of his compositions, and was regarded in Vienna as well as elsewhere as a pianist of first order, when, at the end of the last century there appeared Woelffl, a rival of equal rank.[1] There was a renewal of the old feud in Paris, between the Gluckists and the Piccinists, and the numerous art lovers in the imperial city formed two parties. At the head of the Beethoven-admirers was the charming Fuerst Lichnowsky, while the very cultured Baron Raimund von Wetzlar belonged to the many ardent admirers of Woelffl.

The Baron's lovely villa[2] on the Gruenberg, next to the imperial castle of Schoenbrunn, was a favorite resort of recreation, which he — with true British generosity — threw open to all foreign as well as domestic artists during the summer

---

[1] Joseph Woelffl, born at Salzburg in 1772, died in London in 1812. He was one of the most colorful personalities of his time. Not only a great pianist but also an adventurer who gained his reputation of being a rather obscure gentleman because of fake card-playing.

[2] This castle, which was preserved until this day, had the inscription: "Chairé" (Joy).

months. There it was, that the very interesting competition of
the two rivals brought an indescribable artistic pleasure to the
musical world of Vienna. Each would reproduce the last products of his genius, then one or the other would allow his
imagination to run away with him, and give free vent to
momentary inspirations. Then again both would sit down to
the pianoforte, change off improvising on different themes,
and thus create many a duet-capriccio, which, had it at the
moment of birth been put on paper, would surely have withstood transitoriness.

It would have been difficult, perhaps impossible to give
to either one of the contestants the palm of victory for mechanical skill. Woelffl had been presented by a kind nature
with an enormous hand, that could span ten keys as easily as
other mortals can span an octave, and this enabled him to
execute running chords with lightning rapidity. As far as improvisation went, Beethoven, even at that time, did not belie
his gloomy character: once in the realm of music, he was
removed from everything earthly. The spirit had burst all
fetters, had thrown off the yoke of servitude; and flew, exu-
berantly rejoicing, into aerial spheres. . . . Now his playing
would rush along like a wildly roaring cataract, and later
the magician would force the instrument to an expression of
power, which the strongest structure could barely withstand. . .
Then he would sink back, exhaling soft laments, dissolved
in grief . . . . But soon the soul again rose, triumphing over
transitory earthly suffering, turning upward in devout sounds,
and finding soothing consolation at the sinless bosom of nature. . . . But who can depict the sound of the depth of the
sea? . . . It was a mysterious, a Sanscrit language, the hiero-
glyphics of which only the initiated could decipher . . .

Woelffl, however, educated in Mozart's school, always
remained the same: never shallow but always clear, and
therefore more easily understood by the majority. Technique
for him was only the means to art, and not a gorgeous display

of dry scholarship. He always knew how to arouse interest and to force it into the realm of ideas.

There was another pleasure granted to the unprejudiced, uninitiated listener, namely watching the two protectors in their silent reflection on both the artists, listening intently to the products of their two protegés, sending each other approving glances, and, finally, with old knightly courtesy, giving full credit and justice to the merits on both sides.

The two pianists, however, paid no attention whatsoever. They did respect one another because they knew best how to tax each other; and as candid, straightforward Germans, followed the idea that the road of art was broad enough for many, without enviously obstructing the path to fame for another.

Ign. Ritter von Seyfried
"Beethoven Studien" (1832).

Beethoven and the United States
Written Conversation Between the Deaf Master and Grillparzer

Censorship is death to me.
One must go to North America to give free vent to one's ideas.
Some time ago I had a most disagreeable affair with the police. Merely on account of a few Jews.
Aren't you going to the country this year?
What do you expect from the opera under Barbaja (Domenico Barbaja, 1778-1841).
There is still some hope for the opera at the "Theater an der Wien"; if only we were left alone.
And yet, outside of Vienna, where is there anything of importance done for the opera?
I believe, the Berliners care more for the accessories of the opera than for the music.

190

Does Weber's "Euryanthe" please you? It is more poetry than
music.
The world has lost its innocence, and without innocence no
work of art can be created or enjoyed.
'Criticism' is the password of our day.
Weber is a critical composer. He has even paid court to
Castelli. I am benumbed.
The musician has no censorship.
Foreign literary writers are prejudiced against everything that
comes from Austria. There is a regular league against
Austrian writers in Germany. But in spite of everything
I am in love with Austria.
On the whole my works are pleasing less and less.
Have you read 'Ottokar'?
I have the misfortune to be a hypochondriac. That explains
many things.
My work gives me no pleasure.
If I had but a thousandth part of your energy and firmness.
Was there ever a time when the events of life prevented you
for any length of time from working? Love affairs, for
instance?

From Beethoven's "Conversation Books".

The Creative Process as Described
by Two Great Masters

MOZART:

When I am at peace with myself, and in good spirits,
for instance on a journey, in a carriage, or after a good meal,
or while taking a walk, or at night when I can't sleep: then
thoughts flow into me most easily and at their best. Where
they come from and how — that I cannot tell; nor can I
do anything about it. I retain the ideas that please me in my
mind, and hum them, — at least so I am told. If I hold fast

to one, that I think is suitable, others, more and more come to me, like the ingredients for a pâté, from counterpoint, from the sound of the various instruments, etc. That warms my soul, that is, if I am not disturbed, and keep on broadening these ideas and making them clearer and brighter until the whole thing is fully completed in my mind.

BEETHOVEN:

I carry my thoughts around with me for a very long time before writing them down. My memory is so true, that even after years have gone by, I never forget a theme that I have once made my own. I make many changes; I discard some things, and try again and again, until I am satisfied with what I have found. Then my mind begins to work — in breadth, in height and in depth — and since I know what I want, the basic idea never leaves me: it rises, it grows, and I see and hear the picture in its entire range as if molded in one; and then there is nothing more to do but to write it down. This process is a rapid one if I cannot give it time, for I sometimes have more than one theme working in me. But I am always sure not to confuse one with the other. From where do I get my ideas? That I cannot with certainty say. They come uncalled, directly, indirectly, I could grasp them with my hands: in the open, from nature, in the forest, in the quiet of the night, in the early morning. Sometimes moods which the poet expresses in words come to me in tones: they ring, storm and roar until they finally stand before me in notes.

Beethoven Admires Shakespeare
An English Lady Visits the Master in Baden

THE Imperial Library is the most beautiful I have ever seen, and the librarian was kind and most obliging. What would you say if I told you that after endless trouble, he succeeded in arranging a visit to Beethoven for me, to him, who is so exceedingly difficult to approach, and who answered a note, in which he was asked to receive me thus: "Avec le plus grand plaisir je recevrai une fille de . . . . ., Beethoven."

We went to Baden, a pretty little city in the Archduke-dom of Austria, situated about fifteen English miles from Vienna, and very popular because of its hot baths (from which derived its name, like our Bath), and where the "giant of living composers" (as Mr. . . . . has always, to my great amusement, called him) spends the summer months.

The people seemed astounded at the great pains we took; for, as incredible as it may seem to those who have knowledge of music, his reign is over, except in the hearts of a few elected ones. And these, incidentally, I have not yet met! I was re-peatedly advised to prepare for a rough and impolite recep-tion. When we arrived he had just come out of the rain and was changing his coat. After what I had heard of his brusque manner, I was beginning to fear that he would not receive us very kindly, when he came out of his sanctum with hurried but very firm steps. He addressed us in such a gentle and polite fashion, and with so much sincerity in his kindness, that I know of no other, except may be only one with whom he could be compared: it is Mr. . . . . (a literary personality known for his kindness and simplicity of manner) whom — by the way—he resembles in face, figure and carriage as well as in views. He is small, thin, and peculiar as to his ap-pearance.

He remarked that Mr. . . . thinks a great deal of Han-del, that he, himself loves him too, and continued for a while to praise this great master. I had to communicate with him in writing, for I found it impossible to make myself understood, and although this was a very blundering way of conversing, it did not matter much, since he always continued to speak freely and unasked, and neither waited for questions nor ex-pected to get long answers. I dared to express my admiration for his compositions, and, among others, lauded his "Adelaide" in words that, to my thinking, were not too strongly expressive of these songs of beauty. He modestly remarked that the poem was very beautiful.

Beethoven speaks French very well — at least compared with most other Germans—and conversed well with . . . . . They also conversed a little in Latin. He told me that he would have spoken English, but that his deafness had hindered him from making progress in our language, except in reading. He said he preferred English writers to the French, for "ils sont plus vrais." Thomson is his favorite, but his admiration for Shakespeare is indeed very great.

When we prepared to leave him, he asked us to stay: "Je veux vous donner un souvenir de moi." He stepped up to a table in the adjoining room, and wrote a few lines of music, —a little fugue for the piano forte, and handed it to me in the most courtly manner. Thereupon he asked me to spell my name for him, so that he could write it correctly over the short impromptu. Then he took my arm and led me into the room where he had written that little composition (so to show me his living quarters). They were very neat and — although not indicating the sumptuousness of great wealth — showed no want, either of necessary furniture or of pleasing interior arrangements. But it must not be forgotten that this is his country home, and that the Viennese are not so extravagant or so particular as we are. I carefully led him into a room at the other side, where his large piano stood. It was given to him by Mr. Broadwood, but the master — who seemed to be overcome with melancholy at sight of it — said it was in bad condition, because tuners out here in the country were not so good. He touched a few keys to prove it to me; nevertheless I placed the little script that he had given me, on the stand, and he played it through, quite simply, and added some chords as a prelude. What a handful of notes! How it would have touched the heart of M. . . . . ! Then he stopped, and

I, under no circumstance would have asked for more, for I felt that he was playing without taking any pleasure in it.

We bade each other farewell in a manner that, in France, would indicate lasting friendship, and he said of his own accord, that, should he ever come to England, he would visit us.

From a letter, dated
October 1823, Vienna.

Beethoven to His Imperial Pupil

LET Your Imperial Highness continue his practising, and let him write down his ideas while still at the piano, sketchily and abbreviated. There should be a small table beside the piano. This practice not only strengthens your imagination but you also learn to retain your ideas. It is likewise necessary to write without the piano, and to carry through a simple melody, or a chorale with both simple and varied figures, according to counterpoint. This will assuredly not give a headache to Your Imperial Highness, for it is rather a pleasure to do this, in the midst of artistic occupation — a great pleasure indeed. The capability to represent only what we wish, and feel, — so essential a need to the truly noble — will grow.

From a letter, dated: Vienna, July 1, 1823,
to Archduke Rudolph.

Beethoven's Last Hours
Anselm Huettenbrenner to Alexander Wheelock
Thayer, American Consul in Trieste and
Outstanding Beethoven Biographer

Your Honor: Hallerschloss, Graz, August 20, 1860.

Dear esteemed friend:

Your esteemed letter of July 17th, from Vienna, gave me great pleasure. Although corresponding is not so easy for me as it was thirty years ago, and I do not like to look back on past sad events, in which I at one time took part, I will endeavor to grant your wish, to put down as much of Beethoven's last moments as my memory has retained. I have often desired to send an article on this subject to some review, but never got to carrying out this resolution, because I like to get away from myself as much as possible and very reluctantly speak of myself and of my experiences.

When, on March 26th, 1827, at about three o'clock in the afternoon, I entered Beethoven's bed-room, I found with him Herr Hofrat Breuning, his son, and Frau van Beethoven, the wife of Johann van Beethoven, from Linz, and also my friend Joseph Teltscher, portrait painter. I believe that Professor Schindler too was present. All these gentlemen after a while, left, and they had but little hope of ever again seeing the dying tone poet.

During the last moments of Beethoven's life, Frau van Beethoven and myself were the only ones present. Beethoven, from three o'clock until five, had been lying unconscious, in a struggle with death, when suddenly a stroke of lightning, accompanied by an immediate thunder clap, illuminated the room brightly. Snow was lying on the ground in front of Beethoven's door. After this unexpected phenomenon of nature, which struck me strangely, Beethoven opened his eyes, and with grim mien, and gazing fixedly upwards, he raised

196

his right hand, tightly clenched, as though to say: "I defy you, you hostile powers. Get you hence, God is with me." It seemed as though—like a daring general—he wanted to call to his men: "Courage, soldiers, onward! Trust me! Victory is surely ours!"

When his raised hand fell back on the bed his eyes were half closed. My right hand was under his head, my left rested on his breast. No breath, no heart beat, any longer. The genius of the great master had flown from this world of appearances into the realm of truth. . . .

I closed the eyes of the departed, kissed them, then his forehead, mouth and hands. Frau van Beethoven, at my request, cut off a lock of his hair, and gave it to me, as a sacred remembrance of Beethoven's last hour.

After that, deeply moved, I rushed to the city, and brought the news of Beethoven's death to Herr Tobias Haslinger; then some hours later, I returned to my home in the Steiermark.

Beethoven's personality was more forbidding than attractive; yet the sublime spirit that breathes through his wondrous works, has made a mighty, irresistible magic impression on all highly educated music-lovers. We must esteem, love and admire Beethoven.

It is not true that I asked Beethoven to take the last sacrament; but I did, upon request of Frau von Haslinger, persuade Frau van Beethoven in the tenderest manner, to urge him to gain strength by taking Holy Communion. It is pure invention that Beethoven said to me: "Plaudite, amici, Comoedia finita est". I was not even present on this occasion, March 24th, 1827. Nor do I believe that he made a remark so contrary to his straight-forward nature to any one else. But Frau van Beethoven did in truth tell me that her brother-in-law, after having received Holy Communion, said to the priest: "Father, I thank you. You have brought me comfort."

I must give praise to Herr Johannes van Beethoven and

his wife, as well as to Professor Schindler for their very kind and obliging manner to me.

Hoping, dear friend, to see you in Graz, before you return to America, and to embrace you, I remain with best regards

Your truly devoted friend

Anselm Huettenbrenner

P.S. Will you now, honored friend, be content with what I related to you and only to you, about Beethoven's last hours in this letter? They are probably the last words I will ever write on musical matters.

Austria's Greatest Poet on Beethoven

"I AM reading a tract by Ludwig Rellstab, entitled "Beethoven" in which my relations to the great master — particularly pertaining to the libretto that I wrote for him — are treated in a not quite correct manner." This accusation is not meant for Rellstab, who undoubtedly wrote down word for word what Beethoven told him. The cause of this was probably the sad condition of the master during these last years, which has prevented him from distinguishing between what really happened and what he merely thought.

Everything that happens to a great man is always interesting. I will therefore relate, with all possible veracity, everything about our meeting and what resulted therefrom. Or rather, it is a pleasure for me to bring back to my mind my memories of him, and to set them down herewith.

I was a boy when I saw Beethoven for the first time. It may have been in 1804 or 1805, at a musical soirée in the house of my uncle Joseph Sonnleithner, at that time head of an art and music firm in Vienna. Together with Beethoven were present Cherubini and the Abbé Vogler. Beethoven was, at that time, slender and dressed in black and with great elegance. He wore spectacles, which I so well remember, because in later years he never used this aid to sight. I can not remember whether he or Cherubini played at this occasion, but I do know that, when the servant had already announced the supper, the Abbé Vogler sat down to the piano, and played endless variations on an African theme, which he himself had found and brought along. The company gradually drifted into the dining room during his playing, except Cherubini and Beethoven. At last also Cherubini left, and the great master alone stood by the hard working man. Finally even he lost patience and joined the others, and the Abbé, now left quite alone, still continued to caress his variations in all kinds of ways. I, astounded at the monstrousness of the affair, had stayed behind with him. At to what has happened later, my memory —as it is often the case with youthful reminiscences—fails me altogether. Who was Beethoven's neighbor at table, did he or did he not converse with Cherubini, did the Abbé join them later or not — it would seem that a curtain had been drawn over all this.

A few years later I resided with my parents in the village of Heiligenstadt, near Vienna. Our apartment faced the garden while Beethoven had rented the rooms facing the street. Both apartments were connected by a common corridor, which led to the stairway. My brother and I paid little attention to the queer man — (he had, in the meantime grown stouter and was carelessly, even untidily dressed) — when he shot by, grumbling. My mother, an ardent lover of music, would here and there, when she heard him play the piano, step into the corridor and listen to him with rapt devout attention. This happened several times, when one day the door suddenly opened and Beethoven himself stepped out: seeing my mother, he rushed back and immediately after, his hat on his head, ran out into the street. From this time on, we never again heard him play. In vain did my mother —

since all other discourse with him was cut off — send the servant with a message, asserting that no one ever again would listen to him, and not only that, she assured him that our door would be locked, and that all her family instead of using the common hall, would leave the house by means of the garden — a great detour. But Beethoven remained unmoved and never again touched his piano until in the autumn we finally returned to the city.

In one of the following summers, I visited my grandmother who had her summer residence in Doebling. Beethoven too, at that time, lived there. Opposite the windows of my grandmother stood a decrepit house, owned by a man named Flehberger, notorious for his debauchery. This Flehberger had a daughter, Lise, who was pretty but had not the best reputation. Beethoven seemed to take great interest in the girl. I still see him, coming down the Hirschengasse, his white handkerchief in his right hand, trailing on the ground. He stopped at the portal of the Flehberger court, where the giddy beauty, standing on a hay wagon or a manure cart, was tossing her pitchfork vigorously, and laughing all the time. I never noticed that Beethoven addressed her; he simply stood and gazed at her, until the girl (whose taste ran more in the direction of peasant lads), be it by a derisive word, or by persistently ignoring him, provoked his anger. Then, with a sudden turn he ran away, but never failed to return and to stop at the Flehberger portal the next time. Yes, his interest in her went so far, that, when her father, because of a drunken brawl, was sent to the village jail, he personally intervened with the village community, and pleaded for his release, whereby, however, he so stormily handled the councillors, that he was almost forced unwillingly to share his imprisoned protegé's society.

Later, I saw Beethoven in the street, and once or twice in the "Café" where he was often in company with a poet of the Novalis-Schlegel-guild, long since deceased and forgotten.

His name was Ludwig Stoll. There was a saying that they planned to write an opera. It is difficult to understand how Beethoven could ever have expected anything — except fantastic versifications — from this floater.

In the meantime, I myself had trodden the road of publicity. The "Ahnfrau", "Sappho", "Medea", and "Ottokar" had appeared, when unexpectedly I received word from the director of the two theatres, Graf Moritz Dietrichstein, that Beethoven had prevailed upon him to induce me to write an opera for him. This request, I must say, embarrassed me not a little. In the first place, the idea of ever writing an opera book was far from my mind; then I doubted whether Beethoven, who by this time was completely without hearing, and whose last composition, despite his great merit, had assumed a rather harsh character, which seemed to be in contrast with the natural timbre of a singing voice, — I doubted, as I said, whether he was still capable of writing an opera. The thought, however, of giving a great man the opportunity for an undoubtedly highly interesting task outweighed all other considerations, and I consented.

Among the dramatic subjects I had noted down for future arrangements were two, that permitted of operatic treatment. One was in the field of supreme emotion. But, beside the fact, that I knew of no singer, competent enough to sing the main role, I did not wish Beethoven, already lying dangerously close to a precipice to draw closer to the last borderline of music — by a half diabolical subject.

I chose the fable of Melusine, eliminated as much as possible all reflective elements, and attempted, by predominance of the choruses, powerful finales, etc., and by keeping the third act in almost melo-dramatic form, to adapt myself to the recent trend of Beethoven's music. I omitted to confer with the compositeur on the subject, because I wished to retain my freedom of opinion, and considered that any required changes could be made later, and finally, that it was up to him to decide whether or not he wished to compose the book. Yes, in order not in any way to exert compulsion I sent him the book the same way in which the request had been made. He was not to be influenced or embarrassed by any personal consideration.

A few days later, Schindler, at that time Beethoven's business manager, and the author of a biography of Beethoven, came to see me, and begged me in the name of his lord and master, who was unwell, to come to see him. I got dressed, and we at once started to Beethoven's home which was somewhere in the suburbs. I found him, in a dirty night dress lying on an untidy bed, a book in hand. Behind the bed, there was a small door, leading, as I later saw, to the food pantry. For, when the maid emerged with butter and eggs, he could not, in the midst of the conversation, refrain from casting a searching glance at the quantities taken out, which gave me a sad insight into the vexations of his domestic life.

When we entered, Beethoven arose from his bed, shook hands with me, overflowing with friendliness, and began to speak of the opera. "Your work is living here", he said, pointing to his breast, — "I am leaving for the country in a few days, and I shall then begin at once to compose it. Only I do not know what to do about the hunter's chorus at the beginning. Weber needed four horns; you see, I would have to have eight: where is that going to lead to?"

Although I could not at all see his point, I explained to him that the chorus could, without harming the whole, be left out, with which concession he seemed very much pleased and neither at that time, nor later did he have any objection to the text, nor did he demand any change. On the contrary, he insisted on an immediate contract. The proceeds of the opera were to be divided between him and me. I explained to him, what was true, that I had never considered any gratuity or anything of that order. At any rate, there should be no such question between him and me. He could do what he pleased with the book and I would make no contract with him. After a great deal of talk or rather writing — since Beethoven could no longer hear anything spoken — I left, promising to see him in Hetzendorf, after he had settled there.

I hoped that he had relinquished the idea of business. But a few days later, my publisher Wallishauser (Franz Wallishauser), came to see me, advising me that Beethoven insisted on a contract. Should I not be willing to be so business-like, I could cede all rights to the book to him, Wallishauser. He would then arrange everything else with Beethoven, who already had been informed. I was glad to be rid of the matter, allowed Wallishauser to pay me a moderate sum, ceded all my rights of authorship to him, and thought no more about it. Whether or not they made a contract — I do not know. I am inclined to believe, however, that they did, because, had that not been the case, Wallishauser would not have failed, as usual, to moan about the money invested. I am mentioning all this, to contradict what Beethoven told Rellstab, namely, that I wanted matters arranged differently from him. He was at that time so determined to compose the opera, that he was already making plans (for its performance).

In the course of the summer, Schindler and I accepted an invitation from Beethoven to visit him in Hetzendorf. I do not remember whether Schindler told me on the way there, or whether I had heard it previously, that Beethoven had been prevented from starting to work on the opera because of urgent orders. I therefore avoided mentioning the subject. We went out walking, and conversed as well as it was possible, half speaking and half writing. I am still deeply moved, when I think of Beethoven himself bringing in five bottles of wine, when we were seated at table. He set one before Schindler's plate, one before his own, and three before mine, probably desiring in his good-natured, wild-naive manner, to give me to understand, that I was welcome to drink as much as I pleased.

When I left without Schindler, who was staying on, Beethoven insisted upon accompanying me. He sat next to me in the open carriage, but instead of getting out at the country limits, he went all the way to the city with me, got out at the city limits, shook hands with me, most cordially, and started off on his long way, back home. After he had descended, I saw a piece of paper lying where he had sat. I thought he had forgotten it, and hailed to him to come back for it. But he shook his head, and laughing out aloud as though at a good joke, ran all the faster in the opposite direction. I unwrapped the paper and found that it contained the exact amount for the fare, that I had bargained for, with the driver. So estranged was he from the customs and manners of the world that he did not realize what an insult might lie in such an act, under different circumstances. I took it as it was meant, and laughingly gave the driver the money thus presented.

Later I saw him again only once. I do not remember where. He told me: "Your opera is finished". Whether he meant, just in his head, or whether he was alluding to the innumerable notations which he was in the habit of making — thought and inventions only comprehensible to himself — possibly the elements of the opera in parts as well, that I cannot say. It is certain however, that after his death, not a single note was found referring to that work, planned by us. I kept strictly to my resolution, not to remind him of it in the slightest way, and did not, since conversing with him by writing was troublesome, come near him again, until, in a black suit and with a burning torch in my hand, I was walking behind his coffin.

Two days before, Schindler had come to me with the news that Beethoven was dying and that his friends requested an oration from me, which the actor Anschuetz was to deliver at his grave. I was all the more shocked as I had not known of his illness. I tried however to collect my thoughts, and the following day I began to write the oration, when Schindler entered and called for the speech, for Beethoven had just died. Tears came to my eyes, — and as it always happens to me, when overcome by feeling, I was not able to finish the speech with the pregnance with which it was begun. It was, however, delivered, the guests dispersed, in deep sorrow, and Beethoven was no longer with us.

I really loved him very much. If I have been able to repeat what I knew but poorly, it was because an artist is not so much interested in what an artist has said, as in what he has accomplished. If words alone could express the value of an artist, then Germany would be full of them as it now is void of them. Yes, only the power of coherent thought innate in talent is to the good of creative force, which expresses what is the source of life and individual truth. And the wider the circle the more difficult the fulfillment. The greater the mass, the more difficult its animation. When Goethe knew but little, he wrote the first part of "Faust"; when the whole realm of wisdom was at his disposal he wrote the second. Of details, expressed by Beethoven, I now can only remember, that he greatly esteemed Schiller, that he considered the lot of the poet a more happy one than that of the musician, because the poet has a wider field. And, finally, he liked Weber's "Euryanthe" which then was very popular. On the whole, I think it was Weber's success that aroused in him the desire, himself to write another opera. But he had so accustomed himself to an unbounded flight of imagination, that no opera book in the world would have been able to keep in given bounds to his effusions. He searched and searched and found none, because there were none for him. Otherwise, surely one of the many subjects, offered by Rellstab, would have attracted him, at least as to the idea.

My libretto, which I could no longer consider my own, later fell into the hands of Konradin Kreutzer, by means of the Wallishauser book shop. If not one of the now existing musicians find it worth their while to compose it, — I can only rejoice. Music is in just as bad a way as poetry, and for the same reason: the lack of knowledge in the field of the various arts. Music, in order to expand itself, strives for poetry, just as poetry strives for prose. To explain this further does not seem timely, so long as, philosophers, and art-historians — (I am thinking of Gervinus and similar half-knowing ones who regard the ignorance in their own province as a qualification for every other, alien to them) — have control of the German sphere of art. As for the rest, it can be expected of the sane spirit of the nation, that it will before long withdraw from the domination of words, and will return to facts and actions.

I am closing with a few lines of verse, which I have lately noted down, and for which I know of no better place:
"A man walks on with rapid stride,
His shadow alas, has gone with him.
He walks through wheat and fields and thicket
And all his striving is ahead;
A stream would stem his forward march —
He dashes in and dares the flood,
Ascends the other shore,
Continues his unconquered pace.
Now has arrived at a cliff,
He takes a run, we breathless wait —
A leap — and lo, unhurt
He has spanned the abyss.
What others dread is nought to him,
A victor, he has reached his goal,

But he, who has left no trail,
Of Beethoven, he me minds."

From Franz Grillparzer's Reminiscences.

Grillparzer's Funeral Oration

As we are standing here, at the grave of the departed, we are, so to say, the representatives of a whole nation, of the entire German people, mourning the passing of the great renowned half of what has remained to us of the past glory of native art and patriotic spirit. Still living — and may he live long — is the hero of songs, in the German language and tongue; but the last master of the song of tones, the sweet tongue of the art of tones, the heir to Handel and Bach, to Haydn's and Mozart's undying fame, has passed away, and, weeping, we are standing before the broken strings of an instrument whose melody has now faded away.

The Melody has faded away—let me call it that. For he was an artist and everything he was, he was through art alone. The thorns of life had deeply wounded him, and as the ship-wrecked clings to the shore, so he fled into thine arms, O thou glorious sister of the good and true, consoler of grief, O, heaven-sent art! Firmly he clung to thee, and even when the door through which thou hadst come to him and spoke to him, was closed, when he had become blind to thy traits because of his deaf ear, he ever carried thy image in his heart, and when he died it was still lying on his breast.

He was an artist, and who is to stand beside him?

As the Behemoth storms through the seas so he flew beyond the limits of his art. From the cooing of the dove to the rolling of the thunder, from the most intricate web of artistic form to the terrible point where culture passes into the uncontrolled violence of battling forces of nature — all that he

207

passed through and perceived. He, who is to follow him, shall not continue: he will have to begin over again; for his predecessor stopped only where art stopped.

Adelaide and Leonore! Celebration of the heroes of Vittoria and the humble song of the mass! Children of the three and four divided voices! Roaring symphony: "Freude, schoener Goetterfunken!"—you swan song! Muse of song and strings! Stand around his grave and bestrew it with laurel!

He was an artist and he was a man, a man in every and the highest sense. Because he withdrew from the world they called him misanthropic, and, because he shunned sentimentality, they called him heartless. O, he who knows himself strong, does not flee. It is the finest point which is most easily dulled, bent or broken. An excess of feeling avoids expression of feeling.

He fled from the world because in the whole realm of his loving heart he found no weapon to combat it. He withdrew from his fellowmen, since they were not willing to reach him, and he was not able to descend to them. He remained a solitary because he found no equal. But to the very end, he preserved a human heart for all, fatherly feelings for his dear ones. His life was a sacrifice to mankind.

So he was, so he died, so will he live for all time.

But you, who have followed us here, subdue your grief. You have not lost him. You have won him. No living man ever steps into the halls of immortality. The body must first perish, then only does immortality open its doors. He, whom you are now mourning for, is standing among the great of all time, unapproachable for ever. Return to your homes, saddened but comforted. And when ever again in life the power of his creations overwhelms you like a storm, when ever a stream of joy will flow for a generation not yet born,—then remember this hour and think: "We were there, when they buried him; and when he died, we wept."

BEETHOVEN

The Two "Kreutzer Sonatas"
Beethoven's and Tolstoï's

THE Count, above all, loved music. Toward the end of May, there arrived in Jasnaja Poljana a young violinist, Lassotta, a pupil of the Moscow Conservatory. He had been engaged for the summer months in the country, to instruct Lew Lwowitsch, the son of the Count, in violin playing. He was lodged in the "pavillon", which was located in the park between the school and the main building. There was a small piano in this pavillon, and, in day time, lessons were given there in piano as well as violin playing.

In the evening Lassotta was usually bidden to the main building, where music was widely practised in the large living room. All those present — the Count himself was never absent — either sat around the large table in the middle of the room, or on the side at a round table in the corner. These soirées, if nothing happened to prevent them, took place almost daily, at least three or four times a week. At the wish of the Count, sonatas by Beethoven were preferably produced.

He seemed to like the "Kreutzer Sonata" best, and asked for it almost every night, so that it was finally executed with great efficiency and well thought-out phrasing. The Count was more and more absorbed in this work. It evidently aroused images in him that his fantasy made more and more vivid to him. At last the work had matured within him, and he decided to work on it. As early as the following winter, it appeared under the name of "Kreutzer Sonata". There were, at first, great difficulties with the censorship, and therefore it was first published in Paris, by the "Bibliothêque des Auteurs Célèbres."

Theodor von Hafferverg:
"Vacation with Tolstoï".

209

Characterization of the Great
Classical Pianists:
* Czerny In His "School of Piano Playing"

Clementi's manner is characterized by a firm touch and tone, clear and correct execution, which is largely calculated to produce great rapidity and dexterity of the fingers.

Cramer's and *Dussek's manner*: a beautiful cantabile, avoidance of glaring effects, an astonishing evenness in runs and passages, replacing celerity, which is less in demand in their work, and a wonderful legato together with the use of the pedals.

Mozart's manner: A clear brilliant style of playing intended for staccato more than for legato execution. Intelligent, vivacious execution. Pedal seldom used, and rarely necessary.

Beethoven's manner: Characteristic of passionate force, relieved by all the charms of a legato cantabile. The means of expression are often carried to extremes, particularly when in a humoristic mood. A piquant manner, standing out in bold relief is seldom applied there. But total effects, partly by a full tone legato, partly by a clever application of the forte pedal are used. Mozart's manner, which has been so well perfected by Hummel, is more suited to the German forte-piano, combining a light shallow touch with great distinctness. This piano is good for general use, as well as for young people. Beethoven, who first appeared in 1790, drew from the forte-piano new and daring effects, by the clever use of the pedal, and by an extremely characteristic method, (distinguished by a strict legato of the chords, and for that reason creating a new sort of touch and tone) — effects, that were new and never before thought of. His playing, while it did not have the clear brilliant elegance of other pianists, was nevertheless of an ingenious grandeur, and, especially in the adagios, full of

* Carl Czerny, 1791-1857, the famous pianist, pedagogue and composer.

feeling and romance. His performances on the piano, like his compositions, were tonal pictures of the highest order, intended for universal effect, regardless of details.

EARLY ROMANTICISM

From Schubert's Diary
(1824)

NO one to understand the sorrow, no one to understand the joy of another. We are always trying to go towards each other, but we only succeed in going side by side with each other. O, agony for him who realizes this. . . .

My productions are the outcome of my understanding of music and of my pain. Those that have been generated by pain alone, give least joy to the world.

O, imagination, greatest treasure of man, you inexhaustible fount, from which artists as well as scholars drink inspiration, O, stay with us a while, even though appreciated and revered but by few, and save us from so-called enlightenment, that ugly skeleton without either flesh or blood.

Enviable Nero, who had the strength to destroy a loathsome people to the sound of music and song.

There is no sunshine anywhere. It is impossible in May to sit in the garden. Terrible, fearful, horrible, for me, the most cruel thing that could happen.

Otto Erich Deutsch "Franz Schubert—
Die Dokumente seines Lebens."

The Viennese Poet Eduard von Bauernfeld Characterizes Schubert's Friends

FRANZ von Schober[1] is the superior of us all,—and how much so in talking. But much about him is artificial, and his powers are threatened with being stifled from doing nothing.

[1] Otto Erich Deutsch calls Schober "a lawyer, poet, painter, actor, pedagogue, diplomat, bohemian, a brilliant personality, dominating the group of friends around Schubert".

Schwind[1] is of a wonderfully pure nature, but in constant fermentation, as though wanting to tear himself to pieces.

Schubert alone has the proper mixture of the real and the ideal. The world to him is beautiful.

Schubert Sings the "Winterreise" for His Friends

FOR a while, Schubert was in a sombre mood, and he seemed exhausted. Upon my asking him what ailed him, he replied: "You will soon see and understand." And on a later day he said to me: "Come to Schobers to-night. I am going to let you hear a wreath of the weirdest songs. I am eager to hear what you will say. They have exhausted me more than any of my other songs."

And he sang for us "Die Winterreise" in a profoundly moved voice. We were stunned by the gloomy mood of these songs. Schober said that he liked only one of them: "Der Lindenbaum". Whereupon Schubert answered that these songs pleased him more than any he had written, and that we also would like them some day.

I am absolutely convinced that the emotional strain under which he composed his most beautiful works, among them "Die Winterreise", was the cause of his early death.

From Josef von Spaun's
"Reminiscences of Schubert"
(Otto Erich Deutsch)

[1] Moritz von Schwind, the famous painter.

A Revealing Love Letter

THE poet Kind is so enthusiastic about me, that he has decided to write an opera for me. The subject is gruesome and interesting: "Der Freischuetz." Satan himself, as the "black hunter" appears, bullets are cast, in a mountain ravine at midnight, and witches flit by. Whew! Are you shuddering?

I must now make a weighty confession to you,—something that you would never have believed of your Carl: a girl has captivated me completely. She is, I must admit it, my bride. She has an irresistible inclination for the theatre which I am going to help her to satisfy, even though I am aware of all the perils connected with it. "O my beloved Agatha, will you always be true to me?" I call out. . . . Now, realizing that she has completely conquered me, may I still write to you? ? ? O! O! O! What now? Etsch, etsch! I shouldn't be surprised, if, for a moment, you had been scared. Yes, it is true, that damned hunter's bride haunts me desperately, and as always with me, when I have before me so gigantic a work, I doubt my ability to accomplish it. But in the end I do succeed, and this experience, so often repeated, consoles me. May God give me His blessing! There are terrific tasks to accomplish and my head will often be buzzing — but no matter!

Curiously enough, everything that in the least is connected with my Lina (Carolina) is of striking success. Aennchen, which would be a role admirably suited to you, attracts me above all, and I am irresistibly tempted to compose these sections first, whereby you are always before my eyes. You will therefore recognize your own portrait in the teasing roguish little "puck".

From Carl Maria von Weber's letters to
his fiancée Caroline Brandt (1817.)

The Fingers Hostile to Creative Power
Weber's Viewpoint

LIFE burdens weigh down on me heavily. How happy I would be to fly from life to art, but as art lives only in life, and life only in art, they both, combined continue to harass me.

My seat at the piano, which I had taken to further my creative work had proved a bad omen.

The composer who gets his subject matter there, at the piano, is nearly always born poor or apt to yield his spirit to the common and low. For it is these hands, these damned piano fingers — having acquired from constant practising, a wilful independent mind of their own — become unconscious tyrants, the despots of creative power. They refuse to invent anything new, — yes, the new is inconvenient to them. Secretly and roguishly — true mechanical workers — they mould into a whole, parts of small tone bits, long familiar to them, because they sound so nice and round to the deluded ear, and seem to indicate the direction, and these are favorably accepted and employed.

But how differently does he create whose inner ear is sole judge of both the invented and the approved matter. The spiritual ear, with marvelous ability, embraces and grasps the tone figures and it is a sacred secret inherent in music, and incomprehensible to the layman.

From Carl Maria von Weber's novel:
"Musician's Life".

London Enthusiastic About Weber
(1826)

THE gorgeous sight of the foaming sea, and of England's chalky coast was most uplifting, and the reception given me in England was much more flattering than that in France. An opera: "Rob Roy", after Walter Scott's novel, was being performed at Covent Garden. As I stepped to the edge of the box, better to see, some one called: "There is Weber!" . . . and though I quickly withdrew, a storm of applause broke out, enthusiastic cries of Vivat filled the hall. I had to show myself over and over again to make my bow. And now they demanded the "Freischuetz Ouverture". Could one expect more enthusiasm, more affection? And are these the "cold English people"?

"Oberon" went very well; tremendous applause; the overture had to be repeated. At the close, I was called out and storms of applause greeted me—an honor never done before to a composer. But my longing for home is indescribable, and I brood for days, which could well be spent in better fashion.

What has become of my former vitality and courage? Why this ever analyzing myself? It is obvious, I can't help it. And then, there is that shortness of breath and that convulsive sickly feeling. . . .

From Weber's Biography, written by
his son Max Maria von Weber.

Wagner's Sermon on the Interment of
Weber's Remains

REST in peace. Let this be the unpretentious spot to hold your precious mortal remains. And had they been laid in a tomb of princes, in the proudest minster of a nation, we yet dare to hope that your choice for a last resting place would have been a simple grave on German soil. You were not one of those, who, filled with cold thirst for fame, have no fatherland and to whom the favorite land is the one, in which their ambition has most luxuriant growth. If a fateful bent drew you to a land, where even genius is put on the market, you, in good time, cast longing glances at your native soil, at the modest country home, where — your beloved wife at your side — song upon song flowed from your heart. "O, were I but with my loved ones!" was probably your last sigh, as you passed away.

If you were a sentimental dreamer, who can blame us if we met you in the same spirit, if we fervently shared it with you, if we often had the hidden wish to have you with us again in our dear homeland? O, this sentimental visionariness, — it has made you the darling of your people. Never has there been a more German musician than you. No matter where your genius carried you, no matter how remote, how boundless was the realm of your phantasy,—you were always linked, with a thousand tender threads to the heart of the German people, with which you wept and laughed like a trusting child, listening to the sagas and fairy-tales of its homeland. Yes, it was this child-like faith, which, like a good angel guided your manly spirit and kept it noble and chaste. And it was this child-like trust that ever distinguished you: as you always cherished this splendid quality and kept it undimmed, you never needed to invent or to reason, — you needed only to feel, and you had already found the original fundaments for all.

And you retained this highest of all virtues until your death. You would never have sacrificed this beautiful heritage of your German birth, you have never denied it, you have never betrayed it. Now, the Briton does you justice, the Frenchman admires you, — but only the German loves you: you belong to him, you are a beautiful day in his life, a warm drop of his blood, a piece of his heart. Who would blame us for wanting your ashes to become a part of our soil, our dear German soil?

Once again, don't bear a grudge, you, who have misunderstood the German heart, that heart which always dreams when it loves. Was it sentimentality that made us ask you to return to us the remains of our dear Weber? If so, it was a sentimentality from which sprang all the beautiful flowers of his genius, for which the whole world admired him, and for which we love him.

It is a task of love, dear Weber, that we are now performing, when we withdraw you, who never sought it, from the eyes of admiration, and are leading you into the arms of love. We have tenderly led you from a world where you shone, into the bosom of your family, into your homeland. What does the hero, returning from battle most long for? Surely for his wife and his children, and for the home where they dwell. And we do not have to speak metaphorically: your wife, your children are, in truth, awaiting you. You will hear, in the beyond, the steps of your beloved wife, who has been waiting so long for your coming, and who now, beside her beloved son, is weeping hot tears of love for the returning friend of her heart.

What means death? And what means life? Life everlasting is where both meet in such beautiful re-union. . . .

Let us too, O dear departed, join this union. We then will know no death, and no decay, only thriving and blossoming. The stone enshrining you will become for us the rock in the desert from which the Almighty once drew the refreshing spring: from it will flow, far into times to come, a glorious stream of ever-creating rejuvenating life.

Thou fount of all being, let us ever be mindful and worthy of this union!

On the occasion of the interment of
Weber's remains, after their transportation
from London to Dresden, 1844

Mendelssohn at the Age of Twelve Meets Goethe

(1821)

THEN Professor Zelter came in: "Goethe is here! The old gentleman arrived!" Quickly we ran down the stairs into Goethe's house. He was in the garden, and was just coming around a hedge. He looks very gracious and none of the pictures one sees, does him justice.

We went in to dine. You would never think he was 73 — he looks no more than 50. After the meal, Frl. Ulrike, Frau von Goethe's sister, went up to him to be kissed; I did likewise.

Every morning I receive a kiss from the author of "Faust" and "Werther"; every afternoon father and friend Goethe gives me two kisses. Just think of it! In the afternoon I play for him for more than two hours: fugues by Bach and improvisations of my own. In the evening whist is played, and Prof. Zelter, who too played at first, said: "Whist means: shut up!" A pithy expression! For the evening meal we use to sit together, even Goethe, who ordinarily never takes supper, joins us. Every afternoon he opens the Streicher-piano, saying: "I haven't heard you play today; give me a little noise." Then he would sit beside me, and when I am through (I improvise mostly), I either would beg for a kiss or just take one.

You cannot imagine how kind he is, and how gracious. I cannot say that I think he is an imposing figure: he is not much taller than father. But his carriage, his language, his name, — they are imposing! His voice is of a marvelous timbre and he can shout like ten thousand fighters! His hair is not yet white; his gait is firm and his speech gentle.

From Wilhelm Bode:
"Die Tonkunst in Goethe's Leben".

Goethe on Music

THE sacred in music is entirely in conformance with its dignity, and it is here that it has its greatest effect on life, which through all time and through all the epochs ever remains the same.

The sacredness of church music, the joyfulness and frolicsomeness of folksongs are the two pivots around which revolves true music. And it is from these two points that it will ever have the inevitable effect: devotion and dance.

From "Rameau's Nephew".

Mendelssohn Plays for Goethe

HIS presence proved beneficial for me, for I found that my relation to music has remained the same. I listen to it with pleasure, interest and meditation, and I love its history. For how can we understand any phenomenon if we do not acquaint ourselves with the course of its development? And, added to this, the principal factor was that Felix, in praiseworthy manner, realized this. Being happy in having a good memory, he can recall all kinds of examples at will. Beginning with the Bach period, he has revived for me Haydn, Mozart and Gluck, and has given me a sufficient idea of the

223

great and more recent technicians, such as Beethoven, and has departed with my blessings.

From a letter of Goethe's to Zelter after a visit of the young composer, June 3, 1830.

Mendelssohn on his "Songs Without Words"

SO much is talked about music and so little is said! I myself am of the belief that words alone are not adequate, and even were I to find them adequate, I should probably no longer write music. People complain that music may be construed in so many ways, and that no one knows how really to interpret it, while words are easily comprehended. But the opposite holds true with me. And not only with entire speeches, — even with single words, — even they seem to have too many meanings, becoming ambiguous and indefinite and therefore easily misinterpreted. Music, on the other hand, fills one's soul with a thousand better feelings than words can ever do. Music that I love, expresses to me not vague indefinite thoughts to be put into words—but arouses emotions, such as resignation, melancholy, love of God, or even feelings like the "stirrings of a par-force hunt,"—where one person does not think the same as another: What melancholy means to one, signifies resignation to another; a third does not have much comprehension of either. . . . I could even imagine that for a passionate hunter the sounds of the horns may mean something like a prayer to nature, and, consequently, the true praise of God.

From S. Hensel: "Die Familie Mendelssohn"

Berlioz Admires Mendelssohn

HE is a great master. I would say so even if he hadn't complimented me on my "Romances". Not a word, however, has he said about my overtures or my Requiem.

His "Walpurgisnacht" which he has composed to a poem by Goethe was performed here for the first time. I assure you it is one of the most admirable orchestral compositions you would ever wish to hear.

From Berlioz': "Collected Works"

Mendelssohn's Charming Personality

WHEN speaking of our heroic social accomplishments (official banquets at musical festivals, etc.), he was immensely amused to hear that my fête for Liszt, consisting of only a few people, cost me more than all his grand demonstrations. His laughter then had something childlike and good-natured, and he was never more sociable than when he could indulge in a little mockery.

From Ferdinand Hiller
"Felix Mendelssohn-Bartholdy,
Briefe und Erinnerungen".

Two Germans Are Enthusiastic About Chopin

HEINE:

There is a man of the first order. Chopin is the darling of an elite which seeks in music the highest spiritual gratification. His fame is of an aristocratic order, perfumed by the eulogium of high society, and as distinguished as is his personality. Chopin was born in Poland, of French parentage, and was partly educated in Germany. The influence of three nationalities has had a curious effect on his personality: he has assimilated the best that distinguishes these three nations: Poland gave him his chivalrous thinking, and his historical sorrow; France his grace; Germany his romantic melancholy; and Nature gave him a slim, charming, somewhat delicate appearance and the noblest heart and genius. He is a poet of tones, and nothing can be compared to the delight he gives us, when improvising at the piano. Then he is neither Pole nor Frenchman nor German: then he is a native of the land of Mozart, Rafael and Goethe.

From Bock's "Deutsche Dichter"

SCHUMANN:

Chopin was here yesterday, and, for half an hour played on my piano: phantasies, and new etudes of his own. What an interesting personality! And more interesting still is his playing! He affected me strangely. The overstimulation of his fantastic manner and means is transmitted to the listener: I fairly held my breath. The ease with which his velvet fingers glide over the keys, — I should rather say flee — is admirable. He has enraptured me, I cannot deny it, in a way, that until now has been foreign to me. What overwhelmed me was his childlike, natural attitude, exhibited both in his manner and in his playing.

*From Robert Schumann's "Gesammelte
Schriften ueber Musik und Musiker."*

Nocturnes of Chopin and Field
As Compared by Franz Liszt

FIELD'S inspiration to name his pieces "Nocturnes" was a happy one, for it is admirably suited to these compositions.

PLATE 17.—Jean Philippe Rameau, from the Painting by Greuze, Dijon Museum

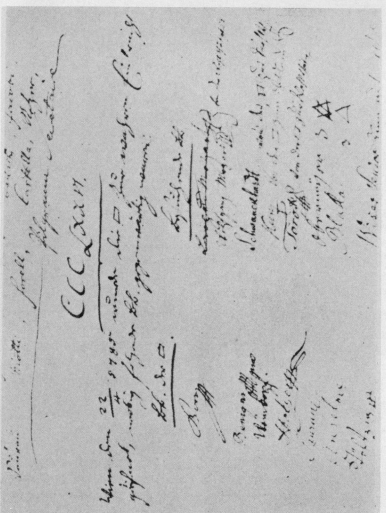

PLATE 18.—Minutes of the Meeting of the Lodge "Zur wahren Eintracht," with Wolfgang and Leopold Mozart's Signatures

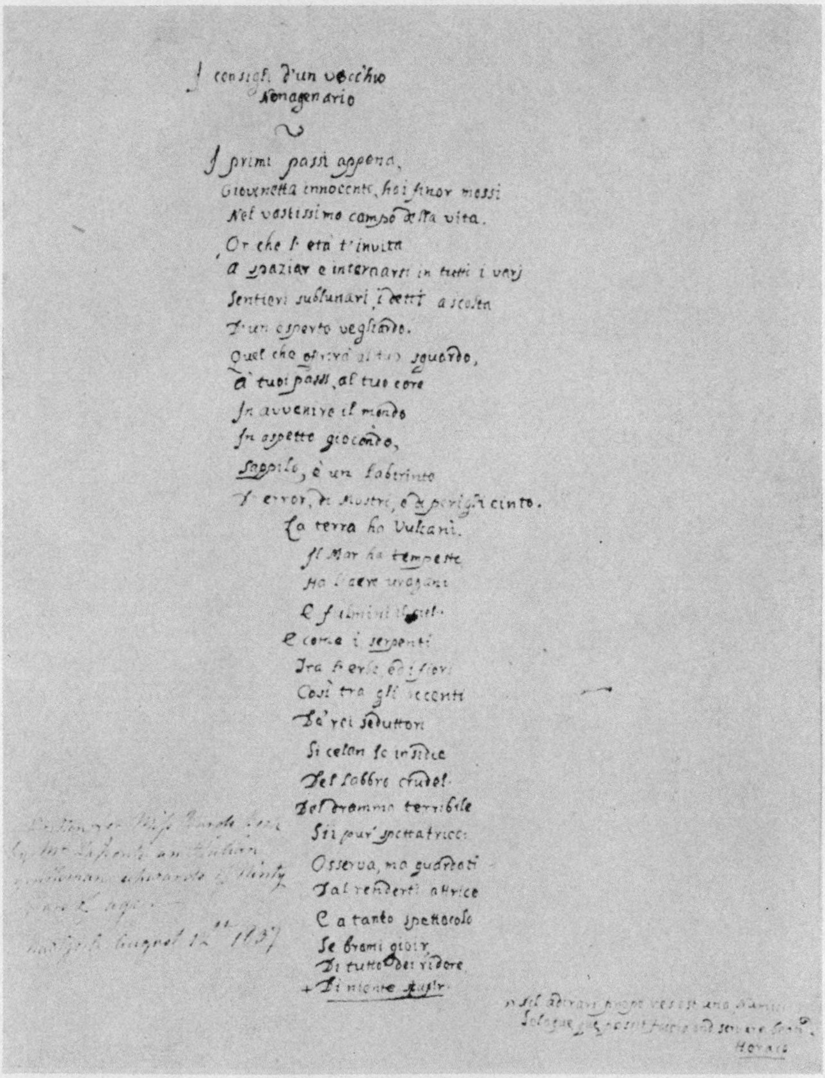

I consigli d'un vecchio
nonagenario

I primi passi appena,
Giovinetta innocente, hai finor messi
Nel vastissimo campo della vita.
Or che l'età t'invita
a spaziar e internarti in tutti i varj
Sentieri sublunari, i detti ascolta
d'un esperto vegliardo.
Quel che offrirà al tuo sguardo,
a' tuoi passi, al tuo core
In avvenire il mondo
In aspetto giocondo,
Sappilo, è un labirinto
d'error, di mostri, e di perigli cinto.
La terra ha vulcani.
Il mar ha tempeste
Ha l'aere uragani
E fulmini ......
E come i serpenti
Tra l'erbe e di fiori
Così tra gli accenti
De' rei seduttori
Si celan le insidie
Del labbro crudel.
Del dramma terribile
Sei pur spettatrice:
Osserva, ma guardati
Tal renderti attrice
E a tanto spettacolo
Se brami gioir,
Di tutto dei ridere
Di niente gustar.

PLATE 19.—Lorenzo Da Ponte's Last Poem, written in New York—1837

PLATE 20.—Portrait of Ludwig van Beethoven by I. G. Waldmüller (1823)

The very first notes put us into the mood where the soul, released from the burdens of the day, and at peace with itself, is carried aloft to the mysterious regions of the starry heavens. Here we feel it to be like Philomel of the ancients, winged and airy, hovering over flowers and scents, with which loveliness it is imbued.

Only one genius has penetrated into this species of music to the very essence of its content: Chopin. Nearer to pain than the nocturnes of Field, they are more sharply accentuated. Their poetry is more sombre but also more captivating. They give us more delight but less calm.

Field, a pupil of Clementi, was initiated by this master into the secrets of the most beautiful method of that epoch, and he has transferred them to a form of poetry, and has created an inimitable example of unconscious grace, melancholy, naïveté, and refined, yet careless elegance. He belongs to that type of preparative schools, which is met with only at certain periods of art when new sources are opened up, — sources, felt and recognized, but not yet exhausted; not yet expanding art to a freer unfoldment; not yet aware of the danger incurred of shattering its wings in this striving.

From Franz Liszt "Gesammelte Schriften"

Music and Imagination

(Ideas of a Romanticist)

T HE compositions of a man who understands Shakespeare and Jean Paul, will be different from one who draws all his wisdom from Marpurg,[1] etc., alone.

Did not Beethoven, on the title page of his overture in C use the expression "Gedichtet von" instead of "composed by"?

1 Friedr. Wilh. Marpurg (1718-1795), famous by his periodicals "Der critische Musicus an der Spree."

There are hidden workings of the soul, which a suggestion in words, by the composer can make more comprehensible, and these should be gratefully accepted.

Very often, unconsciously, and side by side with musical imagination, an idea continues to operate, — and not with the ear alone, but with the eye as well, — and this ever active organ, amid sounds and tones, holds fast to specific outlines, which, with the progressing music, are condensed, and develop into distinct shapes. The more the elements, innate in music, are related to the ideas and shapes thus generated, the more poetic and plastic the composition will become. The keenness of attention paid by the musician to these products of his imagination will determine the effect and the uplift of his work. Why did the thought of immortality stir Beethoven's imagination? Why could the memory of a fallen hero inspire him to a great work? Why was another moved by the remembrance of hours blissfully spent?

I cannot refrain from relating an experience with a friend: who, when playing a Schubert March with me, to my question, whether he did not see very distinct shapes and figures before him, answered: "Why, yes, I found myself in Sevilla, hundreds of years ago, in the midst of promenading dons and donnas with trains, pointed shoes, swords, etc." Strangely enough, our visions, with exception of the city, were identical!

Robert Schumann: *"Gesammelte Schriften"*.

Schumann's Precepts of Art and Life

Ear-training is most important.

Keep time in playing. The playing of some of the virtuosi is like the gait of a drunkard. Do not take these as an example.

Begin early to learn the basic laws of harmony.

Don't ever strum the piano. Go ahead playing and never play pieces half through.

Try to play simple pieces well and perfectly. It is better than to perform difficult ones badly.

You must make enough progress to comprehend a piece of music on paper.

When you play don't mind who is listening, but always play as though a master were listening.

All this stuff of playing runs changes with time. Only inasmuch as technique serves higher purposes is it worthwhile.

You must neither play nor listen — unless forced to — to poor compositions.

Don't let applause, that so-called great virtuosi often receive, tempt you. Let the applause of artists be more your aim than that of the masses.

Everything resembling a fad goes out of fashion. And should you continue cultivating fads in your old age, you will become a fop whom no one respects.

A great deal of playing in society brings more harm than good.

Play fugues industriously. Let Bach's "Welltempered Clavier" become your daily bread.

As a recreation from your studies read good literature.

There is much to be learned from good singers, but don't believe everything they tell you.

Never miss an opportunity to play the organ. There is no instrument so ready to revenge itself for any impurity both in pitch and in playing, as the organ.

Sing diligently in the chorus, especially middle parts. This will improve you musically.

Listen diligently to folk songs. They are a gold mine of the most beautiful melodies, and reveal the characteristics of the various nations.

Never judge a composition after one hearing. What pleases you at first is not always the best. Masters need to be

studied. Many things will become clear to you in your
old age only.

"Melody" is the battle cry of amateurs. Naturally music without melody is nothing. But realize well what is meant
by melody. An easily grasped, rhythmically pleasing,
sweet tune is for some, "melody". But there are melodies of a different character, and when you read Bach,
Mozart, Beethoven, they gaze at you in a thousand varied
ways. The scanty monotony, particularly of modern
Italian opera melodies will, I hope, soon tire you.

When you begin to compose, do it in your mind only. The
fingers must do what the mind wills, not the other way
around.

If heaven has given you a vivid imagination, you will, in
lonely hours, often sit at the piano, as though glued to
it, ready to express your inmost feelings. These are the
happiest hours of youth. But beware of yielding too
often to a talent that may tempt you to waste time and
energy, so to say, on shadowy pictures. The mastery of
form, the power of clear creation, will be gained only
by the firm symbol of script. Therefore write more and
improvise less.

Get a good knowledge of all the other arts and disciplines.

The laws of life are also those of art.

There is no end to learning.

Schumann, "Gesammelte Schriften"

Schumann Rejects Rellstab's Review on the "Kinderszenen"

I have seldom met with anything more clumsy and more
narrow-minded. Suppose he thinks I am going to put a cry-

ing child before me, and choose my tones therefrom? Rell-stab can not see beyond the A. B. C. at times, and wishes for chords only.

From Robert Schumann's
"Gesammelte Schriften ueber
Musik und Musiker".

LATE ROMANTICISM

When Grieg's Talent
Was Discovered By Ole Bull

MY mother was strict, severely so. She was not to be fooled when, instead of diligently practising my exercises, I sat dreaming at the piano. My unpardonable tendency to dream, began, even at that time, to cause me the difficulties that have followed me all my life. Had I not inherited my mother's unquenchable energy and musical talent, I believe, I should never have succeeded in proceeding from dreams to action. School-life was disagreeable to me in the highest degree. But I was always good at singing. When Ole Bull, the Norwegian violin virtuoso, heard, that I was a composer, he made me sit at the piano. All my pleading was in vain. Today, I cannot understand what Ole Bull saw in my youthful pieces, but he very earnestly spoke to my parents. Then he suddenly approached me, and said: "You must go to Leipzig and become a musician." All gazed lovingly at me and I had the feeling that a kind fairy was stroking my cheek. And my good parents! There was not a moment of hesitation or opposition. Everything was arranged, and the whole matter seemed to me, to be the simplest thing in the world. I was then under a magical spell.

G. Schjelderup and W. Niemann
"Edward Grieg's Biography"

"Richard Nordraak, Not Grieg,
was the true Norwegian Genius," says Debussy

I have seen Grieg viewed from the front. He looks like a gifted photographer. From behind he looks — the way he wears his hair — like a sunflower. He is an excellent musician, so long as he stays within the range of his own country, although he does not, by far, use this fact to the same advantage as do Balakirev and Rimsky-Korsakov with their national Russian music. As a matter of fact, Grieg is less an original musician than an ingenious one. It appears, that his real predecessor and contemporary was a young man, a born genius, who promised to become a great musician, but who died at the age of twenty-four: Richard Nordraak. His death is greatly to be deplored: in the first place, Norway was deprived of a hope, and Grieg of an influence, which would have kept him from the wrong path. Grieg seems to pursue a similar aim as that of Ibsen's "The Master Builder": to build houses for men in which they feel at home and are happy.

Debussy: "Monsieur Croche Antidilettante"

"You Have to go to Australia —!"
(1853)

I have written some Norwegian peasant dances, which not one of my compatriots has been able to play properly. When there comes along a young Australian, who is the first to play them as they ought to be played. He is full of the poetry of all the folk songs between Australia and Norway. Percy Grainger is a genius whom we Scandinavians should love.

From Richard H. Stein's
"Biography of Edward Grieg".

Schumann Introduces Young Brahms to the World

I have often, of late, in spite of strenuous productive activity, felt stimulated by noting that so many new and eminent talents announce themselves. I thought, carefully following the career of these elect, that there might be among them one, who, not by gradual development, but like Minerva, springing in full equipment from the head of Zeus, would suddenly appear with the power to give perfect ideal expression to the spirit of our time. And he has come, a young blond, at whose cradle the graces and the heroes stood guard. His name is Johannes Brahms. He came from Hamburg, where he created in solitude and silence, initiated by an excellent, inspiring master into the most difficult fields of art. He bore all the insignia of one to be announced to us: "Behold one of the elect".

Sitting at the piano — and he has a marvelous style of playing — he opened to us wonderful new vistas, and we were drawn, more and more, into his magic circle. He made of the piano an orchestra of lamentation and exultation. There were sonatas, mostly symphonies in disguise; songs, the poetry of which could be understood without knowing the words, for a deep song melody pervades them; various pieces for the piano of sometimes demoniac character but charming in form; sonatas for violin and piano; quartets for string instruments, so diversified, that they seemed to spring from different sources. And were he to touch, with his wand, the mass power of orchestra and chorus, wonderful glimpses into a phantom world might await us.

May his great genius give him this power, which is very probable, since he is invested with another genius — that of modesty. His fellowmen salute him on this, his first march into the world where perhaps wounds may be in store for him, but laurels and palms as well. We welcome him as a strong champion.

From "Gesammelte Schiften ueber Musik und Musiker".

Wagner Versus Wagner
Young Wagner's Opinion About Bellini:

HOW often, on hearing an Italian or French opera, may we have been delighted, but leaving the theatre, with a pitying joke, have purposely laughed away this emotion. Arrived at home, we came to the conclusion that one must beware of too much delight! But should we, for once, not indulge in that joke, should we not come to the conclusion but rather retain what we have just heard, — then we would realize it was Bellini's pure melody, his simple noble song that has charmed us. To retain this and to believe it, can surely not be a crime! It may not even be a crime, to send, before retiring, a prayer to heaven that such melody and such manner of treating the voice may occur for once to a German composer. Melody, and once again, melody, you Germans! For melody is the language in which a musician should express himself. And, indeed, the now prevalent clear comprehension of passion on the stage will be greatly facilitated if it be brought into a clear, easily grasped melody, with a firm stroke, including all secondary sentiments. Rather than having it badly constructed or drowned out by a hundred little commentaries and subtleties, by this or that harmonic nuance, or by the intervention of this or that instrument.

"Rigaer Zuschauer", 1837.

Wagner's Early Development
From Letters To Mathilde von Wesendonck
and Other Friends

I remember that in my thirties, being deeply troubled with doubts as to my qualifications for a highly artistic individuality, I detected imitation and influence in all my work, and uneasily looked forward to my future as a truly original creator.

The phantastic dissoluteness of German student life, after violent excesses, disgusted me very soon. Woman, as such, had begun to exist for me. A yearning, nowhere to be satisfied, found ideal nourishment in the perusal of Heinse's "Ardinghello", as well as in the writings of Heine and other members of the "Young Literature" of Germany. But it was a personal appearance which kindled this longing in me to a noble enthusiasm: I saw Mme. Schroeder-Devrient in a starring performance at the Leipzig theatre. The product of all these impressions and moods was my opera, "Das Liebesverbot, oder Die Novize von Palermo". If you compare this subject with that of "Die Feen", it is obvious that a possibility of development in two basically different directions was existent for me: The solemn earnestness of my innate being here encounters — nourished by the impressions of life — a defiant call for freedom, a wild sensual impetuousness, which seemed in vivid contradiction to the former. I gave up my "Liebesverbot" entirely. I felt I could no longer respect myself as its composer and followed my true artistic faith all the more independently in the continuation of "Rienzi". From now on began my career as a poet, which caused me to leave behind me that of a librettist. I am surely not conceited about my poetic career, and must confess, that it was of necessity only, because no good libretti were forthcoming, and therefore I turned to making my own.

Primarily no subject as such can attract me, that does not present itself to me in both its musical and its poetic significance. Before proceeding to write a verse, or even to design a scene, already overcome by the musical fragrance of my creation,—I have all the tones, all the characterizing motives in my mind,—so that, when the verses are finished, and the scenes arranged, for me, the opera too in its entirety, is completed. Only such subjects should be chosen as are suited to musical treatment; never would I choose a subject which could, by a clever playwright, be utilized for a spoken drama. If it is the mission of the poet of today, from a moral standpoint, to purify and to spiritualize the material interests of our age then it is left to the composer of operas to cast upon us the spell of hallowed poetry, with all its magic fragrance wafted to us from the sagas and tales of olden times. For music here offers a medium for combinations, which is not at the disposal of the poet,—especially not, when faced with our actors.

The period when I started to create from an inner inspiration, began with "The Flying Dutchman". "Tannhaeuser" and "Lohengrin" followed. And if there be in these works a fundamental poetic thought, it is the superlative tragedy of renunciation, the well-motivated, the final of necessity eventuating, and solely redeeming negation of the will. (Schopenhauer). It is this profound train of thought which gave to my poetry and to my music its sacredness without which, what is truly moving therein, could never have been proper to them.

I was not able at the time I created the "Tannhaeuser" to bring about anything inspired from within, anything passionate, or I might even call it "womanly ecstatic". I am now truly horrified at my stagey Venus of that day. Everything fresh and full of life in "Tannhaeuser" is good and I would not make a single change. Everything with the aura of the saga is in itself ethereal: Tannhaeuser's lament and atonement, truly excellent; the grouping requires no change. The action of Tannhaeuser is immeasurably stronger than that of the "Dutchman", developed as it is from interior motives. Every measure of dramatic music is only then justified if it expresses something pertaining to the character of the acting personage. If we are not tuned to deepest compassion for Tannhaeuser, all the rest of the drama has lost its cohesion and reason for being.

As in the course of a drama, the intended fulfillment of a decisive dominant mood can only be attained by a development of the various moods incited, so, of necessity, the musical expression directly affecting sensuous feeling, has to take a decisive part in this development to highest fulfillment. And this was shaped by an at all-time characteristic weaving of the main themes, which was not confined to one scene only,—as was formerly the case to a single vocal section,— but was spread over the entire drama, and so to say, in a most intimate relation to the poetic purpose.

On the day when (after having received notice,—and it became ever more certain that my personal situation was threatened by the most critical matter: an arrest for having supposedly taken part in the Dresden revolt, 1848) I heard Liszt conduct a rehearsal to my "Tannhaeuser", I was amazed to see in him my second ego. What a miracle! The love of the rarest of all friends gave me, at a time when I myself became homeless (banishment and flight to Switzerland), the long yearned-for home for my art, which I had sought so long in the wrong place and never found.

After having driven from my soul all doubts and uncertainties in my writings, I could at last—artistically independent —continue in the course already begun, toward the fulfillment of the ideal form of my own creating. And thus I had gained, by means of my work, a conception of the only possible and suitable future representation.

A Sketch of the "Meistersinger,"
Marienbad, July, 1845

In the manner of the Athenians, who had a tragedy succeeded by a cheerful Satyr Play, I had, on that pleasure trip to Marienbad, suddenly before me the idea of a comic play that could in like manner be affixed to my "Tannhaeuser" as a suitable Satyr Play: "The Meistersinger", headed by Hans Sachs. I conceived Hans Sachs as the last manifestation of the artistic, productive folk spirit, and in this interpretation I set him against the mastersinger philistinism, the comic tablature, the poetic pedantry of which I depicted in the character of the "Merker."

From: "Eine Mitteilung an meine
Freunde", Zuerich, 1851.

Wagner's Acid Attack on Meyerbeer

IN the French comic opera of former days, the poet had alloted to the composer a special field only, which it was up to him to cultivate, while the poet retained for himself the real possession of the land. This condition brought to light what was sanest in the opera as a dramatic genre. The poet sincerely attempted to invent situations and characters, to develop an entertaining, often interesting plot, which he arranged to suit the musicians' composition and style. This charming and clever genre had its home in the "Opera Comique". Scribe and Auber now proceeded to translate this form into the more pompous language of the so-called "Grand Opera", but in the "Mute of Portici" and in "Guillaume Tell", we can still plainly detect a well-constructed plot. The poet, the author, here still held the reins in his own hands, because neither Auber

PLATE 21.—Heiligenstadt—Drawing and Engraving by Joseph Kohl

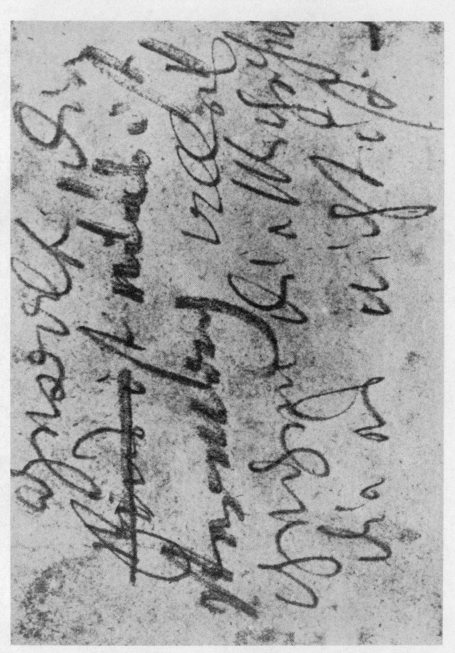

PLATE 22.—From Beethoven's Conversation-Books, 1819, Berlin, State Library

PLATE 23.—Goethe's Dedication to Mendelssohn

PLATE 24.—Frou-Frou Wagner—Caricature on the Publication of the "Milliner's Letters" from "Der Floh," Vienna, 1877

nor Rossini themselves cared to dispense with the comfort of sitting musically and melodically, in the gorgeous theatrical coach, without much concern as to how and where the well-trained driver was going.

Here now comes Meyerbeer, who, not having this desire for a luxurious and melodious comfort, did not hesitate to grab the reins from the driver, and by the consequent zigzagging in the driving to arrive at the sensation, which he, seated in the coach alone with his musical ability, could never hope to achieve.

While Scribe, with great natural skill, continued to write for other composers, clever, light and flowing poems with easily comprehended situations,—this experienced writer now manufactured for Meyerbeer the most unhealthy bombast: action without any plot; situations of the most absurd confusion; characters of a ridiculous grotesqueness. Scribe himself must have been of distorted mind when he brought to light "Robert Le Diable". He must have lost all sane sense of a dramatic plot, when in the "Huguenots" he lowered himself to becoming merely a compiler of decorative nuances and contrasts. He must have been forcibly initiated into historic roguery, before he allowed himself to become a "Prophet" of villains.

We here detect the same determining influence that Weber exerted over the authoress of the "Euryanthe" libretto:* but how different the motives! Weber wanted a drama into which could be merged his noble soulful melody; Meyerbeer, on the other hand, desired a tremendously mottled, historic-romantic, diabolically-religious, sentimentally-roguish, bigoted-voluptuous, frivolous-sacred, mysterious-impudent hodge-podge, to gain the subject for an extremely curious music, which, because of the leathery nature of his musical ability, was never quite successful. What he demanded of his poet, was a setting into scene of a Berlioz orchestra, but note it well—with most

* Hermine von Chezy.

humiliating debasement to the shallow basis of the song trills and fermatas of a Rossini—all for the sake of the "dramatic opera".

"Oper und Drama", 1851.

Richard Wagner,
The Fascinating Conductor
Anton Seidl's Impressions

HE was a man of iron. Almost small in stature, he rose to the height of a giant before the orchestra. His huge head, with its strongly accentuated features, enlivened by beautiful piercing eyes, the play of the muscles of his face, controlling every minute movement, every expression of feeling, will ever be unforgotten. He stood there, his body immovable but his eyes, glowing, glimmering, pricking, his fingers nervously whisking about. The air seemed fevered with his personality and reached every single musician. An invisible force invaded the soul of each of his co-workers. The fever was transmitted to each and every one and no one could escape the influence of this great man.

Everything went topsy-turvy at the beginning of the rehearsals, due to the impatience of the master. He wanted everything to be perfect from the first. The strange illustrative movements of the baton startled and confused the musicians, until they realized that it was not the baton, that was here the ruling force, but the phrase, the melody, or the expression. It was his look that fascinated them, a magnetic fluid ensnared them, and the master had them all in hand. The weakest orchestra under him played superbly. The most rigid rhythm, the loftiest expression of feeling reigned supreme, and all this was reflected in Wagner's face.

I once sat next to a famous actor, who for the first time had seen Wagner exercise the mimic power of his gaze, and watched the play of his facial muscles. This man stared at Wagner as at a phantom appearance, and could not take his eyes off him. He later told me that Wagner's face expressed more than that of all the greatest actors of the world.

"Bayreuther Blaetter"

The Philosophical Background of the "Ring"
From A Letter to Liszt

MY head is full of grand ideas on the subject of "Siegfried." Three dramas with a three-act "Vorspiel" (Prelude). If all the theatres in Germany were to break down, I would build a new one on the Rhine, and raise an assemblage,—and I would accomplish the whole thing in one week.

When I imagine the audience, I can only consider an assemblage of foreigners, who have come from anywhere just to become acquainted with my works. I should prefer some beautiful desert, far away from the smoke and fumes of industrial civilization,—and in this sense, Weimar might do, but certainly never a large city.

Wotan soars to tragic heights, in the end to will his own downfall. This is all we can learn from the history of mankind: the will, ourselves to bring about the inevitable. The culminating creation of this lofty self-destructive will is Siegfried, —fearless, everloving man. That is all. In the meantime, inherent with disaster and power, the true poison of love, is concentrated in the gold, corrupted and wrested from nature: the "Ring of the Nibelungen". The curse resting on it will never be lifted until it has been restored to nature and the Rhine. This too Wotan only learns at the very end: he has entirely, in his lust for power, lost sight of what Loge, in the very beginning has so urgently impressed on him. He then recognizes the power of the curse, in Fafner's deed: fratricide. Only when Siegfried too is destined to ruin, does he realize that the restoration of the stolen gold alone can exterminate the evil, and he makes his own downfall conditional on this extirpation of an age-old wrong. Experience is everything. Even Siegfried, by himself, is not perfect, he is but a half. He becomes the savior only when united with Bruenhilde: one man alone cannot do it all, it is the seeing, suffering, self-sacrifice of a woman, which can at last bring true salvation. For love, in its essence, is the "Eternal Feminine" itself. ("Das Ewig-Weibliche").

Because of the mythical subject I had to resort to a kind of "Sprachmelodie". This is the alliterative verse, which, following the accents of speech in natural vivid rhythm, proved most suitable. It is the verse in which the poets of old composed their poetry, when they themselves were the poets and creators of myths. As regards the innovations that I, in the opinion of many, will have introduced, I am conscious of the advantage gained, if not definitely developed, making the dramatic dialogue the subject of the musical work,—while the opera proper, hitherto has regarded the action, with its arbitrarily inserted moments of lyrical pause, as alone suitable.

While antique tragedy had to limit the dramatic dialogue, because of the necessity of interspersing it with choruses and completely separating them,—this unproductive element of music, which gave to the ancient drama its higher significance,—has now become inseparable from the modern orchestra (the greatest artistic achievement of our age), and is ever side by side with the action,—thus bearing in its womb the motives of action in a deeper sense.

"Tristan and Isolde"

I SHOULD like herewith to designate the art of transition as the most subtle and profound feature of my art. I am repelled by what is abrupt and sudden. It is often unavoidable and necessary, but it should not happen without having first created a mood, that, preparatory to this sudden transition, would make it seem imperative. My masterpiece in this fine art of a gradual transition is undoubtedly the great scene in the second act of "Tristan and Isolde." The beginning of the act reveals life in its most overpowering emotional aspect; the close, is filled with the most fervent sanctified yearning for death. These are the two pillars, and note how I have combined them. This now is the secret of my musical form, and I have the temerity to affirm that its perfect harmony, its clear interpretation of every detail, has hitherto not even been dreamed of. If you could but know how this guiding precept has inspired me with musical inventions of rhythm, harmonic and melodic development, which formerly would never have occurred to me,—you would fully realize how, even in the most specialized branches of art, nothing true can be invented that does not arise from prime motives.

Wagner's Statement, 1854.
From his "Gesammelte Schriften"
(Breitkopf & Haertel, 1911).

Nietzsche Ridicules Wagner

THERE is nothing that Wagner has so profoundly thought about as salvation. His operas express this idea. There is always somebody who wants to be saved: here a man, there a woman—that is his problem. And how rich and manifold are the variations of this "Leitmotiv"! How rare and full of thought his modulations! Who, if not Wagner, taught us that innocence has a predilection for saving interesting sinners (as in Tannhaeuser); or that even the Wandering Jew becomes sedentary (if he gets married) as in the "Flying Dutchman"; or that old corrupt women prefer to be saved by chaste youths (Kundry in "Parsifal"); or that young hysterics desire to be saved by their physicians (as in "Lohengrin"); or that young girls like to be saved by knights (who are Wagnerians, by the way), as in "The Meistersinger"; or that married women too, like to be saved by a knight (the case Isolde); or that the old god, after having compromised himself morally in every possible respect, is at last redeemed by an atheist and immoralist (In the "Ring"). . . .

Friedrich Nietzsche: *"The Case of Wagner".*

Richard Wagner and Mathilde von Wesendonck

THE one thing that has these last six years sustained, consoled and strengthened me, so that I could, in spite of the enormous difference of character, bear with Minna, has been the love of a young woman which approached me timidly, with doubt and hesitation, at the beginning; but which, as time went on, grew ever more sure and positive. Since there could never be the question of a union between us, our love took on a deeply sorrowful character, renouncing every low and base wish, and seeing the source of joy in the happiness of others alone.

She has from the beginning of our acquaintanceship cared for me in the most considerate untiring manner and has won from her husband many things to make my life an easier one. And this love which remained an unspoken one, at last had to find open expression when I composed "Tristan" and dedicated it to her. She then, for the first time, broke down,

248

and declared that she must die. Can you imagine, sister, what this love must have meant to me after a life of suffering and sacrifice? But we always realized that there could never be a union between us and so we became resigned, renouncing every selfish wish. We suffered, endured,—but we loved.

To his sister Klara.

Another Face of Richard Wagner:
"Wie gleicht er dem Weibe"
(*Richard Wagner's Letters to a Milliner*)

IN a recently published catalogue there was offered for sale a highly interesting collection of "Original Musical Manuscripts". Among them were sixteen letters of rather curious content, written by Richard Wagner to a milliner. The price was too high for me, but the "Neue Freie Presse" shared my curiosity, and buying them, enabled me to release them for publication.

These letters were not written to a German youth, nor were they addressed to Cosima or to von Buelow;—they are epistles sent to a Viennese milliner, who, efficient in her field, fully justified the confidence placed in her by the master, when he ordered the innumerable satin dressing-gowns and quilts, mentioned in the letters.

Wagner here spares his readers the boredom, the vagueness, the obscurity, which characterizes his usual style. He avoids the "mental agitation", when he gives a detailed description of how a satin dressing-gown should be lined; nor does he indulge in philosophical maxims which might mar the clarity of expression in ordering a bed-quilt. And nowhere is there a sign of the "impassioned confusion" which might befog the explicit directions given, of how the ribbons, laces, satins, etc. were to be applied. For, after all, he was addressing a mere milliner and had to use more care than when writing for readers of aesthetic treatises.

Dear Fraeulein Bertha:

Unfortunately I am unable to send you money this week, for my affairs are not going as well as I should wish. I am leaving Vienna to settle matters in person elsewhere. Do not worry on that score, however, and rest assured that I most urgently desire to compensate and satisfy you at the earliest possible opportunity. You can rely on it.

Respectfully your devoted

Richard Wagner.

From Starnberg.

Dear Frl. Bertha:

When I last saw you in Vienna, you expressed the desire for further orders. But I feel that I must make a part payment. You are well acquainted with the models I should like to have for my house-robes, etc. The materials which I prefer to have specially ordered for me are difficult to get here. I shall therefore be very pleased to have you serve me. I should like you to send me an annual accounting, itemized, so that I will always be advised of the price of the materials used. I will herewith give you some orders, and will ask you to get the material for me, as follows:

1. I am enclosing a sample of the light brown satin I shall require. A fine heavy quality.
2. Could you get some dark pink satin?
3. Can the enclosed shade of light pink, in a good quality, be obtained at about 4 or 5 flrs.?
4. The same in blue, preferably a little lighter, but not in any case darker.
5. Has Szontag enough of the new red or carmoisin, as enclosed? And the same heavy satin with which you

lined the white dressing-gown with the flowered pattern?

6. Have you some of the dark yellow material with which we made the curtains for the little table?

Please procure for me the material in the shades mentioned, and at the same time let me know whether the offer I made, is acceptable to you. I am hoping that you still have the patterns for my robes. Hoping for an early answer

Yours respectfully

Richard Wagner.

Excerpt: . . . I was not prepared for the payment of such large sums, so you must see now how you can best manage. Let me know and send me the bill in full, so that I am advised of what I still owe you.

Greetings and best wishes

R. Wagner.

Dear Frl. Bertha: (With enclosed sketch for robe)

Now, how much will a dressing-robe, a sketch of which I herewith enclose, cost? Pockets quilted, same shade as the robe, with ruching of the same material.

The gown: pink satin, interlined with eiderdown and stitched in squares. The bottom of the robe, very wide,—six widths of the material. A ruching, as shown in the drawing, of the same material, is to be inserted, not sewed on. From the waist on, let the skirt with ruching, flare out at the bottom, getting gradually wider and wider.

The sleeves, very wide, and very rich (as in sketch, with ruching). A scarf, five ells long, ending in the full width of the material. The shoulders narrow, so that the sleeves don't pull,—you know.

Dear Frl. Bertha:

I am very much surprised not to have heard from you. In your last missive you do mention my letters, but nothing about the dressing-gown; you pay no attention to my orders. Nor do you say anything about the quilt I have ordered. And what about the satin robe? Did you receive the 25 Thalers I sent you?

Yours respectfully,

R. Wagner

Note of Daniel Spitzer, the editor of these letters:

In order to note a contrast, I should like to mention here a little tailor idyl in the life of Schiller. In his diaries, published by Fr. von Gleichen-Russwurm, we find among other household expenses, the modest item:

My clothes, 75 Thaler.

Contrast this with 2500 Gulden that Wagner spent for houserobes alone!

From Daniel Spitzer's
"Gesammelte Schriften"

(Edited by Max Kalbeck & Otto E. Deutsch)

Beethoven Blesses the Young Liszt
(1823)

I WAS about eleven years old when my esteemed teacher, Czerny, took me to see Beethoven. He had for a long time spoken about me to the master, and had asked him to hear me play. But Beethoven had always such a horror of youthful prodigies that he violently opposed to receive me. But, at last, he yielded to the irrepressible Czerny, and impatiently said: "Well, in God's name bring the rascal to me."

It was ten o'clock in the morning, when we stepped into the two-room apartment of the "Schwarzspanierhaus" where Beethoven lived. I was very shy, but Czerny kindly encouraged me. Beethoven was at work at a long narrow table. He gazed at us grimly, spoke a few fleeting words to Czerny, and remained silent when my good teacher beckoned me to the piano. I played a short piece by Ries. When I had finished, Beethoven asked me whether I could play a Bach fugue. I chose the D minor fugue from the "Well-tempered Clavier."

"Could you transpose that fugue into another key at once?" the master asked me. Luckily I could do it. After the final chord I looked up. The dark glowing eye of the great man was on me penetratingly. But suddenly a mild smile overspread the gloomy countenance. Beethoven came close to me, bent over me, put his hand on my head, and gently stroked my hair. "You are a devil of a fellow", he whispered, "what a rascal!" I at once gained courage: "May I now play something by you?" I asked audaciously. Beethoven smiled and nodded. I played the first movement of the C major concerto. When I was through, he grasped both my hands, kissed me on the forehead and softly said: "Go, you are one of the happy ones, for you are going to make many people rejoice and be happy. There is nothing better, nothing more beautiful in the whole world."

This event of my life is my greatest pride, and has ever remained so — the palladium for my entire artistic career. I seldom relate it, and only to good friends.

From Frimmel: "Beethoven-Studien".

VIENNA, A CENTER OF MUSIC

"Music Is Form Moving in Sounds"
The "Formal Aesthetics" of Eduard Hanslick

IN the critical and aesthetic treatment of music, not nearly enough stress is laid on the main theme of a composition. The theme itself already reveals the spirit in which the whole work has been created. When Beethoven begins his "Leonore", and Mendelssohn his "Fingal's Cave", every musician will surmise, at once, without knowledge of a single note of the later development, what the palace before which he is standing is like.

German theory and practice dwell too much on the musical construction of a composition, to the detriment of its thematic content. Nothing can be later developed that not already lies hidden in the theme. However, when the question of the content of a tonal work arises, we must beware of using the word in too extolling a sense. If a musical composition does not have "subject-matter", it does not follow that it is wanting in substance. The partisans who with such zeal are advocating "subject-matter" in music, evidently mean "spiritual content". The composer thinks and "poetizes". But he thinks and poetizes in tones, apart from all objective reality. Those zealots, however, regard composing as merely the means of translating a given subject into music, forgetting that the tones in themselves are the primal language.

The very fact that the composer must think in tones, proves the art of tones devoid of "subject-matter"; inasmuch as any comprehensible content must of necessity be expressed in words. Nevertheless, the abstract form of beauty does not exclude the imprint of individuality on a musical creation. The manner of treatment, as well as the invention of a theme is, in any case so unique, that it could never be lost in a higher generality, but would always stand on its individuality. A melody of Mozart, or Beethoven, stands solidly on its own feet, as does a verse by Goethe, a citation by Lessing, a statue of Thorwaldsen, a painting by Overbeck. The original thoughts or themes of a musical composition have the permanence of a proverb and the clarity of a picture: they are individual and personally eternal. It is only by a relentless elimination of any other "subject-matter" in the art of tones, that its essence can be preserved. Because of the vagueness of the feelings from which at best the subject is drawn, it can never have the spiritual significance which must be accorded to a specifically beautiful formation of tones, freely created from spiritualized material.

"Vom Musikalisch-Schoenen" (1854)

Vienna Silhouettes

A Contemporary on Hugo Wolf, Johannes Brahms, Anton Bruckner

ANY one, taking a walk in Vienna, in the eighties of the 19th century, through the inner part of the city, and roaming through its streets, could easily, within a period of one or two hours meet with three of the greatest masters since Beethoven's and Schubert's death: Hugo Wolf, Johannes Brahms, and Anton Bruckner.

Hugo Wolf, at that time, was a youth of about 25 years, slender and small in stature, with a blond goatee and the sparse remnants of a mustache, the hairs of which he was in the habit of pulling out, one by one. He had shining brown eyes in a pale face, reminding one of Lawrence Sterne and was often seen, deeply absorbed, talking to himself, rushing along, always with books under his arm, well dressed—mostly in a brown velvet coat and with a broad black lavalière.

Brahms, on the other hand, stout, with his gray thick hair and full beard, his face very red, and wearing a loose comfortable suit and broad shoes, rather gave, to a superficial observer, the impression of a distinguished Hamburg merchant. This, too, was confirmed by his slow deliberate gait, which I had observed untold times, when he passed me: when, seated by a window in the "Café Heinrichshof", at 3 o'clock in the afternoon, I saw him drinking black coffee, or, also very often, fast asleep, his face and beard pressed against the window pane.

Anton Bruckner, finally, in his black peasant loden suit, with his shorn Roman pate and the enormous hooked nose, the long neck of a vulture, enclosed by a wide lay-down collar, surely made a strange appearance. In one hand he carried a slouch hat, in the other an enormous blue handkerchief with which he alternately wiped his brow and cranium or tried to remove the traces of a late pinch of snuff.

Friedrich Eckstein:
"Bruckner Festschrift", Vienna 1924.

Diploma of Honorary Citizenship to
Johannes Brahms
(1889)

W E, the Senate of the Free Hansa City of Hamburg, herewith make known that we, in agreement with the community have accorded to the highly esteemed artist of tones, whose creative genius and noble work have made him prominent in his own as well as other countries

Herr Johannes Brahms

the worthy son of the city of Hamburg, in which the art of tones has ever been cultivated, and where he too has received his first inspirations for an artistic career as well as his first instruction,—with full appreciation of his fame as an artist, and in recognition of the love he has always borne for his native city and which he has often displayed,—the highest honor and dignity of our community: the Honorable Citizenship of the Free Hansa City of Hamburg.

Hamburg, June 14th, 1889.

History Proves Brahms Wrong

I HAVE gone far: I am respected both by my friends and my opponents. Even though I am not loved by all,—I am respected, and that is the main thing. I ask for no more. I know very well what my position in the history of music is going to be: the position that Cherubini had, and still has today. That is my lot, my fate. . . .

(From a letter to Koessler, 1894).
Max Kalbeck: "Johannes Brahms".

Brahms, An Emotional Bruckner Opponent

NIETZSCHE at one time made the statement that it was only by chance that I became famous: I was greatly needed as an anti-pope by the anti-Wagnerians. That, of course, is nonsense. I am not the one to be placed at the head of a party, for I must go my own way alone and in peace and have never yet crossed the path of another. Of Bruckner it would be true. After Wagner's death, his party was in need of a "pope", and none could have been better fitted for this job than Bruckner. Do you really believe, that a single person in this mass of immature listeners understands the least bit of those symphonic monster serpents, and don't you think that I am the musician who, today, understands Wagner's works best,—better anyway than his so-called followers, who would like to poison me? I, myself, told Wagner once, that I was the best Wagnerian of the day. Do you consider me so narrow-minded that I should not be charmed by the gaiety and the greatness of "Die Meistersinger"? Or so dishonest as to deny, that in my opinion a few bars of this work are more precious than all the operas together, that have been written since then? And I an "antipope"? That is too stupid. And Bruckner's works "immortal" or even real symphonies? That makes me laugh.

Max Kalbeck

Tchaikovsky Meets Brahms (1887)
Critical But Impressed

HIS beautiful aged head reminded me of that of a handsome Russian priest. He has nothing of the characteristic Germanic type about him, and it is therefore incomprehensible to me, that a learned ethnographer has chosen his head for the title plate of a work, depicting the original Germanic traits. Brahms himself told me about this, when I remarked upon his appearance. A certain mellowness in his general expression, his long scanty hair, his good-natured gray eyes, his gray full beard,—all this completed the portrait of a Russian Grandduke, as is specially found among our clergy. Brahms is incredibly simple in manner, serene and most unassuming. The hours I spent with him have left a very pleasant memory.

I must confess, however, that I have not been able to arrive at a comprehension of this most eminent representative of German music, even though, in Leipzig, we had a long sojourn together. The reason for this, can be traced to the fact, that I, like my Russian musical contemporaries, honor, in Brahms, the honest convinced and energetic musician, without being able to love his music. In Germany, a "Brahms Idealism" is extraordinarily prevalent. There are a great number of authoritative personages and institutions of music, who have exclusively dedicated themselves to a "cult of Brahms", whom they esteem as a star of greatest magnitude, and whom they place beside Beethoven. There are, it is true, "Anti-Brahms-ianers", and especially in other countries, except England. In London, a very efficient Brahms propaganda of the incredibly popular violinist, Joachim, has brought Brahms' fame to the notice of all music lovers. Everywhere else, I maintain, there is a certain unacquaintance with Brahms, but nowhere is he so emphatically ignored as he is in my fatherland.

There is something dry, cold, undefinably veiled in the music of this master that repels the Russians' heart. According to our Russian standpoint, Brahms is wanting in any melodious feeling, while his musical ideas never reach fulfilment. Hardly has an easily-grasped musical phrase been indicated, when he has already fallen into a flood of inferior harmonic runs and modulations, as though aiming to be particularly profound and unintelligible. He irritates and exasperates musical feeling, since he does not wish to meet his obligations; he is practically ashamed of the tones that might touch the heart! Hearing Brahms, one asks oneself: is he profound or does he want to mask his poverty of fantasy? But this question will never find a final answer.

Never could one designate Brahms' music as weak or insignificant. The style of the composer is elevated, and unlike all of us, contemporary tone poets, he does not strive for superficial effects, he does not try, by means of brilliant instrumental combinations, to surprise and startle,—no, everything is serious and noble, and far from any banal imitation. And he is, it would seem, quite independent. Yet the principal element is missing: beauty.

From Otto Keller: "Peter Tchaikovsky."

A Most Humble Dedication

Bruckner to King Ludwig II of Bavaria, 1885

Your Royal Majesty:

Deeply moved and with the greatest feeling of joy, I most humbly beg Your Majesty to permit me to express my most deeply felt gratitude for having deigned to honor me with Your Majesty's most gracious generosity, to accept my most humbly dedicated Seventh Symphony, which I lay at your feet. . . .

Maestro Wagner who has always treated me with marked distinction, has decided to perform all my symphonies.

Your Royal Majesty, the truly kingly patron of Wagner, has ever been for me the ideal of a German monarch.

Therefore I am happy that the golden rays of Your Royal Favor also fall on me, since I, almost 61 years old, am forced, beside the many lessons at the Vienna Conservatory, to give many private lessons, so that little time is left to me for musical composition. Since I now feel strong enough to create my best work and would like to turn to dramatic composition, this lack of time fills my heart with worry. . . .

The Rhythm Power of the Viennese Waltz

Hector Berlioz, 1838

IT is a curious fact, that, in a city like Paris, where the most eminent virtuosi and composers of Europe are heard, the arrival of a German orchestra, which in its essentials makes claim only to fine performance of Waltzes, should be an event of such significance.

We knew the name Strauss, thanks to the music publishers, who have disseminated his waltzes in thousands of copies, but that was all. Of the technical perfection, of the fire, of the rare feeling for rhythm, which distinguishes this orchestra, —of all this we had no inkling.

Its great success, I think, is to be ascribed more to the rhythmical accents of the German waltzes than to the charm of their melody and the brilliance of their instrumentation. There is, in the realm of music, an unexplored field, which has been opened up by Beethoven and Weber, a field that will soon attract to itself everything that a young musical generation has exhibited of vitality, and intelligence. This is the field of rhythm. It is immeasurable and fertile, and the only question is now, to cultivate it well.

From the "Memoirs".

Johann Strauss Goes to Boston

THE Strauss visit to the United States was in connection with the hundredth anniversary of the signing of the American Declaration of Independence. A kind of local celebration in 1872 preceded it in Boston, since Massachusetts, as early as 1772, had proposed separation from England. Boston planned concerts of gigantic proportion and what more natural for a feast of joy than that the songster of love and happiness should be invited for this purpose? People were quite liberal and hospitable and Johann Strauss himself an epicure in the best sense of the word, was not averse to such hospitality. In fact, free passage and paid expenses were furnished during the whole trip for the master himself, his wife and servants. And in addition $100,000 in advance, deposited in a Viennese bank, were allotted to him—certainly no trifle, not even for a waltz king!

On the first of June the adventure began with the departure from Bremerhaven. Johann had an insane fear of seasickness, but was, nevertheless, the one person least susceptible to it. He even arranged a ball on deck. A Prussian band was travelling on the same boat and since he himself, one can scarcely believe it, was not a dancer, his servant had to take over the role of cavalier, and dance the waltzes for him.

The impression on Boston was tremendous. At all street corners there were posters with his picture, a king enthroned on the terrestrial globe and bearing the baton as a scepter. But this shrieking advertisement had a grain of truth in it for to the direction of his baton millions of people moved rhythmically, and he could boast of having caused the whole world to become acquainted with three-quarter time in its Viennese version.

Strauss, according to contract, was to give fourteen concerts in Boston. No trifle! A gigantic wooden hall had been built to seat one hundred thousand. Six policemen cleared the way to the Director's box for him and his servant, who carried his violin. Women kissed the seam of his coat. Autograph collectors besieged his house, and many young women pushed their way up to Stephan, the servant, to get a lock of hair from the handsome Johann. The sly servant, however, had thought up a trick that enabled him to satisfy the women, even if a certain handsome Newfoundland dog began to look somewhat mangy.

Twenty thousand people sang the Danube Waltz. To keep them half way under control Strauss had to station one hundred sub-directors to take the beat from him and pass it on, but Strauss, himself, reported in a letter: "I could only make out those closest to me, and in spite of rehearsals in ensemble, real presentation or artistic achievement is not to be thought of. Now just consider my position, before a public of one hundred thousand Americans. There I stood on the highest director's box. How would the matter get under way and how would it end? Suddenly there was a cannon shot, a delicate hint for the twenty-thousand of us to begin the concert. I gave the sign. My one hundred sub-directors followed me as well as they could, and now a pandemonium was let loose which I shall never forget as long as I live. Since we all started at approximately the same time, my whole attention was directed only toward finishing at the same time as the only possible thing to do, and—God be praised!—I accomplished it."

In addition to the fourteen concerts in Boston, two great balls and four concerts were arranged in New York. Strauss had made America, Viennese.

From Paul Nettl: "Story of Dance Music".

Lanner's Manners Are Not As Good As His Waltzes

THE Arch-Duchess Sophie stepped up to Lanner and most graciously addressed him: "You have certainly worked hard." Lanner was busy wiping off the perspiration with his handkerchief and answered her in the purest Vienna dialect: "Yes, Your Imperial Highness, I surely did". Then, throwing back his swallow tail, he said: "Look, how I am sweating". Whereupon he was relieved of his duties for some time.

From Decsey: "Johann Strauss".

FRENCH AND ITALIANS

Heinrich Heine: Italy is the Home of Music

MUSIC here in Italy is not represented by individuals, it manifests itself in the entire population: music has become the people. With us in the North it is quite different: music there has become man only, and its name is Mozart or Meyerbeer. And besides, if we examine the best the Nordic masters offer us, closely, we find that it too contains Italian sunshine and the fragrance of oranges, and belongs more to beautiful Italy, the home of music, than to our Germany. The despisers of Italian music, who pass judgment on this species of music, will not escape their well-deserved punishment in hell, and will perhaps be damned, all through eternity, to listen to nothing but Bach's Fugues. I pity so many of my colleagues — for instance Rellstab (omnipotent critic in Berlin, in the period of the classics and the romanticists)—who will not escape this damnation, if he does not, before his death, become converted to Rossini.

Rossini, divino maestro, Helios of Italy, you, who send your rays all over the world, pardon my country-people who slander you in writing—as well as copy paper; who do not realize your depth because you have covered it with roses, and for whom you are not thorough enough and not enough weighted down with thought because you flutter so lightly and are so divinely winged.

From Alfred Bock: "Deutsche Dichter
in ihren Beziehungen zur Musik".

Rare Meeting With Paganini
(*As told by Hector Berlioz*)

WHEN an improvement in his health—he was suffering from tuberculosis of the throat—permitted, he, at rare intervals, would arrange a secret gathering, the participants of which were also the sole audience. There he would seize his violin to join them in playing trios and quartets. Then again, when playing the violin became too tiring, he would produce an unknown collection of duets, composed by himself for violin and guitar, and choosing for partner some able German violinist, he would play the guitar part and draw from this instrument incredible effects.

From his Memoirs.

Paganini's Macabre Appearance

AFTER a long wait, in religious silence, at length there appeared on the stage a dark figure that seemed to have risen from the underworld: Paganini in his black gala dress: a black dress-coat and vest of hideous cut, probably prescribed at the court of Proserpine by an infernal etiquette; black trousers hanging loosely and uneasily around his thin legs. His arms, already very long, seemed elongated, inasmuch as he held his violin hanging down in one hand, and the bow in the other, almost touching the ground, when he exhibited his incredible bows before the audience. A ghastly woodenness in the angular writhings of his body gave him something animal-like, so that a queer impulse to laugh overcame us all. His face, illumined by the lights from the orchestra, was of a cadaverous lividness, and bore an expression so incredibly humble and idiotically stupid, that a horrible feeling of pity suppressed our impulse to laugh. Did he learn these compliments from an automaton or from a dog? Is this pleading look that of a man, sick unto death, or is it the mockery of a shrewd miser lurking behind it? Is that a living man, about to pass away, who is to regale an audience in the arena of the arts, with his last convulsions, like a dying gladiator? Or is it a dead man, risen from the grave, a vampire with a violin, who, if not sucking the blood from our hearts, is, to say the least, drawing the money from our pockets?

> *From Heinrich Heine's "Memoirs of*
> *Herr von Schnabelewopski".*
> *(On the occasion of a concert in Hamburg, 1829).*

Rossini, An Admirer of Marchesi's[1] Voice Teaching

Most honored Madam:

If I have hesitated to thank you for the very flattering dedication of your twenty-four solfeggi, you must pardon me: only the state of my health was to blame. Excellent, my dear Signora. Your vocalises which I have perused with greatest interest, are written with a full knowledge of the human voice, and with clarity and elegance. They contain everything belonging to an art that I have seen for a long time treated as though there were question of seizing barricades.

May your interesting work be of use to a youth, which seems to have been driven away from the right path. Be true to your mission, to teach the beautiful Italian singing. It excludes neither the expression of feeling nor dramatic song, which I am sorry to say is fast on the way of becoming merely a question of lungs,—without any study whatsoever, for that is easier.

> *From G. Monaldi's "G. Rossini".*

---

[1] Mathilda de Castrone-Marchesi, 1826-1913, was one of the greatest voice teachers of the 19th century.

Beethoven Holds Cherubini In Highest Esteem

Honored Sir:

It is with great pleasure that I seize this opportunity to approach you by letter. I am often with you in the spirit, as I esteem your theatrical works above all others. Unfortunately, the beautiful world of art has been deprived, at least here in Germany, of a new great theatrical work of yours. Highly as your past works have been valued by true connoisseurs, it is a loss for art not to possess a new product of your great mind.

True art is imperishable, and the true artist takes keenest pleasure in genuine, great products of genius, and therefore I too am delighted when I hear of a new creation of your genius, and take greatest interest in it, more than in my own works. In short, I honor and love you. If it were not for my continued ill health, how delighted I would be to see you in Paris, and talk over matters of art with you. And now I must add, with enthusiasm, that I always address myself to every artist and art lover; otherwise you might think, that, because I am about to ask a favor of you, this was but an introduction to so doing. But I hope that you do not attribute to me so low a way of thinking. This is my request:

I have just finished my sacred Mass, and I wish to send it to the European courts, because I do not want it published in print just yet. I have, therefore, by way of the French Embassy, sent an invitation to His Majesty, the King of France, to subscribe to this work, and I am convinced the King would accept it upon your recommendation. Ma situation critique demande que je ne fixe pas seulement comme ordinaire mes pensées au ciel; au contraire, il faut les fixer aussi en bas pour les nécessitées de la vie. (My critical situation demands that I not only keep my thoughts fixed on the sky, as I ordinarily do; I must as well fix them on matters here below, for the necessities of life).

No matter what happens to my request to you, I shall

ever love and admire you, et vous resterez toujours celui de mes contemporains, que j'éstime le plus. Si vous voulez me faire un extrème plaisir, c'était si vous m'écrirait quelques lignes, ce que me soulegera bien. L'art unit tout le monde, wie viel mehr wahre Kuenstler, et peutêtre vous daignerez aussi de me mettre, mich zu rechnen unter diese Zahl. (And you will always remain the one among my contemporaries, whom I esteem most. If you wish to give me a most profound pleasure, you will write me a few lines, which would bring me great comfort. Art unites the world, and how much more so true artists, and perhaps you deign to number me among them).

Avec le plus haut éstime (With the highest esteem)
Votre ami et serviteur (Your friend and servitor)
Beethoven.

Letter to Cherubini,
Vienna, March 15, 1823.

Dictator Cherubini and Student Berlioz

WHEN Lesueur thought me far enough advanced in my study of harmony, he wished to establish my position and to enter me into his class at the Conservatoire. He spoke about it to Cherubini, who was at that time director of that institution, and I was admitted. Luckily I was not asked to introduce myself, on this occasion, to the formidable composer of "Medea", for the year before, I had roused his wrath to white heat under circumstances which I will now relate.

Cherubini had hardly taken the place of the deceased Perne (François Louis Perne, 1772-1832) as leader of the Conservatoire, when he wished to make an impression by an unheard of severity in the administration of the school, where Puritanism had not been the order of the day. Planning to

273

make meetings of pupils of both sexes impossible, he ordered the men to leave by the portal of the Rue Poissonière, and the girls to enter the one giving on the Rue Bergère; the two entrances were at opposite sides of the building.

When, one morning, in ignorance of this newly issued moral regulation, I entered, as had been my habit so far, by the portal on the Rue Bergère,—the virginal portal—and had almost reached the library, a servant accosted me in the courtyard, ordering me to turn back and to re-enter by the men's door. I thought this demand so ridiculous, that I told the argus in livery to mind his own business, and went my way. The funny fellow wished to ingratiate himself with his new master by being as strict as he was. He did not admit defeat, and hurried to tell the director what had happened. I had been in the library a full quarter of an hour and was engrossed in the study of "Alceste", thinking no more about the incident, when Cherubini, followed by my denouncer, and with more cadaverous mien, with hair more dishevelled, and eyes more malicious than ever, entered the library. They walked all around the table, at which several readers were sitting. After having scrutinized all of them, the servant stopped before me, and announced: "There he is." Cherubini, at first, was so enraged that he could not utter a word. "Ah, ah, ah! So it's you, is it?" he said at last, with his Italian accent, which made his rage seem funnier than ever, "it is you who came in by the entrance that I have forbidden?" "M. le Directeur, I didn't know of your order. I will obey it another time." "Another time, another time! What are you doing here?" "I want to study the Gluck scores, as you see." "And what are these scores to you? And who gave you permission to come into the library?" "M. le Directeur," (I was beginning to lose my temper) "the Gluck scores are among the most beautiful I know in operatic music, and I don't have to ask any one's permission to study them here. The library is open to the public from ten until six, and I have the right to make use of that." "The

274

right?" "Yes, the right." "And I forbid you ever to come here again." "But I will come again, just the same." "What is your name?" he shouted trembling with rage. And I, now too, pale with anger: "M. le Directeur, you may some day know my name,—but today, you shall not hear it." "Hold him, Hottin (the name of the servant), so that I can take him in charge." Whereupon he and the servant, greatly to the astonishment of those present, chased me all around the table, throwing down chairs and desks, without catching me. I got away, and laughingly called out to my persecutors: "You are not going to get either me or my name, but I shall come back to study the Gluck scores."

And that was my first meeting with Cherubini. I do not know whether he remembered it, when later I was introduced to him "officially". It is at any rate droll, that after twelve years, and in spite of him, I became custodian, and finally librarian of the very library from which he had wanted to chase me. As far as Hottin is concerned, he is to-day my orchestra servant and of greatest devotion to me,—the most violent partisan of my music. . . . He even insisted, during the last years of Cherubini's life, that I alone should be considered as successor of the great master, for the post of director of the Conservatoire. However M. Auber was not of his opinion.

I could relate other similar anecdotes about Cherubini, from which can be gathered, that, if he dished up, to me some vipers, I in turn served him with a few rattlesnakes, whose bite he certainly felt.

From Hector Berlioz' "Memoirs".

Strange Opinion of a Frenchman on France

I HAVE long since wanted to go into mourning for France, and the last July Revolution has made my decision to do so firmer and more irrevocable, more unalterable than ever.

Even under the old regime, I was forced to battle against the hatred aroused by my feuilletons on the inefficiency of the theatre directors on the indifference of the audiences. We will now see a large number of great composers appear on the scene in this republic, with popular, philanthropic, national and economic music. In France, I have found that the arts are dead, and in a musical sense it is a land of scamps and cretins. In France, I have found nothing but stupidity and dishonor, for the spirit of the French people is narrow and limited, when there is question of higher art and literature.

His Opinion on Germany

Accept the tribute of our gratitude and admiration, thou homeland of Goethe, Schiller, Beethoven, Gluck, Weber and Mozart; thou ancient German soil where faithfulness is as old as the oaks of thy forests; land, where princes fearlessly live among their subjects and together with them applaud the great artists: those other princes and priests of the peoples.

Berlioz in his "Memoirs".

The Magic Power of Berlioz' Baton: Anton Seidl

HE brought to the rehearsal of his works a wide technical knowledge, and in addition, a most sensitive ear for concord of sound, effect and beauty of tone, a magical, rapturously transporting power which indelibly impressed all those who played under his baton. And as his music—though rugged and mostly full of mighty contrasts and daring effects, has also its calm and soothing moments—so was his conducting. At times he was way up in the air, then again almost under the pulpit. At one time he weirdly threatened the big drummer,

276

then again turned cajolingly to the flutist. Then he drew long strings from the violinists, then he would thrust the air with appeals to the contra-bass, until — with a daring leap — he assisted the cellists to draw out the sweetest cantilenas from their big-bellied instruments. We were all afraid of his demoniac sarcastic visage, and were glad to get out of his clutches.

Anton Seidl in
"Bayreuther Blaetter" (1900).

Glinka's Enthusiasm About Berlioz's Music

ONE of the most eventful experiences I have had is without a doubt my meeting with Berlioz. My intentions to study his compositions — as loudly censured by some as they are praised by others — was one of the musical objects of my visit to Paris. Not only have I heard his music in rehearsals and concerts, but I have come closer to this (in his specialty, of course) first composer of our time. Personally close to the man, too, as far as it is possible to come close to so eccentric a personality. And this is my opinion: In the phantastic field of musical art no one can touch his colossal and ever novel ideas. Greatest uniformity, homogeneity, and, in addition, a minute development of all details; a logical accuracy, in the harmonious weaving; and finally, a stupendous mastery of instrumentation, (always bringing something new) — characterize the music of Berlioz. In the drama he — always carried away by the phantastic aspect of a situation — is (it must be admitted) unnatural, and therefore insincere. Of all the pieces I heard, the overture to the "Francs-Juges", "The March of the Pilgrims" from the symphony "Harold in Italy", the "Scherzo" from "Queen Mab", also the "Dies Irae" and "Tuba Mirum" from the "Requiem" have made an indescribable impression on me.

N. Findeisen: "Glinka's Memoiren" (1887).

Berlioz Dedicates His "Faust" to Goethe

Dear Sir:

For the past years "Faust" has become my regular reading, and, although I have become acquainted with this astounding work only by means of a translation, having meditated on it profoundly, it has taken lasting possession of my soul, and has fascinated my mind, to such an extent, that, within me, musical ideas have formed themselves around your poetic ones; and although I was firmly resolved that my feeble musical fancies should never be associated with your inspirations, born of the highest genius,—I nevertheless, could not resist the temptation to put into music a few of the scenes.

I have now published the score, and although I know it to be unworthy of being offered to you, I nevertheless have taken the liberty to dedicate it to you. I am convinced that you already have a goodly number of compositions, inspired by your divine poem. I therefore, have every reason to fear that I, being the last of many, may be troublesome to you. Even if, in the light of the renown, in which you are now living, the expressions of one, unknown to you, can hardly impress you, I hope you will extend forgiveness to a young composer whose heart is filled with your genius, whose imagination has been inspired by your spirit, and who can no longer conceal from you his great admiration.

Letter of Hector Berlioz to Goethe, 1829.

Berlioz's Colorful Picture on Roman Life and Art

AGAIN and again I returned to the Eternal City to be more and more convinced that of all lots none is sadder than that of a foreign musician who is condemned to live there. He experiences all the Stations of Calvary, when he sees his poetic illusions, one by one, vanish, and the beautiful picture of his imagination crash down before a despairing reality. Each day brings new experiences, all leading to new disappointments. Amidst all the other arts, resplendent with vitality, greatness, majesty, miracle—he sees music, lowered to the role of a serf, who, benumbed with misery, in a hoarse voice, sings songs for which the masses throw him a bare morsel of bread.

I soon realized this in the course of a few weeks, after my arrival in Rome. Following my first impulse, I hastened to St. Peter's—immeasurable, sublime, overwhelming—to find Michelangelo, Raphael, Canova! I tread on the most precious marble flagstones, on the rarest mosaics. There is solemn stillness, the cool atmosphere, the rich, harmoniously tempered coloring, the aged pilgrim—kneeling in solitude, in the vast space. . . .

A slight noise is heard, starting from the darkest corner of the temple, and rolling through the mighty vaults, like distant thunder. I am awe-stricken: I was in truth in the House of God, which I had no right to enter. Then however, as I meditated on how weak mortals like myself had succeeded in erecting a monument of such grandeur and daring, a sensation of pride overcame me; and my heart began to beat at the thought of the great task, awaiting my beloved art, in this atmosphere. Oh, well, I said to myself, without doubt these paintings, these statues, these columns, this gigantic architecture,—they are but the body of the edifice; music is its soul. Only through music will it come to life, music alone embodies the eternal song of the other arts, and lifts it, in grand reverberating tones, to the throne of the Almighty.

Where might the organ be? The organ, not much larger than that of the Paris Opera, was on rollers! A pillar had prevented me from seeing it. Never mind; that poor little instrument probably serves to give the pitch to the singing voices, and must suffice, since all instrumental effect is banned. How large can the number of singers be?—I then thought of the small hall at the Conservatoire in Paris, which would fill St. Peter's Cathedral fifty or sixty times. I thought if there a chorus of ninety voices was daily presented, the choristers of St. Peter's must be counted by the thousands.

Yet, ordinarily there are but eighteen, on festival days, thirty-two. I heard (in the Sistine Chapel) a Miserere sung by only five voices. A very meritorious German critic only recently had words of approbation for the Sistine Chapel. . . . "Most travellers", he said, "when they enter here, expect a music more ravishing, I might almost say, more entertaining, than that of the operas that have charmed them in their own country. Instead of which, the papal singers give them a simple, ancient, devout church-song without any accompaniment whatsoever. The disappointed friends of music then vow, upon their return to their country, that the Sistine Chapel offers nothing of the least musical interest, and all the beautiful accounts you hear, are but fairy tales."

I am not of the same opinion, as these superficial judges, mentioned by the writer. Quite the contrary: those harmonies of past ages, which, without the slightest change in style and coloring have come down to us, are of the same interest to the musician, as the Pompeiian frescoes are to the painter. I am far from longing for an accompaniment of drums and trumpets to this music, an accompaniment which has become so prevalent among Italian composers, that, without it, (at least, so they think) the singers and dancers would be deprived of their well-earned applause. I must admit, it is a relief, to find in the Sistine Chapel—the only place in Italy not yet to have adopted this regrettable abuse—a refuge from the artillery of the cavatine manufacturers. I agree with the German critic, that the thirty-two papal singers who would hardly be heard in any of the large cathedrals of Europe, are sufficient, for the performance of Palestrina's works in the limited space of the Papal Chapel. I will also admit that the pure, calm harmony of this music transports the hearer into a sort of trance. In this harmony there is much charm, and the pretended genius of the composer is not its cause. I wonder whether one can give the name "composer" to a musician, who has spent his life in stringing together a row of successive chords, such as occurs in Palestrina's "Improperia". In these four-part psalmodies, the musician has been actuated by good taste and a certain technique; but melody and rhythm therein are almost non-existent; and the harmony is limited to triads intermingled with suspensions. And as to genius? Along with you: that is a joke. . . .

And besides, those people who honestly believe, that Palestrina consciously, and in conformance with the sacred text, has composed pieces with the sole purpose of raising them into a sphere of religious feeling, are very much mistaken. They evidently do not know his Madrigals, with their gallant frivolous words, which he has put into a music, entirely resembling that with which he has clothed his biblical words. For instance, he has the text: "A handsome shepherd on the shores of the Tiber sighed" sung by a chorus in a slow tempo, which in its effect and harmonic style, in no wise differs from his so-called sacred compositions. The truth of the matter is, that he could write no other music. He was so far from pursuing a heavenly ideal, that among his works can be found a large number of those logogryphes, which, before his time, had been brought into vogue by musicians, the brilliant adversary of whom he is supposed to be. His "Missa ad fugam" proves this point.[1]

What part then have these contrapuntal difficulties, be they ever so cleverly overcome, in the expression of religious feeling? What degree of consideration by the composer to the subject at hand, is revealed in this patient play of interweaving chords? None at all, and that is the truth. The expression of a musical creation is neither more powerful nor more true

[1] Berlioz rightly observes that Palestrina was not a revolutionary, but only the climax of a previous development—a fact recognized by modern musicologists.

because it happens to be written in an endless canon. It does not add either to its truth or its beauty, which to find the composer has surmounted a rare difficulty; not any more, than if he had been overcome by physical pain or some material obstacle from writing.

If Palestrina had lost the use of his hands, and had been compelled to write with his feet, and had acquired skill in making use of them, his works would not have been more valuable, nor more nor less religious.

Yet the German writer, before mentioned, did not hesitate to call Palestrina's "Improperia" sublime.

"The whole ceremony", he continues, "the subject itself, the presence of the Pope, with all the cardinals, the excellent performance of the singers, whose delivery is of admirable exactitude and understanding,—all this makes the representation one of the most imposing and impressive of Holy Week". Yes, most assuredly, but all this does not make this kind of music the creation of a genius.

If on one of these dreary days, foreboding the end of the year, and which the blowing of the icy north wind makes still more gloomy, you take up the "Ossian", and at the same time listen to the Aeolsharp on a leafless tree-top—its phantastic harmonies of deep sadness, a vague, unutterable yearning for another world and immeasurable disgust for the present, seize you, in short, you succumb to a violent attack of spleen with suicidal bent. This effect is surely greater than that produced by the harmonies heard in the Sistine Chapel. Yet, no one has thought of counting the manufacturers of aeolian harps among the number of great composers.

But the musical church service in the Sistine Chapel has at least preserved its dignity, and its proper sacred character, while the other Roman churches, in this respect, have sunk to a state of degradation, I might even say demoralization, that is beyond description. Some French priests, who were witness to this scandalous abasement, were horrified.

At a celebration of the King's birthday, I attended a solemn mass, with a large chorus and orchestra, at which our Ambassador, M. St. Aulaire had asked the best Roman artists to assist. A large podium, erected before the organ, was occupied by about sixty performers. They began to tune their instruments with great noise, as though in a theatre. An organ, much too low in pitch, supported the ridiculous orchestra. One single part was still to be taken, and was entrusted to the organ. But the organist was not satisfied with this arrangement. He wished to earn his money, the good man, and surely did, this I can vouch for. For never in my life have I laughed so heartily! Following the Italian custom, he used the high register only during the ceremony. The orchestra, being louder than the music of small pipes, pretty nearly drowned it. But when the instrumental body was supposed to bring a short chord, followed by a pause, the organ, as is well known, being a bit slow and not able to break off as easily as the other instruments, continued alone, and emitted a chord, which, being more than a quarter of a tone lower than the other instruments, was a most excruciating howl. . . . During the pauses, when the priests were chanting a liturgical song, the musicians, unable to control their musical demon, continued with their preludium, loudly, and all at once, with unbelievable cold-bloodedness: the flute launched forth scales in D; the horn sounded a fanfare in Eb major; the violins indulged in lovely cadenzas, delicate groupetti; the bassoon swollen with its importance, let loose its low tones; while the chirping tones of the organ completed the lustre of this unheard of concert, worthy of a Callot. And all this happened in the presence of civilized people,—the French Ambassador, the Director of the Academy, a large body of priests and cardinals, before an assemblage of artists of all nations. As far as the music is concerned: it was worthy of such an execution. Cavatines with crescendi; Cabalette,[1] Fermate and runs; some work

---

[1] Cabalette: a pompous operatic stretto.

without name, a monstrous march: to begin with, a melody by Vaccai, in between bits of Piccini, a ballet by Gallenberg.[2] And to crown it all, imagine the solos of this curious church music, sung in a soprano voice by a fat wag, whose copper-colored face was decorated with a pair of enormous black whiskers. "Truly, everything is possible in this happy land. Did you ever see a castrato with such a beard?" I said to my neighbor who was convulsed with laughter. "Castrato"—vivaciously interrupted an Italian lady, sitting next to us, and turning around indignantly at our remarks and our laughter. "D'avvero non è castrato" (in truth he is no castrato). "You know him, Signora?" "Per Bacco, non burlate. Imparate, pezzi d'asino, che quel virtuoso maraviglioso è il marito mio." (Devil, no! You better learn, asses that you are, that this wonderful virtuoso is my husband!)

Operatic music, which is as dramatic as the church music is religious, is in the same brilliant condition. The same power of invention, the same purity of form, the same charming style, the same depth of thought. . . .

The singers I heard during the theatrical season, had, on the whole, good voices and that ease of vocalization characterizing Italian singers. They were, with the exception of the German primadonna, Mme. Ungher (whom we have often applauded in Paris), and Salvatore, a very good baritone, but slightly above mediocrity. The chorus, as far as precision, purity and warmth are concerned, are one degree below that of our "Opera Comique". The orchestra, imposing and terrible —like the army of the Prince of Monàcco—is, without exception, possessed of those qualities, that are generally designated as boners. At the "Teatro Valle", the body of the violoncelli is represented by—one single player, he, by profession, being a goldsmith. Still, he is better off than one of his colleagues, who is obliged to weave baskets for making a living.

In Rome, the word symphony as well as overture is ap-

[2] Wenzel Robert, Graf von Gallenberg, a composer of cheap ballet music.

plied to a noise produced by the orchestra, before the rise
of the curtain, and to which no one pays the slightest attention. Weber and Beethoven are names unknown here. A learned Abbé of the Sistine Chapel once said to Mendelssohn: "I
hear, you have in your country a young man of unusual promise, called Mozart".

Of course, the worthy cleric associates with few world-
lings, and his whole life is occupied with the works of Palestrina. He is therefore, as far as concerns his life and views, an
outsider.

It is only fair to state, that there is quite a number of cultured music-lovers, who have heard more of Mozart than that
he is a "young man of great promise". They at least know
that he is dead, and that he (although he can, of course, not
be compared with Donizetti) has written a few scores of great
excellence. I became acquainted with one of them, who had
procured the "Don Giovanni" and, at the piano, had made
quite a study of the score. He told me: "In strict confidence,
the 'old music' is of a higher order than that of 'Zadig and
Astartea' by Vaccai, which was then being produced at the
Apollo Theatre." Instrumental music is to the Romans a closed
book with seven seals, and they haven't a notion of what we
call a symphony.

The one thing that struck me in Rome, was the instrumental folk music, which I am very much inclined to think is
a remnant of antiquity: I am speaking of the "Pifferari".
This is what they call the wandering musicians who, around
Christmas time come down from the mountains in groups of
four or five, furnished with bagpipes and pifferi (a sort of
oboe), to give pious concerts before the images of the Ma-
donna. They usually wear wide mantles of brown cloth, peaked
hats, the headdress of robbers, and are marked by a peculiar
mysterious air of savagery. I spent hours in the streets of Rome,
watching them, as they stood, almost immovable as the image
of their devotion, their heads slightly bent toward their shoul-

ders, fervent faith and reverent love in their shining eyes, gazing at the Holy Mother of God ... A big pifferer blows the second part to the bagpipe, in a harmony of two or three notes, accompanying another pifferer of medium size, playing the melody. Added to them are two small pifferers, usually played by children from twelve to fourteen, which chirp in trills and cadenzas, flooding the rural song with a round of curious flourishes. Sequences of gay, lively tunes, often repeated, a solemn slow prayer of very patriarchal pathos ends the childlike symphony. Its song is contained in several Neapolitan collections, for which reason I refrain from describing it more fully here. Close by, the music is so loud, that one can hardly stand it; but from a certain distance this unique orchestra is of an effect, which few people can resist. Later I heard the pifferari in their homeland, and if I found them curious in Rome, how much more vivid was the impression I got in the wild mountains of the Abruzzi, to which my wanderings had taken me. Volcanic cliffs, black pine forests, formed the natural background to this primitive music. When, in addition to this, the view of the so-called "Cyclops Walls"—these mysterious monuments of a former age—and shepherds in the Sabinian garb (consisting of a sheepskin turned inside out) caused me to dream that I was a contemporary of ancient peoples, in whose midst the Arcadian Evander, high-minded host to Aeneas, also was seen.

One must, as you have noticed, renounce all ideas of hearing music in Rome. I had even reached the point where I could no longer compose in this unmusical atmosphere. What I wrote at the Academy was confined to three or four pieces: 1) An overture to "Rob Roy", for one. It was long and not concise, and was badly received in Paris a year later. I burned it, that same day, after my return from the concert. 2) A rural scene from my "Symphonie Phantastique," which, during my stay at the "Villa Borghese", I completely revised. 3) "The Song of Happiness" from my monodrama "Lelio" which was inspired by a dream which I had, when my secret enemy, the South Wind, had maliciously lulled me to sleep, in the thick wall of hedges formed by the trimmed boxtrees of our classical garden. 4) The melody of "The Prisoner", the fate of which I could, in no wise, foresee. I am mistaken when I say it originated in Rome, for it is dated as from Subiaco. It now occurs to me, that in the inn at Subiaco, where we were living, my friend, the architect Lefèbre, one day, with his elbow, knocked down a book from the table at which he was sitting and drawing. I picked it up. It was a volume of Victor Hugo's "Oriental Women". It turned open at the page with "Prisoner", and I read the precious poem, turning to Lefèbre: "If I had staffed paper handy, I would write the music to it, for I hear it."

"If that is all you want, I can give it to you". Lefèbre took a ruler, and a pen, and in a short while he had drawn a few staffs, on to which I jotted down a vocal part and base for the short air. Then I put the manuscript into my wallet and no longer gave it a thought. Two weeks later, when I had returned to Rome, and there was singing going on at the home of our director, I again thought of "The Prisoner". "I should like to show you", I said to Mlle. Vernet, "a song which I improvised in Subiaco, to see if there is anything to it. I don't remember anything about it." A quickly scribbled piano accompaniment permitted us to execute it tolerably well. It made such a hit, that a month after, M. Vernet, besieged and persecuted, called me to him, and countered me with the words: "Should you again go to the mountains I wish you would bring some other song; for your "Prisoner" is beginning to make me sick and tired. I can not take a step in my house, in my garden, in the woods, on the terrace, in the halls, but what I hear is the singing, humming, grunting, of your tune. It is enough to drive one crazy. To-morrow I am going to send one of my servants home and shall only engage a new one on condition that he does not sing 'The Prisoner'."

I developed this melody later, and arranged it for the orchestra. I believe it is one of my best.

From Berlioz's "Memoirs".

Two Gallicized Italians Clash

Napoleon: Paesiello's music is soft and pleasing, but you are instrumentally too strong; and while Paesiello soothes me agreeably, your compositions make too many demands on the listener.

Cherubini: I understand, you demand music, that does not prevent you from thinking of state and politics. (Napoleon greatly resented this reply).

According to Ludwig Schemann's "Cherubini"

Obituary on Cherubini's Death[1]

CHERUBINI has just drawn his last breath. He, whose works have charmed all Europe, is no more. Immortality now has come to this great spirit. Few musicians have had so marvelous, so successful a career as he had. During the last half of the past century and the beginning of this, his name has always been mentioned with esteem. His works were used and praised by musicians of all schools; their purity, their classicity, raised them far above all platitudes of fashion, above all concessions made to the taste of the public.

Rossini, Auber, and Meyerbeer, representatives of the French, Italian and German schools bowed down to Cherubini whose works they eagerly studied. They bowed to him, whose renowned career had begun long before theirs, and who perhaps did show them the way, and opened it up for

[1] March 15, 1842.

them. Although Cherubini's style leans more to the German than to the Italian school, he cannot be said to belong to the first. His style is less Italian than that of Mozart, purer than Beethoven's. He belongs rather to the old Italian school, but one, which has recognized and utilized the advantages and the achievements of the teachings of harmony: so-to-say a Palestrina of modern times. Indeed, I believe, that if Palestrina had lived in these days, he would have been Cherubini. We find the same purity, the same wise use of the means of aid, the same success, that was achieved in mysterious ways.

The works of this master will ever be used as an example, because they are carried out according to a rigid and almost mathematical plan.

Adolphe Adam (Composer of
"The Postillon of Lonjumeau").

National Rhythm and Melody in Auber's
"Mute of Portici" : Franz Liszt

THIS species of French Opera, the "Grand Opera" is, so to say, a compromise between poetry and music. "La Dame Blanche" by Boieldieu, the subject being taken from a novel, was one of its happiest results. Auber borrowed his subject from history. Emphasizing the historical interest with the sure calculation of an experienced talent—he wove into his work a new and untried element—(national rhythm and melody) and made his opera a brilliantly striking piece of work. The subject of "The Mute of Portici" taken from picturesque Naples finds a most sympathetic response in opinions and feelings absolutely opposed to each other—so striking is the character of this complex.

From Ad. Kohut: "Auber".

"Carmen" — A Fiasco

Halévy's Impressions of the First Performance, 1875

FIRST act: very effective. Crowds on the stage. Bizet is surrounded and warmly congratulated.

The second act proceeds less happily. The beginning brilliantly effective. The Toreador song is very impressive. Then —coolness—. From that point on, Bizet leaves behind him the traditional form of the Opéra Comique, and the audience wonders and doesn't know what to think.

In the entr'acte fewer people collected around Bizet. The congratulations are less sincere, have a more formal character. Increasing coolness in the third act—applause for Micaëla's song only, since that is still written in the old manner—

Still fewer people on the stage, and, after the fourth act, which, from beginning to end, has been received with icy coolness, the stage is empty: only three or four friends are with Bizet. They try to console him, but there is sadness in their eyes. Carmen has been a fiasco.

From Adolf Weissmann: "Georges Bizet."

Two Enthusiastic Statements on "Carmen"

1881:

HURRAH! I have come across something very fine: an opera by Georges Bizet, "Carmen". Sounds just like a novelette by Merimée: clever, strong, at times deeply stirring. A genuine French comic opera talent, not at all disorientated by Wagner, but, on the other hand, a true pupil of Berlioz.

As for dramatic music, it would appear that the French are on a better road, and they have quite a headstart on the Germans in one important respect, i.e.: passion with them is not far-fetched, as for instance, in Wagner.

1888:

This music seems perfect to me. It flows along easily, flexibly, with "courtoisie". It is charming,—and does not perspire! Whatever is good, is light. Everything godly seems light-footed: this is the first sentence in my "Aesthetics".

This music is "diabolique", "raffinée", fatalistic, but always remains popular. Not the "raffinement" of a race, nor of an individual. It is rich, it is precise.

Friedrich Nietzsche
"Gesammelte Schriften".

Are Michelangelo and Beethoven Refined?: *Bizet*

WE have all kinds of music: music of the past, the present, and the future. We also have the melodious, the harmonious and the scholarly,—the last being the most dangerous of all. For me, there are but two kinds of music: the good and the bad. Is not genius born in all countries and at all times? The good and the true never dies. A painter, a poet, or a musician gives all his intelligence, his inner self to the creation of his work. He believes and wavers, he is elated or in despair, he alternately suffers and rejoices, until, at last, in fear and trembling, like a criminal, he says to us: "See, listen and judge." And what do we do—instead of being moved—we ask him for his passport! We inquire about his manners, his connections and his artistic antecedents. But isn't that more than criticism? Yes, it is police. An artist has neither name nor nationality, he is enthusiastic or not, he has genius or talent or he has none. Where a great artist is concerned, don't let us judge him by the qualities he has not, but let us understand those that he possesses. If we come across a passionate, violent, even brutal temperament,—when a Verdi presents us with a work that is made up of filth, gall and blood,—don't let us coolly say to him: "But my dear Sir, that is not refined." Refined? Have Michelangelo, Cervantes, Rabelais, Homer, Dante, Shakespeare, Beethoven always been refined?

From a statement by Bizet
(according to "Bizet" by P. Voss).

What Bizet's Death Meant to French Music
(Debussy's Opinion)

HE died too young, and although he left a masterpiece, French music has a doubtful future. Like a young widow, who no longer has any one to guide her, French music is now delivered up to alien influences, which threaten to throttle it.

It most assuredly can not be denied, that in art certain international relations are necessary, but it is not always necessary to follow him who can scream the loudest. All "mariages de convénience" in the long run turn out badly. We gladly accept all that is good in art, but we do not wish any surprise attacks, nor should we let ourselves be engulfed in an intoxication of enthusiasm. We only arouse a foreign officiousness which in its very nature is ridiculous,—all the more so, since we ourselves have called it forth.

Debussy in
"Monsieur Croche Anti-dilettante"
(Paris, 1923)

FRENCH AND ITALIANS

Two French Antipodes
(Debussy on Gounod)

HE deserves praise for having separated himself from the dictatorial genius of Wagner, as well as from his precepts regarding the combination of the arts. Gounod is a well-educated musician. He knows his Palestrina, he tries to follow Bach. His reverence for tradition is very evident: you don't even have to mention a name like that of Gluck. He takes to his heart the youth of Mozart without imitating Mozart himself. From Mendelssohn he learned how to construct a melody. The means he uses to be kept in mind by posterity are manifold and sometimes not to be explained. To have stirred the hearts of his contemporaries is one of the best among them and it cannot be denied that Gounod has, to an astounding degree, made use of it.

"Monsieur Croche Anti-dilettante"

Saint-Saëns Still Believes in the Older Form
of the Opera

HAVING tried to release lyrical drama from the fetters, which caused all clear-sighted spirits to sigh,—one now has gone so far as to declare all other music outside of the modern lyrical drama as unworthy of the attention of intelligent people. Furthermore one has distorted music by completely suppressing singing in favor of declamation, and by placing the real musical element into an orchestra, developed to excess. Whereby the latter has been robbed of balance, all equilibrium, it has gradually been shorn of all beauty of ‘form and has transformed it into a liquid unfathomable pulp, which is in-

293

tended to arouse sensations, to affect the nervous system. And now they are even trying to make us believe that that too is already a standpoint of the past. We are presented with a picture of a musical drama (the term lyrical drama is no longer adequate), as it should be conditioned to reach perfection. A subject, essentially of a symbolic order, little action, the persons regarded as personified ideas, rather than as acting beings of flesh and blood. And from one deduction to another, they have finally come to the conclusion that the ideal drama is a chimera not to be realized, and it is no longer proper to write for the theatre—meaning the stage as it now exists—but for an ideal stage alone, after the pattern of Bayreuth. With such exaggerations, we should arrive at feeling nothing for the old Italian opera but deep pity. That was a poor flat thing, but it was nevertheless a finely chiselled, more or less gay golden frame, in which appeared from time to time wonderful singers who had had an excellent schooling. That, at any rate, was better than nothing. If we have no ambrosia, it is better to eat dry bread than to die of starvation.

From Unger:
"Musikgeschichte in Selbstzeugnissen".

An Opinion on Debussy's "Pelleas and Melisande"

DEBUSSY asked Maeterlinck for the libretto to this drama. The idea of fatality, of death, which pervades the play of the Belgian poet, the atmosphere of a sad legend that envelops it like a flimsy veil: everything is contained in it of the mysterious, the unreal, the shadowy figures,—poor kings, poor people, poor guests from unnamed lands, whom fate takes by the hand, leading them through a mist to the inevitable. The resigned naive, gentle or serious dialogues of these suffering unhappy people,—all this corresponds with the temperament of Debussy, which has fully measured up to all that is expressed in "Pelleas and Melisande". He has assigned melodies to the symbols of his congenial librettist, which are augmented to the highest conjuring power. He has never given the melodies to the singing voices, but entrusts them to the orchestra,—a muffled, softly undulating orchestra, that seems wrapped in wool, and above which rise the words.

Alfred Bruneau: "La Musique Française".

The Kind Character of César Franck, As Revealed by his Pupil, Paul De Wailly

TEN months of the year César Franck gave lessons, running up and down stairs. For ten months he had to carry the work he meant to finish during his vacation, around with him. All his compositions had to be completed in the summer.

It must be stated, that only the greatest technical ease, and a super-abundance of precious musical ideas could make possible a creation of masterpieces in this manner. But he worked on them long enough in his mind, and filed away at his themes, before he put them down, which then he could easily do.

Franck loved to admire and never criticised. In spite of many disappointments, never a bitter word passed his lips. At one time, when speaking of a pupil who had left him, he said to me, very softly: "he has gone to study with Massenet and he has done wrong." That was the hardest word I ever heard him utter.

He could not make a show of himself. He did not trumpet his genius out to the world, he did not even in soft tones mention it. Although fully conscious of his worth he was very modest. When one day, he showed me one of his compositions, I naively said: "there is something similar somewhere in Wagner". Franck answered outright: "I don't have to know how Wagner did it". But this utterance must not be regarded as an expression of annoyance,—he knew and loved all of Wagner's works. It simply expressed his self-confidence.

Debussy's Achievements as seen by Romain Rolland

HE, a French character through and through, moody, poetic, witty, of lively intelligence, independent, reckless, spread new ideas and paradoxical conceits, scrutinised the judgment of centuries with the impudent mockery of a Parisian gamin, inasmuch as he attacked the greatest, the heroes of music: Gluck, Wagner, Beethoven — stopping only at Bach, Mozart and Weber, — and strongly stressed his preference for the old French masters of the 18th century. He recalled to French music its true nature and its forgotten ideals: clarity, elegant simplicity, naturalness, and above all, charm and plastic beauty. He wanted music to free itself from literary and philosophical assumptions, which burdened the German music of the 19th century. Music should be free from musical rhetoric, which it has been dragging about for centuries, — this heavy structure, these symmetrical constructions, these harmonic and rhythmical formulas, this delight in rhetorical diffuseness. He wants everything in music to be poetry and painting, in order to express in direct and translucent form, pure feeling, and that melody, rhythm, and harmony unfold according to their own primal laws, no longer following a pretended logic of intellectual constructions. He led the way with "Pelleas and Melisande", breaking with all the fundamental principles of the drama in Bayreuth, therewith giving the paradigma of the new art which he had dreamt of.

From "Musicians of Today".

Lecocq's Laments on the Decline of the Operetta

THE operetta is dying, because there are no longer any libretto writers. The operetta has come to be but a shadow of its former grace; it has been automatically mutilated, and it was the great success it had that caused its degeneration. Any dramatic work, of a lighter nature, was put to music, and called operetta. Heaven only knows what was dished up under this name. So, gradually this free, gracefully sparkling genre was killed, the style of which — I say it without reservation — was once so pure. In its place appeared a bastard genre, neither fish nor fry, the Vaudeville with couplets, the operetta in city dress. I, at least, cannot understand and will never permit an actor to sing little stories, attired in a jacket-suit, wearing a felt hat on his head. I feel as though I were attending a rehearsal, without decors and costume. The couplet vaudeville carries within itself two perils: one part of the audience is only interested in the dialogue, the other in music. Some yawn when the music sets in, others, when it stops. And that is quite contrary to the spirit of the true operetta. The music must not appear as unnecessary, patched on a piece of jewelry, but must be a part of the text. Therefore the operetta requires, as its main feature, musical situations.

From an interview with a reporter of "Le Temps"
(Otto Keller: "Die Operette")

Verdi Foresees A World War

THE disaster of France fills my heart, as well as yours, with despair. Yes, the blague, the impertinence, the presumption of the French was and is (in spite of all their mis-

fortunes) unbearable. But after all France gave the modern
world its freedom and civilization. And if it falls, let us not
deceive ourselves, all our liberties will fall, and then falls
our civilization as well. Let our litterateurs and our politicians
praise the knowledge and science and even (God forgive
them) the art of these victors. But if they would only look
a little below the surface, they would see that the old blood
of the Goths still flows in their veins, that they are mon-
strously proud, hard, intolerant, rapacious beyond measure
and scornful of everything that is not German. A people of
intellect without heart — a strong people but they have no
grace. — And that King who is always talking about God
and Divine Providence, with whose help he is destroying the
best part of Europe! He thinks he is predestined to reform
the morals and punish the vices of the modern world!!!
What a fine messenger of God he is!

Old Attila (another emissary of God!) halted before
the majesty of the capital of the old world. But this one
here is about to bombard the capital of the modern world!
And now that Bismarck is trying to make us believe Paris will
be spared, I am more afraid than ever that it will be at least
partly laid in ruins. Why? . . . I cannot imagine. Perhaps
so that there may no longer be any such beautiful capital,
since they themselves will never succeed in building its equal.
Poor Paris! And last April I saw it still so gay, so beautiful,
so shining!

What now? . . . I should have preferred to have our
government follow a more generous policy, and pay a debt
of gratitude. A hundred thousand of our men might have
saved France. Anyhow I would rather have signed a peace
after being defeated along with France, than to have been
a passive spectator. That we are doing this will expose us to
contempt some day. We shall not escape the European war
and it will engulf us. It will not come tomorrow, but it is
coming. An excuse is easily found . . . perhaps Rome . . .

the Mediterranean . . . and then, what about the Adriatic, which they have always proclaimed a German sea?

The business in Rome is a great event, but it leaves me cold, perhaps because I feel that it might lead to internal as well as external disaster; because I can't reconcile the idea of Parliament with the College of Cardinals, a free press with the Inquisition, civil law with the Syllabus; and because I am frightened at the way our government just goes ahead any old way, hoping that time will take care of everything. If tomorrow we should have a shrewd, adroit Pope, a really crafty fellow, such as Rome has often had, he would ruin us. A Pope and a King of Italy — I can't bear to see the two together, even in the letter.

The paper is giving out. Forgive this tirade! It is a release for me. I am very pessimistic. Even so I haven't told you half my qualms and fears. Farewell!

A letter to Clarina Maffei of September 30, 1870, after the defeat of France.

The Future of Music

I COULDN'T tell you what to do, to find a way out of this crisis in music. One would be a melodist like Bellini; another a harmonist like Meyerbeer. I should like neither the one nor the other. If I had my say, a young man who is beginning to compose, should never think of being a melodist, harmonist, realist or idealist, futurist, or any other of the pedantic formulas invented by the devil. Melody and harmony should only be the means in the hands of the artist to bring about a piece of music. And if at some future time, the day will dawn when there is no longer mention of melody and harmony, of German or Italian School, of the past and the future of music, — that might mean just the be-

299

ginning of the realm of art. It is another evil of our time that all the works of young people are generated by fear. No one writes what is in his heart! When these young people begin to compose, they have but one thought in mind, namely, not to offend the audience and to be the darlings of the critics . . .

You tell me that I have to thank the combination of both these arts (melody and harmony) for my success. I have never thought anything of the kind. That, by the way, is an old story, — only it repeats itself with others and after a certain time.

And don't worry, my good Arrivabene: art is not going under. And rely on it, — even modern art has already achieved something.

> *From a letter of Verdi's to Opprandino Arrivabene, the Italian patriot, who participated in the Resorgimento. Verdi corresponded with him for fifty years and sometimes they wrote to each other in the persons of their dogs.*

Verdi is Disgusted by Musical Journalism

Dear Mr. Filippi:[1]

What I am now going to say to you may seem strange, very strange, for I cannot refrain from giving you my impressions. You are going to Cairo? That is a mighty publicity for Aida. I am under the impression that an art, for which one has to beat a drum, is not art at all, but a craft, that an artistic event sinks to the level of a hunting party, to something after which one runs, to gain, if not success, but notoriety.

My feeling about all this is disgust, humility. I always

---

[1] Filippi was invited to attend the first performance of "Aida" in Cairo, December 24, 1871.

like to remember the joys of my early days, when I, almost without friends, without any one having spoken to me, without any influences, offered my work to an audience, and was happy if I had made a good impression. But now, — what a show! Journalists, artists, choristers, directors, professors, etc. — they all must add their little stone to the building-up of my publicity, and to help form a picture of little miseries that add nothing to the worth of an opera, but cover up its true significance. That is to be regretted, — deeply to be regretted.

Letter to the Milan critic Filippi, December 8, 1871.

But He Believes in His Own "Falstaff"

FORTY years ago I wished to write a comic opera, and I have for fifty years been acquainted with the "Merry Wives of Windsor"; however, the usual "buts" that always enter into everything have withstood my desire. But now Boito has removed all the "buts", and has written for me a lyric comedy, which can be compared to none other. It gives me great pleasure to write the music for it, but I do not know whether I will ever finish it. Note what I said: "great pleasure". Falstaff is a villain, who is up to tricks of all kind—but always in an amusing way. He is a type. And they are so rare,—types are! The opera is purely comic. Amen—.

Verdi's Self-Confidence is Affected by Wagner's "Walkuere"

The "Walkuere" is a miracle that fills me with awe. But should not he, who still has some self-confidence in his heart, be saddened, when a work of that order makes him conscious of the limitations of his own creations?

From "Verdi, the Man in his Letters",
Edited by Franz Werfel and Paul Stefan.

The African Climate of "Aida"

1871

I MUST compose a new opera. Ismael Pasha has ordered it for the festival to be given, on the opening of the Suez Canal.

I have been in Egypt to gather the material for it! In Luxor on the Nile, with its Egyptian temples! The marvelous impressions collected there are going to be used in my opera. I am going to call it "Aida". And the graves of the Pharaohs in Luxor, gave me the idea for the last act of the opera, in which Aida, of her free will, will enter the tomb before Rhadames, who is condemned to die there. Sombre graves, over which sacrifices to the gods were made, and over which now the arid winds of the desert are blowing. . . .

The sight of the Nile, with its gentle splashing, its desolate shores gave me the inspiration for my third act so full of mystery and hidden desires. Folk melodies with their characteristic features, will lend local coloring to my music. Meditation on the former greatness of this land and the gentle melancholy that seized me at the sight of the ruins of its primal mighty architecture, inspired me to musical thoughts of my own which only a midday hot climate can incite. And the ruins of Luxor have given me the idea for the decors that I have planned for my "Aida".

Since the first performance is to be at Cairo, it would not do to have these representations falsified in any way, nor must the music lack suggestions of the music of the land— of the true Egyptian folk music.

From his letters.

Il Toscanini Furioso
The Master at Rehearsals

ARTURO Toscanini is the foremost of the Italian conductors, or rather he stands alone, he is a class by himself, and one of the most distinguished conductors of the whole world. His memory is phenomenal, more unshakeable even than that of Hans von Bülow. His brain takes in the most difficult works as the record of a phonograph takes in the tone vibrations.

At one time a discussion arose between him and his orchestra as to the meaning of a certain notation and the score was not in the theatre and had to be sent for. And, naturally, the Maestro was right!

Once, on a very warm day, Toscanini had stuffed a handkerchief between his neck and his collar. The rehearsal goes on. Hours pass. Musicians are hanging in their seats—exhausted. "Rhythm" yells Toscanini at a certain phrase, and angrily throws the wet handkerchief on the floor. He makes the orchestra repeat that phrase. "Rhythm" he screams again, and, in a rage, pulls off his collar and throws it into the orchestra. And when after a third repetition he still is not satisfied, a kick hits the stand of the first cellist and the conductor revolves around himself a few times, roaring: "Rhythm, rhythm,

rhythm". . . . At last the passage sounded as he wished and conceived it. . . .

Krebs: "Masters of the Baton".

Puccini in Love with Butterfly

FROM the stage, last night, I heard the storm raging. I cannot renounce "Butterfly". I wrote it with so much of my heart's blood. I do not like my operas, except perhaps, the last act of "La Bohème." I love my little Butterfly, because she entertains and interests me. I have the feeling that "Butterfly" is the most modern of all my operas. Yes, the most modern.

From "La Vita di Giacomo Puccini"
by Arnaldo Fraccaroli.

Two Composers and One Libretto

THEY were both of good faith, and were greatly shocked when they suddenly found out about their plans.

They were in friendly conversation about their work in the beerhall Trenk in Milan, when Puccini said: "I have long been looking for a good libretto subject to inspire me and I have found it. I am more than happy." "And that is?" asked Leoncavallo. "It is from a French novel by Murger, 'La Vie de Bohème.' "

Leoncavallo jumped up from his seat, all excited and yelling: "But that is the subject I have chosen." "Misericordia!"

In order not to lose his first right, Leoncavallo immediately ran to the editor of the "Secolo" who, the following morning, announced that Leoncavallo was writing an opera to the libretto of "La Bohème". By noon of the same day, the

"Corriere della Sera" brought the news that Puccini too was putting this libretto to music.

Thus began the competition. Two twin sisters were born, but only one had a long life.

Arnaldo Fraccaroli

RUSSIANS AND CZECHS

"No Puppets — Human Beings" — Tchaikovsky

YOU may be right in saying that my opera is not for the stage. The fact that I am lacking in the vein for the stage has long been established. What then are stage effects? If, for instance they are to be found in "Aida", I can assure you, that not for all the treasures in the world would I write an opera on a similar subject. I want living people, no puppets. I shall always be pleased to write an opera, wanting in any effects, but in which there are beings with the same feelings and thoughts that I myself have and can understand. I know nothing about the feelings of an Egyptian princess, a Pharaoh, or a crazy Nubian,—I don't understand them. My instinct tells me that they feel differently, act, speak differently, and express their feelings quite otherwise than we do. Therefore my music, which, without my desiring it, is pervaded with Glinkism, Berliozism, Schumannism, Wagnerism, and many of the other isms—would harmonize as badly with acting persons in an "Aida", as the beautiful gallant speeches of the heroes of Racine, who address one another with "vous", which is his conception of an appropriate conversation between Orestes and Andromache. Such music would be a lie. Now you will ask what it is that I really want. Very well, I will tell you: above all, I want no kings, no tumults of the masses, no gods, no marches,—in short, nothing of all pertaining to the attributes of "Grand Opera". I am looking for an intimate moving drama, based on the conflict of situations, which I myself have experienced or witnessed, and which have the ability to stir me. I have no objection to a phantastic element, for it does not hamper one, but offers unlimited freedom.

From a letter to the composer Taneiev.

Tchaikovsky is Deeply Impressed by Bayreuth, 1876

I HAVE already mentioned that guests came to Bayreuth from all over the world. The most prominent musicians, however,—Verdi, Gounod, Thomas, Brahms, Anton Rubinstein, Joachim, von Buelow,—preferred to "shine in absentia", for not one of them had come. Of the great virtuosi, outside of Liszt—whose presence was a foregone conclusion, owing to his close relationship to the family and his long friendship with Wagner—only our Nicholas Rubinstein was present. The pilgrimage of the artists and music lovers to the "Festspielhaus" began at 3 o'clock in the afternoon.

The theatre is quite a distance away from the town (about an hour's walk), and this hour was the hardest of the day, even for those fortunate enough to have secured a dinner, for it meant a gradual climb in the burning heat of the sun, without the slightest protection. At 4 o'clock sharp, the loud sound of the fanfare is heard. The masses stream into the theatre. At the second sound of the trumpet, there is complete silence: the lights are out, and all conversation has ceased. The house is in complete darkness, and from the covered invisible orchestra resound the first tones of the beautiful prelude.

Wagner's tetralogy, in its gigantic volume, so complicated and so finely thought out a work, that it takes a great deal of time to study it, must be heard several times. I must say that all believers in the civilizing power of art must have taken away a most refreshing impression of this grandiose artistic undertaking, which, because of its inner merit and its effect, will prove to be a milestone in the history of art. In face of this edifice, this unheard of dramatic-musical festival, how absurd, how silly and deplorable are the preachings of those who would call our century the era of absolute decadence of art! Whether or not Wagner was right, when, in the service

310

of his art he went to the extremes, whether or not he has neglected the principle of an aesthetic equilibrium, whether or not art will continue on the path which he designates as a starting point, whether or not the "Nibelungen Ring" will prove to be the point at which will start the reaction,—who can judge that today? But one thing is certain: what took place today, in Bayreuth, will live in the memory of our grand-children and great-grand children. . . .

After the last chord had died out, Wagner was called on the stage. He came, and made a little speech, closing with the following words: "You have now heard and seen what we can do. You have now but to want it, and we will have a German Art." For a few moments there was a dead silence. Then came renewed applause and calls, but much less enthusiastic than before the appearance of the master. I believe the members of the Assembly in Paris, responded in a similar manner, when Louis XIV uttered his famous words: "L'État c'est Moi!" They were, at first silent, and wondered at the immensity of their task, then remembered that the speaker was the King, and shouted: "Vive le Roi!"

From Tchaikovsky's "Collected Criticisms and Reminiscences".

Russia Should Join European Ways of Culture: *Moussorgsky*

IF even in Petrograd, on the soil of decayed human cadavers, at times there flashes a brilliant idea, and the Russian somnolent creativeness awakens,—what must it be like in Europe? Russian creativeness is like an intimidated sparrow who is afraid to move about; but once he has succeeded in a flight up into the clouds, he sits down there to slumber; and

311

when he rushes down headlong back in the valley, he will surely fall into a shopkeeper's booth, and delve in tiny interests, that concern no one; for he, the ever drowsy is never able to free himself from his propensity to do "just as Your Honor wishes".

Moussorgsky on Europe

The gigantic "Te Deum", which in its relation to Beethoven's Second Mass is about the same as that of the Roman St. Peter's Cathedral to our Isaac's Church, could only be generated in the dauntless brain of the European Berlioz. Only the introduction to "Ruslan", the creation of the "Europeanized" (fie! what a word!) Glinka, can be, as far as size is concerned, compared to this colossus. Et nous autres?

We need Europe, not just to make pleasure trips there, but to learn to know it; not to delight in Swiss ice-covered waterfalls or in the view from the Bruehl'sche Terrasse; not to determine where one can eat best: in Paris or in Vienna— that is not what we need. That can be handed to us by the great land-holders (not yet ruined), and stock-brokers (boursiers) with filled pockets. Unhappily, our travelling musicians have not been able to let us hear much more about Europe. And there again is evident the eternal drowsiness of our Russian Empire. In the world of scholars, where minds, of necessity, are more active, the participating powers of all lands are in constant touch with one another. I do not know what the conditions are in the other arts, but in our musical metier, our musicians, who have travelled in Europe, have not yet become conscious of their mission. If our constant relations with the ante-rooms of Europe have brought us some good, a true union with Europe itself might cause us to progress still more.

From Wolfurt: "Moussorgsky"

Smetana's Autobiographical String Quartet

As far as the style of the quartet is concerned, I will gladly leave that to the judgment of the others, and will not in the least be angered if they do not like it. I realize that it is different from any style previously used, but it was not my intention to write after a prescribed recipe, in the form hitherto familiar to us, a form which I have fully learned and mastered, when a young apprentice in musical theory. I believe that the form of a composition should conform to its subject. I wanted to depict the course of my life in tones. *First movement*: Love for art in my young days, a tendency to romanticism, unspeakable yearning for something I could neither express nor clearly define, and also a foreboding—quasi my future misfortune: (b''—b''—e'), the long ringing tone in the finale (e'''—e'''—e'''). This represents the fateful ringing in my ears, which, in the year 1874 indicated my beginning deafness. I allowed myself this bit of foolery, because it was so weighted with destiny for me. *Second movement*: Quasi Polka, leads me to the memories of my gay youth, when I flooded the world with my dance compositions, and when I was everywhere known as an enthusiastic dancer. *Third movement*: Largo sostenuto, telling of my love for a girl who later became my faithful wife. *Fourth movement*: Recognition of the elements of national music; joy over the success of this course; then interruption of this course by the catastrophe so ominous for me! And that was the sole purpose of this composition, which, in a way, is a private matter only. (Remember Beethoven's quartet movement "Dankgesang eines Genesenen an die Gottheit"). It is written for four instruments only, as though in a circle of congenial friends: they converse on what concerns me so deeply. Nothing more.

*From a letter of the composer
to J. Srb.-Debrnov (According
to Rychnovsky: "Smetana").*

Smetana's Gratitude to Franz Liszt

From a letter of Liszt to Smetana, 1880:

Your splendid quartet "Aus meinem Leben" has given us all great pleasure.

Smetana to Hugo Koempel, Concert-Master, after a performance of his E minor quartet:

Permit me, my dear master, to tell you in few words (for, were I to follow my feelings, sheets of paper would not suffice)—how the ever continuing graciousness of my adored grand master Liszt has moved me to tears of heartfelt delight. I should herewith like to make it known that, without a doubt, I have to thank him for everything I have until now accomplished; that it was he, who above all gave me self-confidence, and then, too, has shown me the one and only way I am to go.

Who Was The Better Czech?
(Smetana's Poor Orthography)

WHEN a well-known Czech authoress visited the Smetana exhibit at Horice in 1903, and had come to the bust of Smetana, she exclaimed: "You exhibit that fellow? Why, he didn't even know Czech well." Whereupon Dolansky answered: "Yes, most honored lady, he couldn't write Czech very well, because no one had taught him. And yet he was a better Czech, than you are, a thousand times over, who are minimizing his greatness because you can understand neither his importance nor his strivings. He could not express himself in as clearly cut a manner as you do, and yet he wrote "Libussa" and "Ma Vlast", and a grateful nation will devoutly gaze up at this "know nothing" of orthography, and will bless him, even then, when the most thorough and painstaking antiquary will not find of your activities a trace."

From Ladislav Dolansky's
"Musical Memoirs", 1918.

A Polite Hint

Johannes Brahms Accepts Dvořak's Dedication and

Suggests More Accuracy

I REGRET exceedingly having been away during your sojourn here. All the more so, as on account of my disinclination to write, nothing, on my part, can be hoped for from a written substitute. So I can only repeat that while occupation with your piece gives me greatest pleasure, I would prefer to converse with you about it, critically on certain matters. You write somewhat hastily. If you will now add the many missing sharps, flats and naturals, you will have a chance to look at the notes themselves and at the leading part more closely.

You must pardon me, for it is very presumptuous, in such a matter, and faced with a man like you, to express myself in this way. I would consider the dedication of your quartet as an honor.

It might be practical to hand me both the quartets which I know. Should Herr Simrock (Brahms' publisher) not be inclined to take them, I might try elsewhere.

For today, many thanks for your communication and sincere greetings from your obedient

Johannes Brahms.
From "Brahms' Briefwechsel".

An American Pupil of Dvořak Recollects the History
of the New World Symphony

Dear Dr. Nettl:

I AM afraid, I can not tell you very much, as to what Dvořak's opinion on American music was, for during his stay in this country, the concerts were not nearly as numerous, as they are these days. For instance, the New York Philharmonic, which in these days plays a hundred concerts during the regular concert season, gave only twelve concerts in pairs—the programmes repeated at a second concert—and American compositions were very seldom performed at the time, in fact, I believe he did not hear many.

Besides, there was another thing, very characteristic of Dvořak, he never discussed music—never at home—and in New York only with Anton Seidl, conductor of the New York Philharmonic at the time, a Wagner disciple, whom he used to meet practically daily at Fleischmann's Café, 10th Street and Broadway, which does not exist any more. However, I shall jot down, as tersely as possible, what happened after his arrival in America.

Only a few days, after he had assumed his duties, as director of the National Conservatory of Music, he was approached by Mr. J. G. Huneker, piano teacher at the institute, and at the same time editor in chief of the "Musical Courier", who handed Dvořak an article on "Negro Melodies", and asked him whether or not the future American music could not be constructed in the idiom of these melodies.

Dvořak examined these songs, found them rather interesting, but also rather primitive, and finally returned them to Mr. Huneker, without any remark.

Soon after, Dvořak got hold of some "Plantation Songs" which he found extremely interesting, and deemed they were very typical of the country. Shortly, the enterprising New York Herald sent one of their representatives, to question Dr. Dvořak, as to whether there was any possibility that America, in the near future, might have music which it might rightly call its own. To that question Dr. Dvořak, answered readily: "Why not? You have a great wealth of Plantation Songs which might well be utilized for the purpose; what I mean is, that the American composers should study these songs, some of them being very simple but very beautiful. Let them construe their themes in the idiom of them, for many of them have become so popular, that you may freely call them folk songs."

Whether or not the representative of the New York Herald grasped the right spirit of Dvořak's expression, is hard to tell, for within a day or two, the New York Herald brought forward views of some European celebrities, upon the subject: Joachim, Reger, Rubinstein, Bruckner, Mandyczewski, Brahms, and others, all, save one, deriding Dvořak's statement. That one, Brahms, expressed his opinion in a peculiar way, saying that after all, he was not familiar with American Plantation Songs, but if Dvořak says "it is feasible, I am, in a way, inclined to believe it."

Dvořak, after reading all these views, simply said: "Well, we shall see!"

Many articles and discussions in all papers, not only in New York, and on May 25th of 1893, the New York Herald brought a statement from Dr. Dvořak that "he has come to the further conviction, that future American music will and must be based on the so-called Plantation Songs, "which he called 'typical American'."

While these discussions were never ceasing—it seems rather odd that on May 24th, 1893, at 9 a.m., on the day before the above mentioned statement, appeared in print,—he had completed the score of the "New World Symphony"! Only goes to show, how little the views of the celebrities worried him. . . .

I may as well add, that among the doubting Thomases, was also Anton Seidl, the conductor of the New York Philharmonic, who wrote a very lengthy article for the "North American Review", which was perfectly in accord with the opinions of the European celebrities,—which in plain words meant: not possible! However, when the New York Philharmonic decided to perform the work in December 1893, I was delegated to bring the score to Mr. Seidl. Left it with him, and the following afternoon, at the usual meeting of Seidl and Dvořak at Fleischmann's Café, not one word was said about the Symphony,—but, at parting, Seidl said to me (in German, of course): "Wissen Sie, die Symphonie ist lauter Indianer Musik!" (You must know, the symphony is throughout Indian music).

Well, here was one convert. I may say that witnessing the first performance of the work, while the composer was absent, Seidl simply outdid himself, for it was not only a marvelous performance, but stupendous! Cheers and cheers for the absent composer. Next evening, the composer being present, enthusiasm knew no bounds.

As soon as cable reports of the tremendous success of the Symphony had reached Europe, Dvořak received a cable from his publisher Simrock in Berlin, demanding the Symphony at once for publication. Rather funny, for, for about two years they were "on the outs", or, to put it mildly, not on speaking terms. At the same time Simrock said: "Send me everything you have in your desk".

Thus, at one stroke, Dvořak was—shall I say vindicated for stressing the Plantation Songs to the point, that the European celebrities were silenced, his publisher (at odds before) demanded all he had in his desk, and last but not least Brahms, who, during Dvořak's stay in America, read all the proofs of Dvořak, as quickly as Simrock was turning them out,—became convinced of Dvořak's American achievement.

Brahms, after finishing his task, wrote to Dvořak: "My dear Friend, let me thank you for the privilege of getting acquainted with your works before any one else. I assure you that I have spent many many pleasant moments going over your works".

And now, in conclusion, I may add, that even to this day, the majority of the musical scribes and others, do not really know just when and where the New World Symphony was composed.

Very sincerely yours

Jos. J. Kovařik
An American pupil and assistant of
Anton Dvořak, Mr. Jos. J. Kovařik to
the author of this book, July 22, 1941.

Moussorgsky Hails Glinka

THE decisive step in my career seems justified: in Poltawa, Nikolajeff, Cherson, Odessa, Sewastopol, Yalta, are heard in exemplary manner the creations of the immortal founder of the Russian musical school: Glinka, and of his excellent followers. They were heard for the first time in these places, and one realized—I at least hope so—the great power of the immortal one who has left to posterity the true, unshakeable heritage of Russian musical creativeness. Hail to our Glinka, who pointed out to us the way of truth. . . .

Our programs consisted mostly of works by Glinka, Dargomyzhsky, Sseroff, Balakireff, Cui, Borodine, Rimski-Korsakov, Schubert, Chopin, Liszt and Schumann. In such company it is profitable to wander the world over.

From Kurt von Wolfurt: "Moussorgsky".

319

Spanish Intermezzo
Glinka's Interest in Spanish Folk Music

IN Spain, I propose to take up my "Phantastic Poems". The originality of the melodies there will be a great help to me, all the more so as this field in music has not yet been explored by any one. But my unfettered imagination requires, beside the originality of the material, a text and other positive foundations. I will see, when there, whether I can venture to tackle an opera in the Spanish manner. At all events, I shall render my impressions of Spain in musical form.

(Trip to Spain, 1845).

Dancing — The True Nature of the Spanish People

DANCING, singing and playing, are all one and the same to the Spanish people. They do not dance without singing and playing an instrument. On the other hand, one never hears a song or an instrument which is not accompanied by a slight swaying movement of the body to the rhythm. But because dancing, playing and singing are practised as one, there is a bar to these gayeties. The dance is never a leaping and the song is never a screech. The accompanying music keeps its simple—not to say crude—character, and has done so for hundreds, for thousands of years. In the proper national dances, the sexes mostly move separately. The couples in question do execute their movements together, but they do so without the slightest bodily contact, since the hands are occupied with tambourins or castanets. This is the national dance of Spain. the delight in rhythm of movement. . . . The Spaniard finds all this so pure, so allowable, so natural, that he even permits religious dances in the churches. At the boys' dances which under the name "Seises" are performed in the Cathedral of Seville, after the Conception of the Virgin, and, in Trinity-Week festivals before the altar, to the glory of the Virgin Maria, resound in sacred sarabandes, sung by children while dancing to the accompanying castanets. And, in the same manner, the bagpipes, the tambourine and the "Zambambas" are played when, the week before Christmas, the music of the shepherds of Bethlehem is heard in the churches.

From: Buecher, "Arbeit und Rhythmus."

Glinka's Opinion on the Russian Soul

W E inhabitants of the North feel somewhat differently (from the peoples of the South). The impressions of life affect us either not at all or they sink deep into our souls. We know only unruly exuberance, or bitter tears. Even love is, with us, always bound up with a certain sadness. No doubt, our melancholy Russian songs are children of the North, that may have come to us from the East. The songs of the Orientals are just as melancholy, even in happy Andalusia.

Czar Leaves Opera House — Première of "Russlan and Ludmilla", 1842

The public was very cool, and the Imperial family left the theatre before the fifth act. It was only after the curtain had dropped for the last time, that a timid applause was heard, but a distinct sound of hissing rent the air. "Shall I leave?" Glinka asked, "I believe they are hissing?" General Dubelt, who was in the director's box with him, said: "Go, Christ suffered more than you!"

From Riesemann:
"Monographies on Russian Music".

Program of a Modern Composition
From Alexander Scriabin's
"Promethean Phantasies"[1]

I.
1) Theme: the sweetness of yearning, that makes the spirit soar. Urge to creation. Dozing and a striving for new sensations.
2) Flight to the heights of an active negation. Creating.
3) Elements of depression, emanating from doubts.
4) Effort with the will to victory.
5) Man as God.
6) Appeasement through activity.

II.
1) The soul yields to the longing for love.
2) . . . .
3) Sudden breaking out of desperation, which fetters the spirit.
4) The awakening of protest.
5) Struggle.
6) Freedom through love, and the consciousness of unity.
7) The enfoldment of a liberated striving.
8) Man as God.

III.
1) . . . .
2) . . . .
3) . . . .

[1] "Poème de l'Extase".

4) . . . .
5) Union of the feeling of revolt with the sweetness of yearning.
6) The last phase of the struggle again leads to a deliverance through love.

IV.

1) Man as God. Realization of the uselessness of all happening.
2) Free play. Intoxication of liberty. Recognition of unity.
3) Perception of the relativity of all phenomena.
4) What formerly depressed, now arouses activity.

The Czech Alois Haba and His Quarter-Tone-Music

OUR scale, as is well known, contains twelve tones within the octave. From one tone to the next there is an interval of half a tone. Neither these half-tone steps, nor the whole-tone steps are, as is generally accepted equal. The interval from C to D is larger than that from D to E. The division of the octave into twelve half tones is not an arbitrary matter, but based on profoundly thought-out mathematical acoustic considerations.

Originally based on sentiment, "irrationally" intoned, these intervals had to disappear before an advanced culture of music, and had to be replaced by definite grades, by "rational" intervals.

The name of the famous Pythagoras is connected with this event. The Pythagorean method of tonal determination differs very little from ours, most essentially, however, in the conception of the third, which Pythagoras counted among the dissonances, while we have (through Zarlino) raised the third to consonance.

I began to play the violin when only a boy. Even at that

323

time, I thought it strange that my ear perceived many tone graduations before the strings were tuned in pure fifths. This simple perception persisted in me. I soon tried to divide the whole tone into two half tones and the half tone into two halves again. That was my first meeting with quarter-tones in my early youth. Years have gone by. I made intense attempts to reach a freedom of expression in the half-tone system. Secretly I sought for sounds, called for by my inner ear, and thus I have gradually worked myself into a new world of sound. I well remember my violent inner agitation when I showed my teacher Franz Schreker, two and a half years ago, my quarter-tone quartet and felt like a sinner, awaiting condemnation. Gradually I regained assurance. I had wanted something new, and I found it. Today the lawfulness of the quarter-tone system is evident to me. I know what lies still hidden between the former half-tone intervals and within the half-tone chords and what seems useful for me for my new method of expression.

Alois Hába: "Von neuer Musik"

Stravinsky Lives Neither in the Past
Nor in the Future

FOR me, as a creative musician, composition is a daily function that I am compelled to discharge. I compose because I am made for that and cannot do otherwise. Just as any organ atrophies unless kept in a state of constant activity, so the faculty of composition becomes enfeebled and dulled unless kept up by practice and effort. The uninitiated imagine that one must await inspiration in order to create. That is a mistake; I am far from saying that there is no such thing as inspiration; quite the opposite. It is found as a driving force in every kind of human activity, and is in no wise peculiar to artists. But that force is only brought into action by an effort, and that effort is work. Just as appetite comes by eating, so work brings inspiration, if inspiration is not discernible at the beginning. But it is not simply inspiration that counts. It is the result of inspiration—that is, the composition.

At the beginning of my career as a composer I was a good deal spoiled by the public. Even such things as were at first received with hostility were soon afterward acclaimed. But I have a very distinct feeling that in the course of the last fifteen years my written work has estranged me from the great mass of my listeners. They expected something different from me. Liking the music of "L'Oiseau de Feu", "Petroushka", "Le Sacre du Printemps", "Les Noces", and being accustomed to the language of those works, they are astonished to hear me speaking in another idiom. They cannot and will not follow me in the progress of my musical thought. What moves and delights me leaves them indifferent, and what still continues to interest them holds no further attraction for me. For that matter, I believe that there was seldom any real communion of spirit between us. If it happened—and it still happens—that we liked the same things, I very much doubt whether it was for the same reasons. Yet art postulates communion, and the artist has an imperative need to make others share the joy which he experiences himself. But, in spite of that need, he prefers direct and frank opposition to apparent agreement which is based on misunderstanding.

Unfortunately, perfect communion is rare, and the more the personality of the author is revealed the rarer that communion becomes. The more he eliminates all that is extraneous, all that is not his own or "in him", the greater is his risk of conflicting with the expectations of the bulk of the public, who always receive a shock when confronted by something to which they are not accustomed.

The author's need for communion is all-embracing, but

unfortunately that is only an unattainable ideal, so that he is compelled to content himself with something less. In my own case, I find that while the general public no longer gives me the enthusiastic reception of earlier days, that does not in any way prevent a large number of listeners, mainly of the younger generation, from acclaiming my work with all the old ardour. I wonder whether, after all, it is simply a matter of generation.

It is very doubtful whether Rimsky-Korsakov would ever have accepted "Le Sacre" or even "Petroushka". Is it any wonder, then, that the hypercritics of today should be dumbfounded by a language in which all the characteristics of their aesthetics seem to be violated? What, however, is less justifiable is that they nearly always blame the author for what is in fact due to their own lack of comprehension, a lack made all the more conspicuous because in their inability to state their grievance clearly they cautiously try to conceal their incompetence in the looseness and vagueness of their phraseology.

Their attitude certainly cannot make me deviate from my path. I shall assuredly not sacrifice my predilections and my aspirations to the demands of those who, in their blindness, do not realize that they are simply asking me to go backwards. It should be obvious that what they wish for has become obsolete for me, and that I could not follow them without doing violence to myself. But, on the other hand, it would be a great mistake to regard me as an adherent of "Zukunftsmusik"— the music of the future. Nothing could be more ridiculous. I live neither in the past nor in the future. I am in the present. I cannot know what tomorrow will bring forth. I can know only what the truth is for me today. That is what I am called upon to serve, and I serve it in all lucidity.

From Stravinsky's "An Autobiography".

A Soviet Composer Speaks: Shostakovich

THERE can be no music without an ideology. The old composers, whether they knew it or not, were upholding a political theory. Most of them, of course, were bolstering the rule of the upper classes. Only Beethoven was a forerunner of the revolutionary movement. If you read his letters, you will see how often he wrote to his friends that he wished to give new ideas to the public and rouse it to revolt against its masters.

On the other hand, Wagner's biographers show that he began his career as a radical and ended it as a reactionary. His monarchistic patriotism had a bad effect on his mind. Perhaps it is a personal prejudice, but I do not consider Wagner an important composer. It is true that he is played rather frequently in Russia today; but we hear him in the same spirit with which we go to a museum to study the forms of the old regime. We can learn certain technical lessons from him, but we do not accept him.

We, as revolutionists, have a different conception of music. Lenin himself said that "music is a means of unifying broad masses of people". Not a leader of masses, perhaps, but certainly an organizing force. For music has the power of stirring specific emotions in those who listen to it. No one can deny that Tchaikovsky's Sixth Symphony produces a feeling of despair, while Beethoven's Third awakens us to the joy of struggle. Even the symphonic form, which appears more than any other to be divorced from literary elements, can be said to have a bearing on politics. Thus we regard Scriabin as our bitterest musical enemy, because Scriabin's music tends to an unhealthy eroticism, also to mysticism and passivity, and escape from the realities of life.

Not that the Soviets are always joyous, or supposed to be. But good music lifts and heartens and lightens people for work and effort. It may be tragic but it must be strong. It is no longer an end in itself but a vital weapon to the struggle. Because of this, Soviet music will probably develop along different lines from any the world has known. There must be a change! After all, we have entered a new epoch, and history has proved that every age creates its own language.

From "The Book of Modern Composers"
Edited by David Ewen.

MUSIC OF RECENT TIMES

Richard Strauss Defending His
"Sinfonia Domestica"

THIS symphony is supposed to portray married life. I know that some people regard it as a comic representation of domestic happiness. But I confess that I did not, in the least, mean to be funny when I composed it. What can be more serious than matrimony? Wedlock is one of the most important events in life, and the holy joy of such a union is heightened by the arrival of a child. This life, of course, also has its humor, which I have introduced into my work, to enliven it. But I want the symphony to be accepted as something very serious and in this sense it has been played in Germany.

From M. Steinitzer: "Straussiana".

Richard Strauss Has Peculiar Ideas on Democracy
(His Statement—1912)

FOR me, there is but one point of view in the matter "Parsifal": the respect for the wish of a genius. Unfortunately, in the question of the protection of "Parsifal", it is not those people interested in the refinement and growth of our culture who have to decide, but only jurists and politicians without any comprehension of the unlimited rights of the spiritual owner.

I attended the session of the Reichstag of the German Reich, where for eight long days, the representatives of the German people, with very few exceptions, enviably ignorant of all material on copyright and its extension, have debated the question. I have heard a man called Eugene Richter, trample in most impudent terms on the rights of two hundred miserable German composers—among them the heirs of Richard Wagner—in favor of two hundred inn-keepers.

Facts like this will never change as long as the stupid general voting system subsists and as long as the votes are counted,—not weighed; as long as, for instance, the vote of one Richard Wagner does not equal that of a hundred thousand other votes, and that of ten thousand porters that of one vote.

Then perhaps I wouldn't in the "Goethe Bund" hear such phrases as: "the rights of the German nation which must be invested with the power to plunder a genius (whom, during his lifetime they scoffed at and decried) thirty years after his death, and to prostitute his work on the smallest stages of the provinces".

We few elect will protest in vain, and the German philistine (middle class bourgeois), will, in two years, of a Sunday afternoon, between his dinner and his "Evening Schoppen", —instead of going to a movie, or a comic opera—hear "Parsifal", for fifty Pfennig . . .

From Max Steinitzer: "Richard Strauss".

Pfitzner Versus Busoni

BUSONI, it is true, is very musical, but he does not love music—at least not ours—(il n'aime pas la musique). He is a cool fluctuating spirit. Art to him is more a matter of intellect than of the heart,—as, generally speaking, the music of the north is warmer than that of the south. He has with his extraordinary musical endowments overcome all technical difficulties. Now he is bored with what he has conquered, and is disturbed by the limitations of what he has acquired. I can well understand that such sentiments take hold of every being, particularly in relation to himself: that a man finds it most boring and unbearable, when, in a mentally and physically bad disposition, he must as long as he lives, day by day, dress every morning and undress every evening. That the body must always take the same place in the same room, that every minute of one's life must be bought with a breath, and that it sickens one to have always the same nose in the same face! Were such sensations lasting, one could hang oneself. And so our aesthetician (Busoni) also desires that our music commit suicide, and it must be seen whether it is healthy enough not to do so.

But truly: if we were to learn to see with his eyes, music could do no better than to disappear altogether. For this is how he sees it: a wild piece of land with uncultivated and dry sedges in an untilled soil, a few half-mouldering stones on the graves of heroes, among them a few sign posts, pointing into the blue—and on all sides beautiful green pastures.

Hans Pfitzner: "Danger of Futurism".
(From his "Gesammelte Schriften",
1929-1934)

Counterpoint is Satan's Gift to the Germans:
Richard Strauss

CLASSICAL opera knows two ways of carrying out the dialogue which forms the action: pure prose, or the so-called "recitativo secco" with accompaniment by harpsichord. Only Beethoven and Marschner made use of the very effective and colorful melodrama.[1] In Mozart's German operas the real ac-

---

[1] "Melodrama" in the German sense: spoken drama with illustrative musical accompaniment.

tion is represented almost exclusively in prose to which are added, as a retarding element, vocal parts in Lied—or Aria—form, free ensembles, finales of broad symphonic structure, and the aria with a recitativo accompagnato as introduction.

I have always paid greatest attention to a declamation fraught with meaning, and a lively tempo of the dialogue,—and this with ever more growing success.

It may be that, as a consequence of a faulty propensity on my part, even this thin and transparent orchestra is still too polyphonic in its action, is too restlessly presented, and so hinders the spoken word on the stage. It may also be that the defective technique of speech of our opera singers, or the throaty tone formation, so prevalent with us Germans, and too strong a timbre also, are to blame. Orchestral polyphony, no matter how soft in coloring, no matter how pianissimo, is the death of the word spoken on the stage, and Satan has laid the counterpoint into our German cradles to prevent our thriving on the opera stage . . .

From the preface to "Intermezzo", 1924.

Pfitzner's "Palestrina"
A Recollection of Thomas Mann

ON a summer night, sitting on a garden terrace we were discussing this work, which quite naturally was compared to the "Meistersinger", both as an artistic drama and as a work of art as a whole. Thus Ighino was contrasted with David, Palestrina, with Stolzing, and with Sachs,—and the Mass with the "Preislied". We spoke of Bach and of the Italian church music as style-forming powers. Pfitzner said: "The difference is most obviously expressed in the closing scenic picture. At the end of the "Meistersinger" we have a brilliantly lighted stage, enthusiasm of the people, a betrothal, splendor and gloria; my "Palestrina", also highly celebrated, however, remains alone in the semi-darkness of his chamber, dreaming under his organ of one departed. The "Meistersinger" is an apotheosis of the new, a praise of the future and of life; in "Palestrina" everything tends toward the past, and sympathy with death is the reigning thought."

We were all silent and—as musicians do—he cast his eyes upward, gazing into the vague.

From Thomas Mann:
"Betrachtungen eines Unpolitischen", (1922).

The World Has Little Understanding For
Mahler's Greatness

Y OU will see: I shall never live to see the victory of my cause. Everything I write is too new, too strange, for the people; they find no bridge across to me, because even the first that I have offered them, in no way is connected with what formerly was. My earliest works, from my study period, in which I still clung to the past, and which were more or less of the past, have been lost, or have never been produced. And what came later—beginning with "Das Klagende Lied", is already so "Mahler-like", so sharply marked by my own style, and so different from anything else, that there is no connection any longer. In addition to that: I have not created much and—except for a few songs—no smaller works. Only at long intervals did I write a few—it is true—enormous works. Even Beethoven was "Mozartish" at first, and Wagner leaned toward the Meyerbeer form of opera. But with me there is nothing of the sort. All understanding between the composer and the listener is based on the convention: that the latter approve of this or that motive or symbol, as the expression of this or that thought, or rather,—in few words—of the spiritual content. That is particularly true of Wagner. But Beethoven also, and more or less every other composer, has his especially accepted expression for everything he wishes to say. The people, however, have not yet accepted my language. They have no idea of what I want to say, and what I feel, and it seems senseless to them and incomprehensible. This also applies to the musicians who perform my works; it takes them quite a time to understand me. Why must I suffer all this? Why take upon myself this fearful martyrdom? And not only for me, but for those who, before me have been crucified, because they wanted to give to the world their best; and for all those coming after me, I feel immeasurable pain.

From Specht: "Gustav Mahler".

Gustav Mahler at Work on his Third Symphony

I HAVE already told you that I am at work on a great composition. Can't you understand how that takes up all of a man? At such times I no longer belong to myself—the labor pains of the creator of such a work are terrible.

My symphony is going to be something, the like of which the world has not yet heard. All nature is voiced therein, and tells of deeply mysterious matters. . . .

I tell you, at certain passages I myself am sometimes overcome with an uncanny feeling, and can hardly believe that I could have written them.

From a letter to Anna Bahr-Mildenburg, 18. 8. 1896.

Gustav Mahler's Music, A "Voice of Nature"

I THINK it is strange how most people, in speaking of nature, only think of flowers, birds, the forest, etc. No one seems to know anything of Dionysos, the great god Pan. There you already have a sort of program, i.e. an example of how I make music: it is always and all over but the voice of nature. This is what I am sure Bülow meant, when he once spoke to me about a "Symphonic Problem". I recognize no other kind of program, than "nature"—at least not for my work. If I have given a sort of title to it, I meant merely to set up some kind of a sign-post for an explanation of its inner meaning. If words are required, we have human articulate speech which can materialize the most daring intentions, by the means of the illuminating world. It is the world itself, nature as a whole, which, so to say, is awakened to tones out of an unfathomable silence.

From a letter to Dr. Richard Batka, 1896.

"Start from the Beginning!"

EVERY composer must start from the beginning. The misapplied slogan "Inner Experience" fools the stupid alone. It is too often forgotten how rigid a school our great masters went through to acquire the mechanics of their art, before they proceeded to break through form, and with wise hands to broaden and to deepen music. It is, therefore, wrong for our young musicians to believe that as composers of Lieder, they can continue where Wolf left off. . . . We must never lose sight of the long course of development, gone through by Wolf. The same applies to the followers of Richard Strauss. What an infinite distance between Strauss's F minor Symphony and Salome. . . .

Max Reger.

337

Aphorisms of Max Reger

"Only a sincerely devout man can write true music."

"The Protestants do not realize how great a treasure they possess in their chorales."

"When thinking in music, I can think polyphonically only. I am, you must know, the "Fugen-Seppl.""

"If I happen to be endowed with more brains than most, please not to forget how many note-heads I have painted. Think of Mendelssohn, Schubert and Wolf. Too little time is given us, and I must see my work completed."

"I can live in Germany only; I know I should succumb to home-sickness elsewhere."

(Speaking of his last works): "But children, I am only just beginning. . . ."

"When you ask me: what is art?—I cannot tell you. Perhaps the knowledge will come to me after my death."

(On the future of music): "I believe we are about to enter a new era in music. The signs of a new dawn are multiplying. For the Liszt-Berlioz program, and that of their followers: Richard Strauss, Nicodé and so forth, being directly opposed to the very essence of music, has missed its mark. True music should not, as does program music, require a medium, such as title, analysis, and so forth, to be universally understood. Music should, by its very nature, be the outflow of pure feeling, untainted by any savor of reflectiveness."

From Hermann Unger "Musikgeschichte in Selbstzeugnissen."

Pro and Contra Mechanical Music

A Statement by Paul Hindemith

WHAT is mechanical music? It is partly "conserved" and "canned" music, i.e., the recording of vocal or instrumental music produced by man; partly also original music, which by the composer himself, or by some one who arranged it, is reproduced by the mechanical apparatus in question. There have at all times been original compositions for mechanical musical instruments. Mozart wrote three compositions for the mechanical organ; and then, there are those pieces written for the Aeolian Co., by Stravinsky, Malipiero, etc., for the mechanical piano.

Only the music written by the composer himself for a roll can be of interest here. That alone, of all recorded music, can meet highest demands, and that alone is true mechanical music.

One of the principal objections to it is that it destroys the charm of music, that charm which is based on the interpretation of a composition by one or another performer. It is said to be the invention of a materialistic age, that stuffs humanity with surrogates, and makes men incapable of appreciating true music. Its merits are said to lie in the absolute fixation of the composer's ideas; independence of the momentary disposition of the reproducer; expansion of technical and sound devices; of a diminishing of concert practice (long overdue); the personal cult; and possibilities for a spreading of good music at little cost.

Reproaches are as unjustified as enthusiasm. It would never occur to any one to deny the need for conserved or for retail music. Folk festivals, balls, pageants, restaurants, etc. are unthinkable without music. They use up the second and third rate scum of classical and romantic music: the greatest abuse is perpetrated with great masterpieces. The "Eroica" ar-

339

ranged for five players with a harmonium; a "Parsifal Phantasy" with a tolling of bells; entire Mozart Symphonies; string quartets; songs (Hildach's "Spring Song" for example!);—these are favorite pieces to be mutilated. Bach to be heard in a silly film, or in a crowded coffee-house,—does this seem right?

But how purely, honestly, precisely and artistically, conserved music can satisfy various demands! It is not at all necessary to have human power put into service for entertainment music, even though the audiences of today are sentimental enough to ask for soul, personality and depth, at all times, and for all occasions. But that is indulging in quite an unnecessary luxury.

From the "Program Notes" to the
"Music Festival" in Baden-Baden, 1927.

Two Apostles of Ultra-Modern Harmony
Arnold Schoenberg

I HAVE demonstrated that the system of chords based on thirds has a breach, and I have exposed this combination of unaligned chords, under the name of "tones foreign to harmony", a badly disguised design to stop up the hole with a considerable amount of garbage, a heap so large, that neither the hole nor the pile is big enough to absorb it. But seeing that there is question of chords of fourths only, this does not, by any means, signify a proposal to replace the old system of thirds by a structure of fourths. These fourth-chords are introduced at first like everything that is later accepted generally: as a technical means only, as merely an impressionistic form of expression. The novel and unusual in a new harmony should be used by the true artist for one reason only: namely to ex-

press something stirring within him, of a new and hitherto
unheard of nature.

For those who are to continue this work, it may seem to
be a new sound, a technical means only. But it is a great deal
more than that. A new sound is a symbol, inspirationally discovered, which announces the new man, now voicing new
ideas. The artist who has courage, follows his own inclinations only; and only he who follows his inclinations has courage; and only he who has courage is a true artist.

This strikes us particularly when considering Debussy. His
impressionism sets down the chords of fourths with such ef-
ficacy that they seem inseparably bound up with what he has
to say as new, and which can rightly be regarded as his spiritual
possession, although it has been proved that before him, and
contemporary with him, similar things have been enunciated.
Perhaps the fact that they express the moods of nature contributed to this, for his music does sound like a pronouncement
of nature. And that everything must yield to this voice is clear.
It is possible, nay, probable even, that others, beside me, have
employed these chords: possibly Mahler, Strauss or Pfitzner.
But I do not know it. Yet I do not wish to claim any priority.
I care too little about it, for I know how little it signifies.

My pupils, Dr. Anton von Webern and Alban Berg have
made use of these chords; and the Hungarian Bela Bartók,
the Viennese, Anton Schreker,—both following in the path
of Debussy; Ducas, and perhaps also Puccini, are not far away
from it either. Even though it may seem that the most gifted
of our younger composers are adopting this method, it would
be of little value to set down a system now, because the fact
that we are not far away enough from these innovations, might
confuse our judgment. But, in the meantime, this structure of
the fourths makes possible the marshalling together of all
phenomena. The list of those who, today in 1921, are resort-
ing to these measures, might be a very long one. It would never
occur to me that my book might have lost in value because

341

I have given it actuality by linking it to events of the day. Nor does either the quality or the quantity of my brethren in arms (modern composers) give me any satisfaction. For them it naturally signifies a "New trend" and they call themselves "Atonalists". I must reject this, for I am a musician and will have nothing to do with what is atonal. Atonal could only mean something that in no way corresponds with the essence of tones. Everything arising from a tone combination means tonality. A musical piece will, of necessity be tonal in so far as there must be a relation of tone with tone, by virtue of which the tones, whether placed side by side, or above one another, as such produce an intelligible result. That then is nonsense. I will except the Viennese Joseph Hauer, whose theories, even where I note exaggerations, are original and profound; whose compositions, while they seem to be examples rather than compositions, do display creative talent, and whose attitude, (in any case, his courage and sacrifice), are deserving of credit. It is a pity that nowadays the idea "One can write everything and anything", keeps so many young people from learning something worth while, to understand the classics, to acquire culture. For "anything and everything could be written in former days" but it never was any good. No master would dare to write "anything",—he writes as he must, to fulfill his task. To prepare for that, with great diligence and with a thousand doubts of his ability and with a thousand scruples as to whether he has properly understood the message received from on high,—this is reserved only for those who have the courage and the fervor to suffer all the consequences of a burden placed on their shoulders without their volition. And that is a long way from the wilfullness of a "trend" and it is far braver.

From his "Harmonielehre", 1922.

Bela Bartók

THE music of our day is definitely striving toward atonal ways. However it does not seem right to have the atonal principle conceived as the absolute opposite of the tonal principle. The latter is the consequence of a gradual development, which proceeds step by step and does not exhibit any gaps or forced leaps.

Schoenberg, in his "Harmonielehre" claims that the development of the sonata-form is to some extent the germ of atonality. That is easily understood; the development excludes the predominance of two keys (as in the exposition) or of one (as in the recapitulation) in place of which it puts a more freely chosen succession of various keys, of which each one—be it only passing—is always conceived as a key. In other words: in the "Durchfuehrung" (development) there prevails a sort of equality of the twelve keys.

The accumulation of altered chords in the post-Beethoven period (Wagner, Liszt), then the freer use of the "Durchgangsnoten" (passing and non-harmonic tones), — (Strauss, Debussy) — over the tonal chords, (still operating tonally, it is true), are two important transitional steps from tonality to atonality. In Strauss and even more in post-Strauss music, we find in works of tonal character, some parts (for example in "Heldenleben", the theme of the "Opponents") in which tonality has already been definitely abolished. The next step to atonality is shown in those works, which with the exception of the beginning and close (tradition of unity), result in being atonal.

The decisive turn to atonality, however, began, when one realized the necessity of equality of the individual single tones of our twelve-tone-system: when one tried to arrange the twelve tones, no longer according to specified scale systems, and to give lesser or greater weight to the individual tones,—but to use these individual tones in any combination, not resting on the scale system, at one's discretion, be it horizontal or vertical. In this procedure, certain tones in their combination do acquire a relative preponderance; but this difference in preponderance is no longer based on this or another scale system, but is the result of the actual combination. The possibilities for expression are increased by the free and equal treatment of the individual twelve tones in a measure hardly yet to be gauged.

"The Problem of New Music" in "Melos".

Modern Music is our Music

THE art of music during the past fifty years has undergone a violent upheaval. Audiences everywhere have shown signs of bewilderment at the variety of styles and tendencies that all pass muster under the name of modern music. Being unaware of the separate steps that brought about these revolutionary changes, they are naturally at a loss to understand the end result. Speaking generally, the lay listener has remained antagonistic, confused, or merely apathetic to the major creations of the newer composers.

For many years a number of fantastic notions were spread concerning the nature of so-called "modern music". (Incredible as it may seem, some of these odd notions are still being circulated by newspaper writers and radio commentators who ought to know better). It was said, for example, that the new composers were admittedly clever, but their music lacked emotion—or worse still, that they deliberately eschewed all semblance of feeling. This is, of course, the sheerest nonsense. No one would deny that there have been modern pieces that were merely clever, others that were only arid, but to suggest that the contemporary composers hold a special brief for music that is "all mind and no heart" is literally untrue. New music, in general, reflects just as much emotion as any other kind of music, but the quality and intensity of emotional expression have changed.

Many lesser misconceptions were current until quite recently. It was said that modern music lacked melody and that its rhythmic structure was so complicated as to result in utter chaos. But if music is not made up of melodies, what does it consist of? I cannot conceive of a music, save by rarest exception, that does not exist primarily by virtue of its melodic content. As for modern rhythm, it can sound chaotic only to those whose rhythmic conceptions are still in an undeveloped stage. Then, finally, there used to be the old reproach about dissonances — that contemporary music was nothing but a cacophonic web of sound. But that complaint is heard much less frequently nowadays. It was probably dispelled by repeated hearings of one typical modern piece. As dissonances become familiar, they lose their terror; thus each repetition drove home the point that dissonance, like consonance, is a purely relative thing. All chords are now judged alike, according to their appositeness to the situation in which they are placed.

True or not, these various charges indicate that the art of music has been passing through a period of revolutionary change. Although this break with the past began more than forty years ago, there are still some people who have not yet recovered from the shock. Music has been changing, but they have remained the same. Nevertheless, inwardly, they know that change in music, like change in all the arts, is inevitable. After all, why should I or any other composer living in a time like ours write music that reflects some other period? Isn't it natural for us to try to develop our own kind of music? In doing so, we are merely following the example of revolutionaries like Beethoven and Wagner. They too sought new expressive possibilities in music — and found them.

The fact is that the whole history of music is a history

of continuous change. There never was a great composer who
left music exactly as he found it. This is true of Bach and Mozart, just as it is true of Debussy and Stravinsky. We can only
conclude, therefore, that the period of change through which
music has recently passed was, contrary to what many people
believe, an inevitable one — part of the great tradition of
music throughout the ages.

At any rate, whether we like it or not, music today is
radically different from what it was fifty years ago. Modern
music, in a word, is principally the expression in terms of an
enriched musical language of a new spirit of objectivity, at-
tuned to our own times. It is the music of the composer of today — in other words, *our* music.

*From Aaron Copland's book
"Our New Music".*

Gershwin About Jazz

THE great music of the past in other countries has always
been built on folk-music. This is the strongest source of musical fecundity. America is no exception among the countries.
The best music being written today is music which comes from
folk-sources. It is not always recognized that America has folk-
music; yet it really has not only one but many different folk-
musics. It is a vast land, and different sorts of folk-music have
sprung up in different parts, all having validity, and all being a
possible foundation for the development into art music. For this
reason, I believe that it is possible for a number of distinctive
styles to develop in America, all legitimately born of folk-
songs from different localities. Jazz, ragtime, Negro spirituals
and blues, Southern mountain songs, country fiddling, and
cowboy songs can all be employed in the creation of American
art music, and are actually used by many composers today.

346

These composers are certain to produce something worth while if they have the innate feeling and talent to develop the rich material offered to them. There are also other composers who can be classed as legitimately American who do not make use of folk-music as a base, but who have personally, working in America, developed highly individual styles and methods. Their new-found materials should be called American, just as an invention is called American if it is made by an American.

Jazz, I regard as an American folk-music; not the only one, but a very powerful one which is probably in the blood and feeling of the American people more than any other style of folk-music. I believe that it can be made the basis of serious symphonic works of lasting value, in the hands of a composer with talent for both jazz and symphonic music.

It is difficult to determine what enduring values, aesthetically, jazz has contributed, because "jazz" is a word which has been used for at least five or six different types of music. It is really a conglomeration of many things. It has a little bit of ragtime, the blues, classicism, and spirituals. Basically, it is a matter of rhythm. After rhythm, in importance come intervals, music intervals which are peculiar to the rhythm. After all, there is nothing new in music. I maintained years ago that there is very little difference in the music of different nations. There is just that little individual touch. One country may prefer a peculiar rhythm or a note like the seventh. This it stresses, and it becomes identified with that nation. In America, this preferred rhythm is called jazz. Jazz is music; it uses the same notes that Bach used. When jazz is played in another nation, it is called American. When it is played in another country, it sounds false. Jazz is the result of the energy stored up in America. It is a very energetic kind of music, noisy, boisterous, and even vulgar. One thing is certain. Jazz has contributed an enduring value to America in the sense that it has expressed ourselves. It is an original American achievement which will endure, not as jazz perhaps, but which will leave its mark on future music in one form or another. The only kinds of music which endure are those which possess form in the universal sense and folk-music. All else dies. But unquestionably folk-songs are being written and have been written which contain enduring elements of jazz. To be sure, that is only an element; it is not the whole. An entire composition written in jazz could not live.

> *This statement is taken from two essays by the composer, which appeared in the books "American Composers on American Music" (ed. by Henry Cowell) and "Revolt in the Arts" (ed. by Oliver M. Saylor).*

George Gershwin, As Seen by a Friend

HE was as simple, as unaffected, as modest, and as charming a youth as one could desire to meet.

There was nothing about him that was forbidding. He wore his unprecedented celebrity as lightly as if it were a cane —that cane which one heard swinging so jauntily in the opening rhythms of "An American in Paris". If one did not fear a word that has been twisted in certain mouths, out of its originally robust meaning, one would say that he created immediately an impression of "wholesomeness". It was, in fact, a genuine pleasure to discover this youngster moving easily, confidently, through the comfort and the affluence that he had won for himself. No affectations. No embarrassing habits that cling to one from earlier, more humble days and surroundings. Simplicity, and even at moments an engaging naiveté. Above all, no desire to make an effect. The man and his music —and this, too, on his part was a form of honesty—were one.

The man had, too, that psychological rarity, the saving

grace of self-knowledge. He was one of the most objective mentalities that I have encountered, and this in a young man whose success was so rapid, so phenomenal, is doubly rare.

I have heard him, when the mood was upon him, talk of his finest things in a manner surprisingly impersonal, and manifestly without the slightest trace of affectation. And to have heard him talk was to understand his music so much better.

He was not only modest, but he was intellectually nervous, keyed ever to concert pitch. The quality appeared almost at the very beginning of his career and remained with him in his greatest triumphs. It is the eagerness of a high-spirited steed. He was driven—there is no question about it—by some inner compulsion, and was protected by his demon against stagnation and mere self-repetition. There were moments when that demon was almost visible in his eyes. He will have been playing one of his songs, and have reached the end of the chorus. It is a moment that his familiar listeners have been waiting for. The pink of his cheeks became a little deeper. The end of his cigar gleamed like another eye. A smile—that questioning smile—lighted up his countenance and he launched into a series of variations that had all the excitement of improvisation. He attacked the keys with conscious power; his wrist, at will, was a hammer driving in spikes, or a brush tinting surfaces. His playing, which enlisted the accompaniment of his entire person, became a quasi-Nietzschean dance of arms and legs. This was not the specialized virtuosity of the concert player; it was a sort of intensified living.

He was fond of parties, and the longer they let him sing and play, the better he liked it. Hosts and hostesses have been known to take advantage of his generosity; George once told Behrman that his mother, a level-headed materfamilias, had cautioned him against overdoing it. "You see", he added in extenuation, "the trouble is, when I don't play I don't have a good time".

349

For the rest, the psychopathology of George's every-day life was the sort that even the less gifted of us can match. He was generous, too generous, not only with his playing, but with his leisure. The veriest little tyro of a high-school girl from the most modest suburb could have a half-hour interview with him for her school paper. With the patience of a Job he sat down, asked her where to begin, and started off for the thousandth time: "I was born in Brooklyn on the . . ." His autograph was almost as free as his advice.

The quotidian Gershwin was not enamoured of card games, unless it be hearts. Poker failed to excite him. Ping-pong, an occasional set of tennis, backgammon, golf . . . these, and especially the open air, seduced him from the more sober tasks of compositions.

His beard was heavy, and very early in the day threatened to take on the hue of Jed Harris's blue patch. A three days' growth and he looked like some hermit who has taken the vows.

You would usually find him dressed in blue or grey; one suit with a white pencil stripe has become famous in the photographs. In the matter of clothes he was not a patriot, preferring foreign makes.

He had the chief nationalities timed. The English rhythm is 6/8; the Viennese, 3/4; New York is 4/4; and Russia (this, with a Tchaikovskian twinkle in his eye), 5/4.

London for quietude, Paris for beauty, and New York (of all places!) for work.

He was a man of mood rather than method. A definite contract stipulating a date of delivery acted as a spur; once thus stimulated, he could work hours on end without interruption.

Outside of his scores he found it hard to be on time.

Politics was a bore.

If he had not had a secretary, or that remarkably efficient brother, Ira, it is unlikely that he would ever have paid a bill

it would indeed be a novelty here, and tend to attract many
the young people away from the Quakers and sects to atter
services where such music was found, even against the wish
of their parents. This would afford a good opportunity
show them the truth and their error.

. . . And it may be assumed that even a small organ-i
strument and music in this place would be acceptable to Go
and prove far more useful than many hundreds in Europ
where there is already a superfluity of such things.

There are in Europe masters enough who would buil
such instruments, and a fine one can be secured for 300 or 40
thalers. Then if an experienced organist and musician cou'
be found, who would undertake so far a journey, he woul
be very welcome here. In case this could not be, if we onl
had an organ, some one or other might be found who ha
knowledge thereof."

From "Our American Music"
by John Tasker Howard.

Music in Latin America

LATIN America possesses well-organized choral societie
of which the "Orfeon Lamas" in Caracas, Venezuela, enjoy
great renown. The largest choral ensemble is the Brazilia
school children's chorus, numbering several thousand boy
and girls, with Villa-Lobos as conductor. Each year, on Brazil'
Independence Day, September 7, this chorus which Villa-Lobo
with his love for neologisms calls "Orpheonic Concentration"
gives a gala performance at the great stadium in Rio d
Janeiro. Villa-Lobos stations himself atop a specially construct
ed platform, fifty feet high and directs the chorus, not with a
ordinary conductor's baton, but with flags of national colors
Before the beginning of each concert, Villa-Lobos "tunes up"

or answered a letter. You wrote to him, you telegraphed, you
even cabled. Yet, like Rhadames thrice questioned in the great
fourth act of "Aida", "he is silent". Then, suddenly, a five-
page, tight-packed missive.

Something of the Hebrew-Christian morality clung to him,
especially where women were concerned. In their presence,
he was quite correct; for that matter, his conversation among
men was masculine, but hardly Rabelaisian. He was known,
before his sister Frances was married, to suggest in company
that she pull her dresses down.

Isaac Goldberg.
(From the "Book of Modern Composers"
edited by David Ewen).

Alexandrian America

MUSICAL America is destined to fulfill a tremendous
mission of conservation, the conservation of Europe's great
cultural values. Indeed, she is already fulfilling it. America
today invites comparison with Alexandria of antiquity. After
Rome had subdued Greece, Greek culture sought refuge in
Egypt. The dynasty founded by Ptolemy, a general of Alexander the Great, made Alexandria a brilliant center of Hellenistic culture in which the Greek tradition was cultivated and
extended.

The outstanding characteristic of that era is not so much
that it created culture, but that it preserved and commented
on it. It was a culture of scholarship, symbolized by the renowned Alexandrian Library. Here historians, physicians,
scientists and other scholars found a new homeland. Here lived
the most important musicologists of antiquity and of the Middle Ages—Claudius Ptolemy, whose teachings of harmony
dominated the musical science of the Middle Ages, Euclydes,

Didymos and others. For eight full centuries this Alexandrian culture maintained itself.

Compared with Europe today, America appears to be a second Alexandria. In the past twenty-five years there has been a tremendous growth of musical activity, but the reproductive element has been much stronger than the creative. The gargantuan, technically perfect radio system surfeits us with elaborate performances of the best, even the rarest works of former centuries, carrying them to the most distant parts of the country, to the isolated prairies, to the Arctic. Millions are now acquainted with music. And the phonograph not only preserves works of art, but preserves them as they are played. A mighty network of musical libraries helps to spread knowledge.

Above all, the gigantic Library of Congress is like the great Library of Alexandria. It has the largest operatic collection of the world. The inter-library loan service, unknown to Europe, has put every book at the disposal of anybody who has need of it. And now all the great musical manuscripts of the masters can even be photographed and made available. The best orchestras with the best artists in the world help to cultivate and spread the music of the past. The most important musicologists at the universities, colleges and other schools teach the history, philosophy and science of music. Musical education begins in the elementary schools and continues through the university. Even the smallest schools have their own orchestras. Music here is not a matter of individual talent —as it was in modern Europe—but it is a goal of general education, as in the Middle Ages.

This enormous, elaborate cultivation of the music of the past on a scale hitherto unknown in the world, has a significance which, in my opinion, at present overshadows the cultivation of native music. Some years ago the German critic Benz forecast the coming century as an era of "Wiederklang", an echoing of the music of former ages. It almost seems as if that prophecy were being fulfilled in America, that America

has become the land of European music. And tha to me, is the significance of the present, the latest migration, which surpasses in importance all previo migrations.

Paul Nettl. (From "Modern

Music, a Civilizing Power in the New

JUSTUS FALCKNER, the first German ministei in this country, was the author of the fine hymns c gregation.

Two years before he was awarded the pastor: "Gloria Dei Church" (near Philadelphia, Pennsylvan ner wrote a letter to Heinrich Muhlen of Holste for assistance for his church. The letter tells of con the colony, and provides an interesting contrast t titude of New Englanders regarding music:

". . . I will take occasion to mention that ma besides myself, who know the ways of the land, mai music would contribute much towards a good Christia It would not only attract and civilize the wild Inc it would do much good in spreading the Gospel trutl the sects and others by attracting them. Instrumen is especially serviceable here. Thus a well-soundii would perhaps prove of great profit, to say nothir fact that the Indians would come running from far to listen to such unknown melody, and on that might become willing to accept our language and and remain with people who had such agreeable th they are said to come ever so far to listen to one w even a reed-pipe: such an extraordinary love have any melodious and ringing sound. Now as the me saturnine, stingy Quaker spirit has abolished all suc or answered a letter. You wrote to him, you telegraphed, you even cabled. Yet, like Rhadames thrice questioned in the great fourth act of "Aida", "he is silent". Then, suddenly, a five-page, tight-packed missive.

Something of the Hebrew-Christian morality clung to him, especially where women were concerned. In their presence, he was quite correct; for that matter, his conversation among men was masculine, but hardly Rabelaisian. He was known, before his sister Frances was married, to suggest in company that she pull her dresses down.

Isaac Goldberg.
(From the "Book of Modern Composers"
edited by David Ewen).

Alexandrian America

Musical America is destined to fulfill a tremendous mission of conservation, the conservation of Europe's great cultural values. Indeed, she is already fulfilling it. America today invites comparison with Alexandria of antiquity. After Rome had subdued Greece, Greek culture sought refuge in Egypt. The dynasty founded by Ptolemy, a general of Alexander the Great, made Alexandria a brilliant center of Hellenistic culture in which the Greek tradition was cultivated and extended.

The outstanding characteristic of that era is not so much that it created culture, but that it preserved and commented on it. It was a culture of scholarship, symbolized by the renowned Alexandrian Library. Here historians, physicians, scientists and other scholars found a new homeland. Here lived the most important musicologists of antiquity and of the Middle Ages—Claudius Ptolemy, whose teachings of harmony dominated the musical science of the Middle Ages, Euclydes,

351

Didymos and others. For eight full centuries this Alexandrian culture maintained itself.

Compared with Europe today, America appears to be a second Alexandria. In the past twenty-five years there has been a tremendous growth of musical activity, but the reproductive element has been much stronger than the creative. The gargantuan, technically perfect radio system surfeits us with elaborate performances of the best, even the rarest works of former centuries, carrying them to the most distant parts of the country, to the isolated prairies, to the Arctic. Millions are now acquainted with music. And the phonograph not only preserves works of art, but preserves them as they are played. A mighty network of musical libraries helps to spread knowledge.

Above all, the gigantic Library of Congress is like the great Library of Alexandria. It has the largest operatic collection of the world. The inter-library loan service, unknown to Europe, has put every book at the disposal of anybody who has need of it. And now all the great musical manuscripts of the masters can even be photographed and made available. The best orchestras with the best artists in the world help to cultivate and spread the music of the past. The most important musicologists at the universities, colleges and other schools teach the history, philosophy and science of music. Musical education begins in the elementary schools and continues through the university. Even the smallest schools have their own orchestras. Music here is not a matter of individual talent —as it was in modern Europe—but it is a goal of general education, as in the Middle Ages.

This enormous, elaborate cultivation of the music of the past on a scale hitherto unknown in the world, has a significance which, in my opinion, at present overshadows the cultivation of native music. Some years ago the German critic Benz forecast the coming century as an era of "Wiederklang", an echoing of the music of former ages. It almost seems as if that prophecy were being fulfilled in America, that America has become the land of European music. And that, it seems to me, is the significance of the present, the latest European migration, which surpasses in importance all previous musical migrations.

Paul Nettl. (From "Modern Music").

Music, a Civilizing Power in the New World

JUSTUS FALCKNER, the first German minister ordained in this country, was the author of the fine hymns of his congregation.

Two years before he was awarded the pastorate of the "Gloria Dei Church" (near Philadelphia, Pennsylvania), Falckner wrote a letter to Heinrich Muhlen of Holstein, asking for assistance for his church. The letter tells of conditions in the colony, and provides an interesting contrast to the attitude of New Englanders regarding music:

". . . I will take occasion to mention that many others besides myself, who know the ways of the land, maintain that music would contribute much towards a good Christian service. It would not only attract and civilize the wild Indians, but it would do much good in spreading the Gospel truths among the sects and others by attracting them. Instrumental music is especially serviceable here. Thus a well-sounding organ would perhaps prove of great profit, to say nothing of the fact that the Indians would come running from far and near to listen to such unknown melody, and on that account might become willing to accept our language and teaching, and remain with people who had such agreeable things; for they are said to come ever so far to listen to one who plays even a reed-pipe: such an extraordinary love have they for any melodious and ringing sound. Now as the melancholy, saturnine, stingy Quaker spirit has abolished all such music, it would indeed be a novelty here, and tend to attract many of the young people away from the Quakers and sects to attend services where such music was found, even against the wishes of their parents. This would afford a good opportunity to show them the truth and their error.

. . . And it may be assumed that even a small organ-instrument and music in this place would be acceptable to God, and prove far more useful than many hundreds in Europe where there is already a superfluity of such things.

There are in Europe masters enough who would build such instruments, and a fine one can be secured for 300 or 400 thalers. Then if an experienced organist and musician could be found, who would undertake so far a journey, he would be very welcome here. In case this could not be, if we only had an organ, some one or other might be found who had knowledge thereof."

From "Our American Music"
by John Tasker Howard.

Music in Latin America

LATIN America possesses well-organized choral societies, of which the "Orfeon Lamas" in Caracas, Venezuela, enjoys great renown. The largest choral ensemble is the Brazilian school children's chorus, numbering several thousand boys and girls, with Villa-Lobos as conductor. Each year, on Brazil's Independence Day, September 7, this chorus which Villa-Lobos with his love for neologisms calls "Orpheonic Concentration", gives a gala performance at the great stadium in Rio de Janeiro. Villa-Lobos stations himself atop a specially constructed platform, fifty feet high and directs the chorus, not with an ordinary conductor's baton, but with flags of national colors. Before the beginning of each concert, Villa-Lobos "tunes up" the children by making them sing a six-part canon in thirds, resulting in a chord of the eleventh, with the following words:

Bondade
Realidade
Amizade
Sinceridade
Igualidade
Lealdade

These words, meaning respectively, goodness, reality, amity, sincerity, equality, and loyalty, form an acrostic spelling:

B
R
A
S
I
L

which is the proper orthography in the Portuguese language.

Opera is universally popular in Latin America, but only two opera houses maintain regular seasons, the "Teatro Colón" (which means, of course, Columbus Theater) in Buenos Aires, and the "Teatro Municipal" in Rio de Janeiro. Pursuing a protective national policy, the Teatro Colón has produced numerous native operas and ballets. However, few of these remain in the repertoire, the maximum number of performances of an opera by an Argentine composer being twenty-five. A list of operas presented at the Teatro Colón, during the first quarter of a century of its existence, is given in the de luxe volume "El Arte Lírico en el Teatro Colón, 1908-1933".

From Nicolas Slonimsky's
"Music of Latin America".

Music Helps to Clear Political Tension

SITTING in a semi-circle in a large room at the Ankara Palace Hotel in Ankara, Turkey, were top Turkish government officials and international diplomats. I had arranged a concert and a reception to break up the tension during the strenuous negotiations with the Turks by our UNRRA mission. String quartets of Schubert and Mozart were being played. The youthful and handsome Soviet Ambassador, Vinogradov, was on my left; the tall blond-mustached British Ambassador, Sir David Kelly, just arrived from the Argentine, on my right. All differences in political ideology were lost for the hour in the universal plaint of this music. Toasts with vodka followed the concert. Later, we stood in a circle with American Ambassador Wilson. All was informal. The music had relaxed tensions. An agreement in principle was reached which led to our successful negotiations with the Turks.

> *Ira Hirschmann (New York Post)*
> *(Mr. Hirschmann completed a special mission for UNRRA in August 1946.)*

Ernst Křenek's Ideas About Modern Theatre

THE mistaken idea of regarding the stage as a moral institution has been supported and strengthened by the misinterpretation of the Aristotelian precept, that tragedy engenders compassion and fear, and that the arousing of these emotions has an ethical effect.

This ethical effect, and that is where the fallacy begins, is made concrete by demanding that the subject-matter contain precise instruction in the form of a tangible moral precept.

356

In reality, the effect of the drama, or any work of art, is never derived from the subject-matter alone (which is but a necessary incentive to artistic form),—but is based on the manner with which this subject-matter is translated and woven into the organism of the work itself. A play may consist of good situations, beautiful verses, well-adapted music, interesting scenic effects, histrionically brilliant presentations,—in short, innumerable valuable details,—and may even contain a pleasing moral: it still will be ineffectual if it isn't a real play, i.e., if the author has not the faculty (called a gift for theatre) to combine all these elements, so that, as though by electric contact, they yield up their individual importance and become one logical whole, thus forming essential parts of the drama.

It is not the function of the theatre to preach that good must be rewarded and evil punished, and to present to us all sorts of historic and actual villains. To bring the events of life into dramatic action may possibly be a rather bare formulation of the mission of the theatre. The true effect, one that brings with it a heightened feeling of life, will not be the outcome of a single beautifully constructed sentence, but the expression of an artistic fulfillment of the work as a whole.

From a statement in the magazine: "Anbruch".

The West Faces the East

Hába, the representative of modern European quarter-tone music, is a Czech and belongs to a musical culture close to the East. In him we have an embodiment of the mutual relation between Oriental and modern Occidental musical practice.

Several years ago, Cairo was host to a congress for Arabian music. The best of all the Arab orchestras participated and there were exhaustive discussions about theory and musical science, as well as much comparative measuring of the intervals in the Arab tonal system. It was evident from start to finish that the East is not inclined to sacrifice its own system of greater and smaller intervals for the glamor of European music. Hába was the main speaker at the congress, and a quarter-tone piano was used, built by the Czechoslovak firm, Foerster, especially with the Arab tonal system in mind. The Egyptian delegates recognized Hába's tempered quarter and sixth tone system as the basis of their own, and in this way gave official sanction to his music.

We do not know what has been the fate of Alois Hába's music in Africa since then. Hába himself, however, has grown more and more interested in Oriental music. Though not a Jew, he was asked by the Prague center for Jewish culture, shortly before the Hitler invasion, to notate the traditional thousand year old "Neginoth" of the Prague "Alt-Neu" Synagogue. Hába carried out the task successfully, being one of the few who, because of an unbelievably sensitive ear, can distinguish the tiny intervals and commit them to writing. Jewish synagogue singing in Europe, so far as it has not been "reformed", is in itself a living monument of Oriental music, just as genuine Gregorian singing is of the Catholic church. Some years ago the musicologist, Heinrich Berl, in his book "Das Judentum in der Musik", advanced the theory, since then hotly contested, that Occidental culture is plastic and spatial, Oriental culture musical and temporal. In musical terms this means that the Occidental product is characterized by simultaneous harmony, the Oriental by pure harmony and rhythm. Until their emancipation, the music of the Jews followed Oriental principles. About 1800, when they made contact with the broad stream of European music, they continued to advance the anti-harmonic Oriental principle of pure melody, as opposed to Occidental chordal music. Mendelssohn and Meyerbeer have shown how creative this linearism can be, just as does

Offenbach who always used the same harmonic turns for his rhythmic and melodic ideas. The true linear principle, however, was carried out fully in Europe for the first time by Arnold Schoenberg, whose twelve-tone school is made up so largely of musicians of Jewish descent. Schoenberg, Berl points out, unlike Debussy and the impressionists, who broke through the system of harmonic thinking, has gone back to the principle of Oriental music. If Berl is right, then Jews in the twentieth century have played a role like that of the enharmonists and chromaticians in Venice and Naples during the Renaissance. They are present-day exponents of the anti-harmonic system. Let us remember at this point that all the Jewish musical traditions of the Middle Ages were of Arabian origin, and were materially bound to the Arabian system of intervals.

In the music of our time, we recognize a continually increasing Oriental influence. Classical and romantic harmony with its principle of suspense and solution, so characteristic of the Occident, is constantly being challenged. The dynamic Faustian tension of spiritual life is perfectly represented by the tension and resolution of dissonance. Of all this the Oriental knows nothing. To him, music, if we may use a metaphor of Hanslick's, is but an interplay of tonally moving forms, a mosaic of ornaments, which corresponds exactly to his contemplative or ecstatic state of mind. Today our own modern music, as exemplified in the twelve-tone system is abandoning the old harmony of suspense. Schoenberg's melodies need no suspensions or resolutions, nor do they have them. The leading tone thus becomes obsolete. The melody despite all loss of harmony and counterpoint, goes its own way, following the laws of pure melody, while the polyphony is frequently relieved by the old, more primitive form of heterophony which is found in the music of the Orient.

On hearing one of the ecstatic dances of the Balinese or Javanese, with their rhythmic complications and counter-rhythms, their heterophony and their daring mixtures of tonal color, one recognizes a fascinating similarity to the works of the French impressionists. The psychological basis is the same; instead of concern with psychological problems, music here is ecstatic, or playful,—music for its own sake.

And finally, with the emerging of the National Schools of Czechs and Poles, Russians and Hungarians, also other elements of Oriental origin have made their way into European music. To a lesser degree, American jazz, partly built on Negro culture—which in turn is related to the culture of the Near East—has exerted its anti-Western influence. The modern emphasis on rhythm and further destruction of the old European tonal system are additional evidence.

Music in the nineteenth century was still predominantly European. In the twentieth it is definitely so no longer. Just as Europe, through America, Russia and the East, has lost its monopoly on so many things, so its hegemony over music also has been challenged by almost all the peoples of the earth.

Paul Nettl. (From "Modern Music")

Americanism: Humanity

THE historian of a distant future will probably evaluate American music as an entity that to our day is still indiscernible. However, if he looks for a historical analogy to the American crucible, he will find it in the musical history of the old Austrian empire. Austrian music developed into a classical style without any ideological support, out of a diversity of national elements. Close to the Hungarian border, in a Burgenland hut, was born the man who wrote the Austrian national anthem. Called derogatorily "the Croatian", he worked on the estate of Hungarian counts and used in his music tunes ranging from Italian to Bohemian, from South Slav to

German, and fused them into the precious idiom that, in a single word, was called "Austrian", and that, as such, has become universal. His name, of course, is Joseph Haydn; on certain manuscripts in his own handwriting, it is Giuseppe Haydn. We see the greatness of Haydn, the good patriot, the friend of many folklores, the arch-Austrian of obscure extraction, the composer of the Austrian national anthem, lies in his musical genius and great humanity, neither of which is dependent upon nationalism in the political or geographic sense.

Likewise, musical chauvinism, the use of Sioux Indian tunes, and accumulation of folklore, will not make great American music. Misuse and misconception of national ideals have played their part in the destruction of the musical culture of Europe. We in America may follow the lead of Roger Sessions, who concluded an address to American musicologists and music teachers in Pittsburgh, in 1937, with these words: "Being American involves, after all, first being human; and what Americanism can have any ultimate value, except the specific and inescapable inherent coloring of humanity?"

From Frederick Dorian:
"The History of Music in Performance".

MUSIC IN A

DEGENERATE WORLD

"Hitler Jugend" — Representing the
Nazi Musical Culture

THE aversion of our youth, observed in an ever-growing degree since 1900, to music of preceding generations is not only an aesthetic one, but is consonant with an aversion to the form of musical life, as it is practiced today; particularly in the larger cities. Form and content of music are indivisibly ONE. The form of music, now, has taken on a capitalistic character. Concert and opera music must be bought. In the metropolis, the love of art has been replaced by a purely social function, paid for according to wealth and station. From this naturally followed an external manifestation of stardom, and an over-estimation of the interpreter, whose place at present has been taken by the baton virtuoso. Stardom went so far that the name of a star-conductor was put on the program in large letters while the name of the composer was entirely omitted. And we have had the bitter experience of seeing our concert practice completely Americanized. . . . The "Hitler Jugend" rejects concert and opera music in its present form, i.e. in its social form and musical content. It is seeking new forms of musical life, new musical content. It has been accused of being antagonistic to great art, and of having no love for it.

To this we answer: No! We do not want antiquated forms of musical culture, for a young generation and an art-hungry people. We no longer have any use for the old music because political ideas have changed.

In the new revival movement, the problems are in direct opposition to the concert practice which makes the listener a passive factor; for what we want is his cooperation, or, to put it correctly, we want this passivity replaced by the activity of a

365

co-producing, co-singing layman. This demand for an active partaking of the hearer, has penetrated to the masses, a thousand times repeated, and logically presented with the soundest arguments. This activity of the layman has become the problem of the musical education of the individual, as well as of the people, and is therefore a social problem.

The Youth Movement demanded community music, and this is our profound problem: to introduce music into popular society. High art has always been considered an individualistic aesthetic art. But the shallowness, the superficiality of its presentation is what the "Hitler Jugend" objects to. A glance into the song books of the "Hitler Jugend" shows how much the music of this movement is carried by creative power of the young generation alone, and how close it is to the present day.

The "Music Days" at Erfurt were arranged by the members of the camp. They practice the teaching of chorus work, and again and again they try for a clarity of intonation, intelligibility of diction, and a feeling for singing. They have courses for the flute, the lute, fanfares, drums; and at evenings small circles produce music of various kinds. And success is not wanting. From the political unison song, framed in by new music of wind instruments, resounds the earnest will for a powerful celebration.

Of highest excellence was a performance of Spitta's "Erntekantate" (text by Roth), which because of its deep and genuine piety disproves the statement of those liars who speak of the godlessness of the Hitler Youth. All the references and speeches made in the camp, served to prove the deepening of the universal work that they are doing. The spirit of musical conformance to this idea fills its life, its marches, its feasts and celebrations.

But the music of the "Hitler Jugend" strives for still more. The Hitler Youth is well aware that there is a kind of music that can be practised by almost any individual: songs of political confession, folk songs, choruses, music for string instruments, fanfares,—in short, music which does not require much technical knowledge. Of course, they know that this kind of music will always be that of dilettantes, but this does not mean a negation of the great works of the past. They desire with deep reverence to combine both ways: practising their own popular and primitive music, and, in addition, enjoying master work concerts. Therefore the doublefold performance of the "Kunst der Fuge" and the orchestral concert of November 11, 1935!

If there has been any danger of a too one-sided practise of music of the past, the Hitler Youth has known how to get around this cliff by its radical acceptance of the music of our time, proceeding from a sound instinct.

From the magazine "Musik Kultur", 1935.

Hitler's Music Education Camp

ONCE a year the musical members of the "Hitler Jugend Bund" and the "Bund deutscher Maedchen" meet in a music camp. Reports about the last year's work are read, experiences exchanged, and exercises for the coming year are prepared. In 1934, the meeting took place in Cassel, in 1935 at Erfurt. The result of ten years of musical education could be noted at Erfurt. Chorus work and folk song form the nucleus of the educational aims of the young people. And how great was the improvement to be seen at Erfurt! The fact alone that all members always appear in uniform; that each morning and each night is heard the sound of marching troops; that each morning the flag is raised before the "Logenhaus", and lowered again at night, while every one stands rigidly in line,—all of this symbolizes their having been sworn in, and emphasizes the character and the spirit of the music-practising "Hitler Jugend". This National-Socialistic Unity, resolving political problems as well, demands the same spirit of the social musical audience.

From "Musik Kultur", 1935.

Music and Nazidom

THE National-Socialistic State has from the beginning recognized how colossal is the task of introducing the culture and practice of the arts. And it has taken hold of each department in the field of art with an energy and buoyancy almost unequalled in the history of art.

We have paid especial attention to music. Music has always been an essential and prominent expression of the German spirit and culture, and the role it has played and is playing in the life of our people is greater and stronger than with any other people. This tendency in the German people is of a peculiar kind. Nordic conception of music manifests itself less in passion and exaltation than in the expression of soul experience and an inner power. Music with the Germans is not a representative art but finds its outlet in folk music. This form of creative power of German music is exhibited not only in the unusually large number of talents among the German people, but also in the inexhaustible treasure of its folk songs. And to nourish and make flourish this treasure is the duty of the National-Socialistic State.

From "Musik Kultur", 1936.

Judaism in the Opinion of a Nazi Musicologist

ALTHOUGH the articles on Jews have already been considerably curtailed in the first edition, it is not advisable to eliminate them altogether, as it is the only way to determine the status of Non-Aryans. Such informative material is indispensable for a cultural-political alignment. If Jewish literature has been cited, it has, of course been done, not for recommendation — particularly as regards foreign literature — but to point out its effects, and, where Aryan efforts are not under consideration, to utilize the facts stated. To treat it as a bagatelle, would minimize the accomplishments of those who have subdued it.

As in all the other arts, Judaism has usurped the field of music in Europe as well as in the United States of America. All important posts of the press, agencies, publishers, have been assigned to persons of their own Jewish race, in this manner forcing their tastes on the "Wirtsvoelker". We cannot deny that their accomplishments, owing to their talent for adaptation, have been noteworthy, especially on the field of reproduction. If, since 1933, they are expelled from our cultural circles, they have to thank the essentially just nature of the Aryan cause for this, now fighting the spiritual as well as economic "Tyrannei" which Judaism had forced on us.

From the preface to Hans Joachim Moser's
Musiklexikon (1943).

Mahler in the Eyes of the Nazis

Mahler's creations include ten symphonies which pro-Jewish sentiment has immeasurably over-estimated. They often show banal invention and long empty stretches.

Moser.

Music in the Theresienstadt Ghetto

HAVING spent three years in Theresienstadt I was in a position to observe the "Freizeitgestaltung". As is well known, the Nazis had erected an enormous Ghetto in Theresienstadt, which, at times, had 60,000 inhabitants, whereas before the Hitler invasion the small North-Bohemian town counted no more than 7180 heads.

As the Jews enjoyed a sort of self-rule, they were able to give concerts and theatre performances. They made free use of this privilege, particularly since a great number of distinguished composers, directors, conductors, and performing artists were among the interned. These performances took place in the "Sokolovna". There were at least two concert and theatre performances a week. The hall was always so crowded that the listeners had to stand in the street. This was not only because no entrance fee was charged,—it was the indescribable hunger for music, and above all for good music of these poor victims of Nazism, that drew such crowds.

There was chamber music as well as instrumental and vocal music. Most of these performances had to be repeated ten and more times, owing to this great demand for them. Lectures on music and on history of music were the order of the day. I remember, among others, the excellent lecture of the Berlin music-critic Kurt Singer, who spoke beautifully on Bach and Beethoven. The pianist, Alice Sommer-Herz, from Prague gave over a hundred concerts, with excellent programs from Bach to Bela Bartók and Martinû.

Of the younger composers interned in Theresienstadt, I recall Victor Ullmann, whose works have been performed with great success at International Music Festivals; Hans Krasa, whose opera "Verlobung im Traum" was very popular in its day; young Gideon Klein, and the conductor Antscherl, the composer Reiner, and many others. Of these, Ullmann, Krasa, and many others were sent to Auschwitz, and were undoubtedly gassed. Hardly any came back.

At one time, a children's opera, "Pan Brundigar" was given. It reminded one of Hindemith's "Wir bauen eine Stadt". Only children took part, children—the most musical among them—directed and conducted the opera. This opera had been so excellently produced as to create a great sensation, not only in the camp itself. Its fame spread far and wide, and had come to the ears of the Nazi commanders. An order was issued to perform the opera for the Nazi lords of the Kommandatur. And so the children played their opera for the group leaders of the "S. A." and the "S. S.". They were all delighted. Some of the children's parents lulled themselves in the belief that they had now won the especial favor of the Nazis. But what happened? After several days came the order that all the children, and all the musicians who had participated in the performance of the opera, were to be sent to the camp of destruction, Auschwitz! And that was the end of the artistic flowering of the ghetto of Theresienstadt. . . .

From a letter to the editor.

Index of Names

INDEX OF NAMES

Field, John—226, 227.
Filippi, music critic—300, 301.
Findeisen, N.—277.
Finkh, Hermann—54.
Fischer, Ludwig—146.
Flehberger—200.
Follino—52.
Fontenet—109.
Forbach, Countess—94, 100, 103.
Fraccaroli, Arnaldo—304, 305.
Franc, Martin le—29.
Franck, César—295, 296.
Franz, Archduke—157.
Frauenlob—26.
Frederic II, the Great—78, 79, 124, 125.
Frederick Augustus, King of Poland and Elector of Saxony—120, 121, 122, 124.
Frescobaldi, Girolamo—53.
Frimmel, Theodor—252, 253.
Fugger, Jacob—43.
Fuss, J. E. (critic)—183.

Gabrieli, Andrea—43.
Gabrieli, Giovanni—43, 53, 57.
Galilei, Vincenzo—37, 38, 39, 48, 49.
Gallenberg, W. R.—284.
Garrick, David—83, 84.
Gellert, Friedrich—138.
Geminiani, Francesco—62.
George I. of Britain—128, 129.
Gerbert, Martin—24.
Gershwin, George—346, 347, 348, 349, 350, 351.
Gervinus, Georg Gottfried—206.
Gessner, Joh. Mathias—123.
Giotto—36.
Giraldus Cambrensis—27, 28.
Glaucon—11, 12, 13.
Glinka, Michael I.—277, 309, 312, 319, 320, 321, 322.
Gluck, Ch. W.—83, 84, 85, 86, 87, 88, 89, 90, 91, 92, 93, 94, 95, 97, 98, 99, 100, 101, 102, 103, 104, 105, 106, 107, 108, 109, 110, 144, 145, 188, 223, 274, 276, 293, 296.
Goerner, Joh. Val.—120, 121.
Goethe, Joh. W.—102, 103, 167, 168, 169, 175, 176, 177, 185,

186, 187, 205, 222, 223, 224, 225, 226, 258, 276, 278, 279, 332.
Goldberg, Isaak—348, 349, 350, 351.
Gonzaga, Francesco—52.
Gounod, Charles Fr.—293, 310.
Gozzi, Carlo—239.
Grainger, Percy—236.
Gregory I.—23.
Grieg, Edward—235, 236.
Griesinger, G. A.—137.
Grillparzer, Franz—190, 191, 198, 199, 200, 201, 202, 203, 204, 205, 206, 207, 208.
Grimm, Baron Melchior—146, 147, 148.
Guardasoni—157.
Guarini, G. B.—52.
Guido of Arezzo—26.

Hába, Alois—323, 324.
Hafferverg, Theodor von—209.
Halévy, J. F.—290.
Handel, G. F.—125, 126, 127, 128, 129, 130, 131, 193, 207.
Hanslick, Ed.—257, 258, 359.
Haslinger, Tobias—197.
Hauer, Joseph—342.
Haydn, Joseph—135, 136, 137, 138, 139, 140, 141, 142, 143, 144, 145, 186, 207, 223, 361.
Heine, Heinrich—225, 226, 239, 269, 270, 271.
Heinse, Wilhelm—239.
Henry IV.—50.
Hensel, S.—224.
Herder, Johann Gottfr.—173, 174.
Hildach, Eugen—340.
Hiller, Ferdinand—225.
Hindemith, Paul—339, 340, 371.
Hirschmann, Ira—356.
Hitler, Adolf—358, 365, 366, 367, 370.
Hoffman, Leopold Aloys (Writer & Freemason)—149.
Homer—292.
Howard, John Tasker—353, 354.
Huettenbrenner, Anselm—196, 197, 198.
Hugbald of Flanders—25.
Hugo, Victor—287.

375

INDEX OF NAMES

377

INDEX OF NAMES

Index of Subjects

INDEX OF SUBJECTS